VBA Functions

Note: If an equivalent VBA function is not available, you can use Excel's worksheet functions in your VBA code. Just precede the function with a reference to the Application object. For example, VBA does not have a function to convert radians to degrees. Because Excel has a worksheet function for this, you can use a VBA statement such as the following:

```
Deg = Application.Degrees(3.14)
```

Function	What It Does
Abs	Returns the absolute value of a number
Array	Returns a variant containing an array
Asc	Converts the first character of a string to its ASCII value
Atn	Returns the arctangent of a number
CBool	Converts an expression to Boolean
CCur	Converts an expression to currency data type
CDate	Converts an expression to date data type
CDbl	Converts an expression to double data type
Chr	Converts an ANSI value to a string
CInt	Converts an expression to integer data type
CLng	Converts an expression to long data type
Cos	Returns the cosine of a number
CreateObject	Creates an OLE Automation object
CSng	Converts an expression to single data type
CStr	Converts an expression to string data type
CurDir	Returns the current path
CVar	Converts an expression to variant data type
CVErr	Returns a user-defined error number
Date	Returns the current system date
DateSerial	Converts a date to a serial number
DateValue	Converts a string to a date
Day	Returns the day of the month from a date
Dir	Returns the name of a file or directory that matches a pattern
EOF	Returns True if the end of a text file has been reached
Erl	Returns the line number that caused an error
Err	Returns the error number of an error condition
Error	Returns the error message that corresponds to an error number
Exp	Returns the base of the natural logarithm (e) raised to a power
FileAttr	Returns the file mode for a text file
FileDateTime	Returns the date and time when a file was last modified
FileLen	Returns the number of bytes in a file
Fix	Returns the integer portion of a number
Format	Displays an expression in a particular format
FreeFile	Returns the next available file number when working with text files
GetAttr	Returns a code representing a file attribute
GetObject	Retrieves an OLE Automation object from a file
Hex	Converts from decimal to hexadecimal
Hour	Returns the hours portion of a time
Input	Returns characters from a sequential text file
InputBox	Displays a box to prompt the user for input
InStr	Returns the position of a string within another string
Int	Returns the integer portion of a number
IsArray	Returns True if a variable is an array
IsDate	Returns True if a variable is a date
IsEmpty	Returns True if a variable has been initialized

Function	What It Does
IsError	Returns True if an expression is an error value
IsMissing	Returns True if an optional argument was not passed to a procedure
IsNull	Returns True if an expression contains no valid data
IsNumeric	Returns True if an expression can be evaluated as a number
IsObject	Returns True if an expression references an OLE Automation object
LBound	Returns the smallest subscript for a dimension of an array
LCase	Returns a string converted to lowercase
Left	Returns a specified number of characters from the left of a string
Len	Returns the number of characters in a string
Loc	Returns the current read or write position of a text file
LOF	Returns the number of bytes in an open text file
Log	Returns the natural logarithm of a number
LTrim	Returns a copy of a string, with any leading spaces removed
Mid	Returns a specified number of characters from a string
Minute	Returns the minutes portion of a time
Month	Returns the month of a date
MsgBox	Displays a modal message box
Now	Returns the current system date and time
Oct	Converts from decimal to octal
RGB	Returns a numeric RGB value representing a color
Right	Returns a specified number of characters from the right of a string
Rnd	Returns a random number between 0 and 1
RTrim	Returns a copy of a string, with any trailing spaces removed
Second	Returns the seconds portion of a time
Seek	Returns the current position in a text file
Sgn	Returns an integer that indicates the sign of a number
Shell	Runs an executable program
Sin	Returns the sine of a number
Space	Returns a string with a specified number of spaces
Spc	Positions output when printing to a file
Sqr	Returns the square root of a number
Str	Returns a string representation of a number
StrComp	Returns a value indicating the result of a string comparison
String	Returns a repeating character or string
Tab	Positions output when printing to a file
Tan	Returns the tangent of a number
Time	Returns the current system time
Timer	Returns the number of seconds since midnight
TimeSerial	Returns the time for a specified hour, minute, and second
TimeValue	Converts a string to a time serial number
TypeName	Returns a string that describes the data type of a variable
UBound	Returns the largest available subscript for a dimension of an array
UCase	Converts a string to uppercase
Val	Returns the numbers contained in a string
VarType	Returns a value indicating the subtype of a variable
Weekday	Returns a number representing a day of the week
Year	Returns the year of a date

COMPUTER
BOOK SERIES
FROM IDG

Excel Programming For Dummies®

Cheat Sheet

VBA Statements

Statement	What It Does
Array	Creates an array
Beep	Sounds a tone using the computer's speaker
Call	Transfers control to another procedure
ChDir	Changes the current directory
ChDrive	Changes the current drive
Close	Closes a text file
Const	Declares a constant value
Date	Sets the current system date
Declare	Declares a reference to an external procedure in a DLL
Dim	Declares an array locally
Do...Loop	Loops
DoEvents	Lets the operating system process events
End	Exits the program
Erase	Reinitializes an array
Err	Sets Err to a specified value
Error	Simulates a specific error condition
Exit Do	Exits a block of Do...Loop code
Exit For	Exits a block of Do...For code
Exit Function	Exits a function procedure
Exit Property	Exits a property procedure
Exit Sub	Exits a subroutine procedure
FileCopy	Copies a file
For Each...Next	Loops
For...Next	Loops
Function	Declares the name and arguments for a function procedure
Get	Reads data from a text file
GoSub...Return	Branches
GoTo	Branches
If...Then...Else	Processes statements conditionally
Input #	Reads data from a sequential text file
Kill	Deletes a file from disk
Let	Assigns the value of an expression to a variable or a property
Line Input #	Reads a line of data from a sequential text file
Lock...Unlock	Controls access to a text file
LSet	Left-aligns a string within a string variable
Mid	Replaces characters in a string with other characters
MkDir	Creates a new directory
Name	Renames a file or a directory
On Error	Branches on an error

Statement	What It Does
On...GoSub	Branches on a condition
On...GoTo	Branches on a condition
Open	Opens a text file
Option Base	Changes the default lower limit
Option Compare	Declares the default comparison mode when comparing strings
Option Explicit	Forces declaration of all variables in a module
Option Private	Indicates that an entire module is private
Print #	Writes data to a sequential file
Private	Declares a local array
Property Get	Declares the name and arguments of a Property Get procedure
Property Let	Declares the name and arguments of a Property Let procedure
Property Set	Declares the name and arguments of a Property Set procedure
Public	Declares a public array
Put	Writes a variable to a text file
Randomize	Initializes the random number generator
ReDim	Changes the dimensions of an array
Rem	Specifies a line of comments (same as an apostrophe)
Reset	Closes all open text files
Resume	Resumes execution when an error-handling routine finishes
RmDir	Removes an empty directory
RSet	Right-aligns a string within a string variable
Seek	Sets the position for the next access in a text file
Select Case	Processes statements conditionally
SendKeys	Sends keystrokes to the active window
Set	Assigns an object reference to a variable or a property
SetAttr	Changes attribute information for a file
Static	Changes the dimensions of an array, keeping the data intact
Stop	Pauses the program
Sub	Declares the name and arguments of a Sub procedure
Time	Sets the system time
Type	Defines a custom data type
While...Wend	Loops
Width #	Sets the output line width of a text file
With	Sets a series of properties for an object
Write #	Writes data to a sequential text file

IDG
BOOKS
WORLDWIDE

. . .For Dummies: #1 Computer Book Series for Beginners

®

COMPUTER BOOK SERIES FROM IDG

References for the Rest of Us! ®

Are you intimidated and confused by computers? Do you find that traditional manuals are overloaded with technical details you'll never use? Do your friends and family always call you to fix simple problems on their PCs? Then the *...For Dummies*® computer book series from IDG Books Worldwide is for you.

...For Dummies books are written for those frustrated computer users who know they aren't really dumb but find that PC hardware, software, and indeed the unique vocabulary of computing make them feel helpless. *...For Dummies* books use a lighthearted approach, a down-to-earth style, and even cartoons and humorous icons to diffuse computer novices' fears and build their confidence. Lighthearted but not lightweight, these books are a perfect survival guide for anyone forced to use a computer.

Already, hundreds of thousands of satisfied readers agree. They have made ...*For Dummies* books the #1 introductory level computer book series and have written asking for more. So, if you're looking for the most fun and easy way to learn about computers, look to ...*For Dummies* books to give you a helping hand.

by John Walkenbach

IDG
BOOKS
WORLDWIDE

IDG Books Worldwide, Inc.
An International Data Group Company

Foster City, CA ♦ Chicago, IL ♦ Indianapolis, IN ♦ Braintree, MA ♦ Southlake, TX

Excel Programming For Windows® 95 For Dummies®

Published by
IDG Books Worldwide, Inc.
An International Data Group Company
919 E. Hillsdale Blvd.
Suite 400
Foster City, CA 94404

Library of Congress Catalog Card No.: 96-75766

ISBN: 1-56884-642-8

Printed in the United States of America

10 9 8 7 6 5 4 3 2 1

1A/SR/QV/ZW/IN

Distributed in the United States by IDG Books Worldwide, Inc.

Distributed by Macmillan Canada for Canada; by Computer and Technical Books for the Caribbean Basin; by Contemporanea de Ediciones for Venezuela; by Distribuidora Cuspide for Argentina; by CITEC for Brazil; by Ediciones ZETA S.C.R. Ltda. for Peru; by Editorial Limusa SA for Mexico; by Transworld Publishers Limited in the United Kingdom and Europe; by Al-Maiman Publishers & Distributors for Saudi Arabia; by Simron Pty. Ltd. for South Africa; by IDG Communications (HK) Ltd. for Hong Kong; by Toppan Company Ltd. for Japan; by Addison Wesley Publishing Company for Korea; by Longman Singapore Publishers Ltd. for Singapore, Malaysia, Thailand, and Indonesia; by Unalis Corporation for Taiwan; by WS Computer Publishing Company, Inc. for the Philippines; by WoodsLane Pty. Ltd. for Australia; by WoodsLane Enterprises Ltd. for New Zealand.

For general information on IDG Books Worldwide's books in the U.S., please call our Consumer Customer Service department at 800-762-2974. For reseller information, including discounts and premium sales, please call our Reseller Customer Service department at 800-434-3422.

For information on where to purchase IDG Books Worldwide's books outside the U.S., contact IDG Books Worldwide at 415-655-3021 or fax 415-655-3295.

For information on translations, contact Marc Jeffrey Mikulich, Director, Foreign & Subsidiary Rights, at IDG Books Worldwide, 415-655-3018 or fax 415-655-3295.

For sales inquiries and special prices for bulk quantities, write to the address above or call IDG Books Worldwide at 415-655-3200.

For information on using IDG Books Worldwide's books in the classroom, or ordering examination copies, contact the Education Office at 800-434-2086 or fax 817-251-8174.

For authorization to photocopy items for corporate, personal, or educational use, please contact Copyright Clearance Center, 222 Rosewood Drive, Danvers, MA 01923, or fax 508-750-4470.

is a trademark under exclusive license to IDG Books Worldwide, Inc., from International Data Group, Inc.

About the Author

John Walkenbach

John Walkenbach is a leading authority on spreadsheet software. He is principal of JWalk and Associates, Inc., a Southern California-based consulting firm that specializes in spreadsheet application development. John is also a shareware developer; his most popular product is the Power Utility Pak add-in for Excel. He has written more than 250 articles and reviews for publications such as *PC World, InfoWorld, Windows,* and *PC/Computing*. He is the author of 14 other spreadsheet books, including *Excel for Windows 95 Bible, Excel for Windows For Dummies Quick Reference,* and *Excel for Windows 95 Power Programming With VBA*. He also maintains The Spreadsheet Page, a site on the World Wide Web (http://www.cts.com/browse/jwalk). When he's not banging away on his computer keyboard, he's probably banging away on one of his guitars, trying to cop a few blues licks from Eric Clapton.

Dedication

This book is dedicated to my sister Pat, who finally discovered the World Wide Web. Welcome to cyberspace, sis.

Publisher's Acknowledgments

We're proud of this book; send us your comments about it by using the Reader Response Card at the back of the book or by e-mailing us at feedback/dummies@idgbooks.com. Some of the people who helped bring this book to market include:

Acquisitions, Development, & Editorial

Project Editor: John Pont

Acquisitions Editor: Tammy Goldfeld

Assistant Acquisitions Editor: Gareth Hancock

Product Development Manager: Mary Bednarek

Editors: Mary Goodwin, Joe Jansen

Technical Reviewer: Ellen Finkelstein

Editorial Manager: Mary Corder

Editorial Assistants: Constance Carlisle, Chris Collins

Production

Project Coordinator: Valery Bourke

Layout and Graphics: E. Shawn Aylsworth, Linda Boyer, Elizabeth Cardenas-Nelson, J. Tyler Conner, Dominique DeFelice, Julie Forey, Todd Klemme, Anne Sipahimalani, Jane Martin, Drew Moore, Mark C. Owens, Tricia Reynolds, Gina Scott, Kate Snell, Jenny Shoemake, Michael Sullivan

Proofreaders: Kathy McGuinnes, Dwight Ramsey, Christine Meloy Beck, Carl Saff, Nancy Price, Robert Springer, Karen Gregor-York

Indexer: Sherry Massey

General & Administrative

IDG Books Worldwide, Inc.: John Kilcullen, President & CEO; Steven Berkowitz, COO & Publisher

Dummies, Inc.: Milissa Koloski, Executive Vice President & Publisher

Dummies Technology Press & Dummies Editorial: Diane Graves Steele, Associate Publisher; Judith A. Taylor, Brand Manager; Myra Immell, Editorial Director

Dummies Trade Press: Kathleen A. Welton, Vice President & Publisher; Stacy S. Collins, Brand Manager

IDG Books Production for Dummies Press: Beth Jenkins, Production Director; Cindy L. Phipps, Supervisor of Project Coordination; Kathie S. Schnorr, Supervisor of Page Layout; Shelley Lea, Supervisor of Graphics and Design

Dummies Packaging & Book Design: Erin McDermitt, Packaging Coordinator; Kavish+Kavish, Cover Design

◆

The publisher would like to give special thanks to Patrick J. McGovern, without whom this book would not have been possible.

◆

Welcome to the world of IDG Books Worldwide.

IDG Books Worldwide, Inc., is a subsidiary of International Data Group, the world's largest publisher of computer-related information and the leading global provider of information services on information technology. IDG was founded more than 25 years ago and now employs more than 7,700 people worldwide. IDG publishes more than 250 computer publications in 67 countries (see listing below). More than 70 million people read one or more IDG publications each month.

Launched in 1990, IDG Books Worldwide is today the #1 publisher of best-selling computer books in the United States. We are proud to have received 8 awards from the Computer Press Association in recognition of editorial excellence and three from Computer Currents' First Annual Readers' Choice Awards, and our best-selling *...For Dummies®* series has more than 19 million copies in print with translations in 28 languages. IDG Books Worldwide, through a joint venture with IDG's Hi-Tech Beijing, became the first U.S. publisher to publish a computer book in the People's Republic of China. In record time, IDG Books Worldwide has become the first choice for millions of readers around the world who want to learn how to better manage their businesses.

Our mission is simple: Every one of our books is designed to bring extra value and skill-building instructions to the reader. Our books are written by experts who understand and care about our readers. The knowledge base of our editorial staff comes from years of experience in publishing, education, and journalism — experience which we use to produce books for the '90s. In short, we care about books, so we attract the best people. We devote special attention to details such as audience, interior design, use of icons, and illustrations. And because we use an efficient process of authoring, editing, and desktop publishing our books electronically, we can spend more time ensuring superior content and spend less time on the technicalities of making books.

You can count on our commitment to deliver high-quality books at competitive prices on topics you want to read about. At IDG Books Worldwide, we continue in the IDG tradition of delivering quality for more than 25 years. You'll find no better book on a subject than one from IDG Books Worldwide.

John J. Kilcullen

John Kilcullen
President and CEO
IDG Books Worldwide, Inc.

Contents at a Glance

Cartoons at a Glance

By Rich Tennant • Fax: 508-546-7747 • E-mail: the5wave@tiac.net

page 77

page 247

page 273

page 9

page 349

page 309

page 29

page 187

Table of Contents

Introduction

● ●

*G*reetings, prospective Excel programmer.

Thanks for buying my book. I think you'll find that it offers a fast, enjoyable way to learn the ins and outs of Microsoft Excel programming. Even if you don't have the foggiest idea of what programming is all about, this book can help you make Excel jump through hoops in no time (well, it will take *some* time).

Unlike most programming books, this one is written in plain English, and even normal people can understand it. Even better, it's filled with information of the "just the facts, ma'am" variety — and not the useless drivel that you may need once every third lifetime.

What This Book Covers

You can find many Excel books on the market (far too many, as far as I'm concerned). This quick overview can help you decide whether this book is really right for you. *Excel Programming For Dummies:*

- ✔ Is designed for intermediate to advanced Excel users who want to learn Visual Basic for Applications (VBA) programming
- ✔ Requires no previous programming experience
- ✔ Covers all the most commonly used commands
- ✔ Is appropriate for Excel for Windows 95 (also known as Excel 7) as well as Excel 5
- ✔ Just might make you crack a smile occasionally — it even has cartoons

While writing this book, I used Windows 95 and Excel for Windows 95. However, most of the material I present also applies to Excel 5. If you use Windows 3.1 or Excel 5, however, the figures in this book may differ slightly from what you see on your screen.

This is *not* an introductory Excel book. If you're looking for a general-purpose Excel book, check out any of the following books published by IDG Books Worldwide, Inc.:

- ✔ *Excel For Windows 95 For Dummies*, by Greg Harvey
- ✔ *Excel For Windows 95 Bible*, by John Walkenbach (yep, that's me)
- ✔ *Excel For Windows 95 For Dummies Quick Reference*, by John Walkenbach (me again)

Notice that the title of this book isn't *The Complete Guide to Excel Programming For Dummies*. I don't cover all aspects of Excel programming — but then again, you probably don't want to know *everything* about this topic. In the unlikely event you want a more comprehensive Excel programming book, you might try *Excel For Windows 95 Power Programming With VBA*, by John Walkenbach (is this guy prolific, or what?).

So, You Want to Be a Programmer . . .

Besides earning money to pay my bills, my main goal in writing this book is to teach Excel users how to use the VBA language — a tool that helps you significantly enhance the power of the world's most popular spreadsheet. However, using VBA involves programming. (Yikes! The *p* word.)

If you're like most computer users, the very word *programmer* probably conjures up an image of someone who looks and behaves nothing like you. Perhaps words such as *nerd, geek,* and *dweeb* come to mind.

Fact is, times have changed. Computer programming has become much easier, and even so-called normal people now engage in this activity. *Programming* simply means developing instructions that the computer automatically carries out. *Excel programming* refers to the fact that you can instruct Excel to automatically do things that you normally do manually — saving you lots of time and (hopefully) reducing errors. I could go on, but I need to save some good stuff for Chapter 1.

Suffice it to say that you need to become an Excel programmer. This could be something you came up with yourself, or (more likely) something your boss decided. In this book, I tell you everything you need to know about Excel programming, so you won't feel like an idiot the next time you're trapped in a conference room with a group of Excel aficionados. And by the time you finish this book, you can honestly say, "Yeah, I do some Excel programming."

Why Bother?

Many Excel users never bother to learn VBA programming. Your interest in this topic definitely places you among an elite group. Welcome to the fold. If you're still not convinced that this is a good idea, I've come up with a few good reasons why you should take the time to learn VBA programming:

- ✔ **It will make you more marketable.** Like it or not, Microsoft's applications are extremely popular. Several already include VBA, and others will soon have it. The more you know about VBA, the better your chances for advancement in your job.

- ✔ **It lets you get the most out of your software investment** (or, more likely, your *employer's* software investment). Using Excel without knowing VBA is sort of like buying a TV set and watching only the odd-numbered channels.

- ✔ **It will improve your productivity (eventually).** Learning VBA definitely takes some time, but you'll more than make up for this in the amount of time you ultimately save because you're more productive. Sort of like what they told you about going to college.

- ✔ **It's fun (well, sometimes).** Some people really enjoy making Excel do things that are otherwise impossible. By the time you finish this book, you just might be one of those people.

What I Assume about You

People who write books usually have a target reader in mind. For this book, my target reader is a conglomerate of dozens of Excel users I've met over the years (either in person, or — more frequently — out in cyberspace). The following points more or less describe my hypothetical reader:

- ✔ You have access to a PC at work — and probably at home.

- ✔ You're running Windows 95 and Excel 7 (or, you may be running Windows 3.1 and Excel 5).

- ✔ You've been using computers for several years.

- ✔ You use Excel frequently in your work, and you consider yourself to be more knowledgeable than the average Excel user.

- ✔ You need to make Excel do things that you currently can't make it do.

- ✔ You have little or no programming experience.

- ✔ You need to get some work done, and you have a low tolerance for boring computer books.

Obligatory Typographical Conventions Section

All computer books have a section like this. (I think some federal law requires it.) Read it or skip it.

Sometimes, I refer to key combinations — which means you hold down one key while you press another. For example, Ctrl+Z means you hold down the Ctrl key while you press Z.

Any text you need to enter appears in **bold**. For example, I might say, Enter **=SUM(B:B)** in cell A1.

Excel programming involves developing *code* — that is, the instructions Excel follows. All code in this book appears in a monospace font, like this:

```
Range("AnnualTotal").Select
```

Some long lines of code don't fit between the margins in this book. In such cases, I use the standard VBA line continuation character sequence: a space, followed by an underscore character. Here's an example:

```
Selection.PasteSpecial Paste:=xlValues, Operation:=xlNone, _
    SkipBlanks:=False, Transpose:=False
```

When you enter this code, you can type it as written, or place it on a single line (omitting the space and the underscore character).

How This Book Is Organized

I divided this book into eight major parts, each of which contains several chapters. Although I arranged the chapters in a fairly logical sequence, you can read them in any order you choose.

Part I: Introducing VBA

Part I has but two chapters. I introduce the VBA language in the first chapter. In Chapter 2, I let you get your feet wet right away by taking you on a hands-on guided tour.

Part II: How VBA Works with Excel

In writing this book, I assumed that you already know how to use Excel. The four chapters in Part II give you a better grasp on how VBA is implemented within Excel. These chapters are all important, so don't skip past them, okay?

Part III: Programming Concepts

The eight chapters in Part III get you into the nitty-gritty of what programming is all about. You may not need to know all this stuff, but you'll be glad it's there if you ever do need it.

Part IV: Developing Custom Dialog Boxes

One of the coolest parts of programming in Excel is designing custom dialog boxes (well, at least *I* like it). The four chapters in Part IV teach you how to create dialog boxes that look like they came straight from the software lab at Microsoft.

Part V: Creating Custom Menus and Toolbars

Part V has two chapters, both of which address *user interface* topics. One chapter deals with creating custom menus; the other describes how to customize toolbars.

Part VI: Putting It All Together

The three chapters in Part VI pull together information from the previous chapters. You learn how to develop custom worksheet functions, create add-ins, and design user-oriented applications.

Part VII: Advanced Stuff

I designed Part VII for the overachievers among you. Not everyone needs to know this stuff, but you should at least take a look at it. In these chapters, I reveal some techniques you can use to make your applications perform magic.

Part VIII: The Part of Tens

Traditionally, books in the *...For Dummies* series contain a final part that consists of short *Top Ten* type chapters. Because I'm a sucker for tradition, this book has several such chapters which you can peruse at your convenience. (If you're like most readers, you'll turn to this part first.)

Marginal Icons

Somewhere along the line, some market research company must have shown that publishers can sell more copies of their computer books if they stick icons in the margins of those books. *Icons* are those little pictures that supposedly draw your attention to various features, or help you decide whether something is worth reading.

I don't know if this research is valid, but I'm not taking any chances. So, here are the icons you'll encounter in your travels from front cover to back cover:

This icon flags material you might consider technical. You might find it interesting, but you can safely skip it if you're in a hurry.

Don't skip information marked with this icon. This identifies a shortcut that can save you lots of time (and maybe even allow you to leave the office at a reasonable hour).

This icon tells you when you need to store information in the deep recesses of your cortex for later use.

Read anything marked with this icon. Otherwise, you may lose your data, blow up your computer, cause a nuclear meltdown — or maybe even ruin your day.

This icon signals a feature that is new to Excel for Windows 95. If you're still using Excel 5, you're out of luck.

This icon tells you to wake up and pay attention. It's not quite worthy of a Remember icon, and not as severe as a Warning.

A Blatant Plug

You might be interested in a shareware product I developed: the Power Utility Pak for Excel. It contains 23 useful Excel utilities and 22 new worksheet functions. The best part is that I developed it using VBA exclusively.

Thousands of people throughout the planet use Power Utility Pack for Excel, which normally sells for $39.95. But because you bought my book, you can get your very own copy absolutely free (well, there *is* a small shipping and handling charge). And if you're curious, you can even get the VBA source files so you can see what goes on behind the scenes (and maybe even snag a useful programming trick or two along the way). Check out the coupon in the back of the book for details.

Wanna Reach Out?

I enjoy hearing from readers, so please don't hesitate to send me your questions, comments, or suggestions. The best way to contact me is by e-mail:

```
jwalk@cts.com
```

And if you're really ambitious, I urge you to point your World Wide Web browser to my very own Web site, which I pack to the gills with even more Excel goodies. The URL is:

```
http://www.cts.com/browse/jwalk
```

If you haven't reached the on-ramp to the information superhighway, you can contact me via traditional mail in care of the publisher.

Now What?

Reading this introduction was your first step. Now, it's time to move on and become a programmer (there's that *p* word, again!).

If you're a programming virgin, I strongly suggest that you start with Chapter 1, and then progress in chapter order until you've learned enough. Chapter 2 gives you some immediate hands-on experience so that you'll have the illusion that you're making quick progress.

But it's a free country (at least it was when I wrote these words); I won't sic the Computer Book Police on you if you opt to thumb through randomly and read whatever strikes your fancy.

I hope you have as much fun reading this book as I did writing it.

Part I
Introducing VBA

In this part . . .

*E*very book must start somewhere. This one starts by
introducing you to VBA (and I'm sure you two will
become very good friends over the course of a few dozen
chapters). After I make the necessary introductions,
Chapter 2 walks you through a real-live Excel
programming session.

Chapter 1

What Is VBA?

*T*his chapter is completely devoid of hands-on training stuff. However, it does contain some essential background information to assist you on your way to becoming an Excel programmer. In other words, this chapter paves the way for everything else that follows and gives you a feel for how Excel programming fits into the overall scheme of the universe.

Okay, So What Is VBA?

VBA, which stands for Visual Basic for Applications, is a programming language developed by Microsoft — you know, the company run by the richest man in the U.S. Excel, as well as a few other Microsoft applications, uses the VBA language. As I write this, VBA is included with Access and Project; it will eventually find its way into other applications such as Word and PowerPoint.

Don't confuse VBA with VB (which stands for Visual Basic). VB is a programming language that lets you create stand-alone, executable programs (you know, those EXE files). Although VBA and VB have a lot in common, they are different animals.

In a nutshell, VBA is the tool you use to develop macros (or programs) that control Excel.

A few words about terminology

With the introduction of VBA in Excel 5, the terminology used to describe the programmable features in Excel got a bit muddy. For example, VBA is a programming language, but it also serves as a macro language. So, what do you call something written in VBA and executed in Excel? Is it a *macro*, or is it a *program?* Excel's online help often refers to VBA code as a macro, so I use that terminology. However, I also call this stuff a program.

By the way, *macro* does *not* stand for Messy And Confusing Repeated Operation. Rather, it comes from the Greek *makros*, which means large — which also describes your paycheck after you become an expert macro programmer.

What Can You Do with VBA?

You're undoubtedly aware that people use Excel for thousands of different tasks. Here are just a few examples:

- ✔ Keeping lists of things, such as customers, students' grades, or Christmas gift ideas
- ✔ Budgeting and forecasting
- ✔ Analyzing scientific data
- ✔ Creating invoices and other forms
- ✔ Developing charts and maps from data
- ✔ Blah, blah, blah

This list could go on and on, but I think you get the idea. My point is simply that people use Excel for a wide variety of applications, and everyone reading this book has different needs and expectations regarding Excel. But one thing virtually every reader has in common is the *need to automate some aspects of Excel*. That, dear reader, is what VBA is all about.

For example, you might create a VBA macro to format and print your month-end sales report. After developing and debugging the macro, you can invoke it with a single command, causing Excel to perform many time-consuming procedures automatically.

Kodak had an advertising slogan, "You press the button, we do the rest." That statement pretty much sums up the appeal of macros. You execute a macro with a single action (perhaps a button click), and the macro automatically does lots of cool things for you.

In the following sections, I briefly describe some common uses for VBA macros. One or two of these may push your button.

Insert a text string automatically

If you often need to enter your company name into worksheets, you can create a macro to do the typing for you. You can also extend this concept as far as you like. For example, you might develop a macro that automatically types a list of all the salespeople who work for your company. This is a very simple — but quite handy — use for VBA.

Automate a task you perform frequently

Assume you're a sales manager and you need to prepare a month-end sales report to keep your boss happy. If the task is straightforward, you can develop a VBA macro to do it for you. Your boss will be impressed by the consistently high quality of your reports, and you'll be promoted to a new job for which you are highly unqualified.

Automate repetitive operations

If you need to perform the same action on, say, 12 different Excel workbooks, you can record a macro while you perform the task on the first workbook, and then let the macro repeat your action on the other workbooks. The nice thing about this is that Excel never complains about being bored.

Create a custom command

If you find that you often issue the same sequence of Excel menu commands, you can save yourself a few seconds by developing a macro that combines these commands into a single, custom command, which you execute with a single keystroke.

Create a custom toolbar button

You can customize the toolbars in Excel with your own buttons, which execute macros you write. Quite impressive.

Create a custom menu command

You can also customize Excel's menus with your own commands, which execute macros you write. Even more impressive.

Create a simplified front end for users who don't know much about Excel

In almost any office, you can find lots of people who don't really understand how to use computers (sound familiar?). Using VBA, you can make it easy for these inexperienced users to perform useful work. For example, you can set up a foolproof data entry template so that you don't have to waste *your* time doing mundane work.

Develop new worksheet functions

Although Excel includes numerous built-in functions, you can create custom worksheet functions that greatly simplify your formulas. I guarantee you'll be surprised by how easy this is (I show you how to do this in Chapter 21). Even better, as shown in Figure 1-1, the Function Wizard displays your custom functions, making them appear to be built-in Excel functions.

Figure 1-1: When you develop custom worksheet functions with VBA, they appear in the Function Wizard.

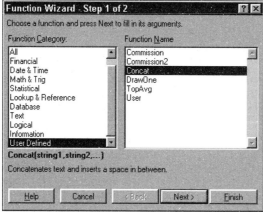

Create complete, turnkey, macro-driven applications

If you're willing to spend some time, you can use VBA to create large-scale applications, complete with custom dialog boxes, online help, and lots of other accouterments.

Create custom add-ins for Excel

You're probably familiar with some of the add-ins that ship with Excel. Most of these were created with Excel macros. I developed my Power Utility Pak add-in using only VBA. With some help from this book, you can create your own add-ins.

What Are the Pros and Cons of VBA?

In the following sections, I briefly describe the good things about VBA. Then I explore its darker side.

VBA advantages

You can automate almost anything you do in Excel. To do so, you write instructions that Excel carries out. Automating a task by using VBA offers several advantages:

- Excel always executes the task in exactly the same way (in most cases, consistency is a good thing).
- Excel performs the task much faster than you could do it manually (unless, of course, you're Clark Kent).
- Excel always performs the task without errors (which probably can't be said about you or me).
- Excel allows the task to be performed by someone who doesn't know anything about Excel.
- Excel helps you do things that are otherwise impossible, which can make you a very popular person around the office.

VBA disadvantages

It's only fair that I give equal time to listing the disadvantages (or *potential* disadvantages) of VBA:

- You have to learn how to write programs in VBA (but that's why you bought this book, right?). Fortunately, it's not as difficult as you might expect.

- Other people who need to use the VBA programs you develop must have their own copies of Excel. It would be nice if you could press a button that transforms your Excel/VBA application into a stand-alone program, but that isn't possible (and probably never will be).

- Sometimes, things go wrong. In other words, you can't blindly assume that your VBA program will always work correctly under all circumstances. Welcome to the world of debugging. . .

- VBA is a moving target. As you know, Microsoft is continually upgrading Excel. You may discover that VBA code you've written doesn't work properly with a different version of Excel. Take it from me — I discovered this the hard way (see the following sidebar).

VBA in a Nutshell

The following is a quick and dirty summary of what VBA is all about. Of course, I describe all this stuff in excruciating detail later in the book:

- **You perform actions in VBA by writing (or recording) code in a VBA module sheet.** You store VBA modules in an Excel workbook, and a workbook can hold any number of VBA modules.

- **A VBA module consists of subroutine procedures.** A *subroutine procedure* is basically computer code that performs some action on or with objects. The following example shows a simple subroutine called Test:

```
Sub Test()
    Sum = 1 + 1
    MsgBox "The answer is " & Sum
End Sub
```

- **A VBA module can also have function procedures.** A function procedure returns a single value, and you can call it from another VBA procedure, or even use it as a function in a worksheet formula. Here's an example of a function named AddTwo:

A personal anecdote

Excel programming has its own challenges and frustrations. My book, *Excel 5 For Windows Power Programming Techniques*, includes a disk containing the examples I discuss in the book. I compressed these files so they would fit on a single disk. Trying to be clever, I wrote a VBA program to expand the files and copy them to the appropriate directories. I spent a lot of time writing and debugging the code, and I tested it thoroughly on three different computers.

Imagine my surprise when I started receiving e-mail from readers who could not install the files. With a bit of sleuthing, I eventually discovered that the readers who were having the problem had all upgraded to Excel 5.0c (I developed my installation program using Excel 5.0a). It turns out that the Excel 5.0c upgrade featured a very subtle change that caused my macro to bomb. Because I'm not privy to Microsoft's plans, I couldn't anticipate this problem. Needless to say, this author suffered lots of embarrassment and had to e-mail corrections to hundreds of frustrated readers.

```
Function AddTwo(arg1, arg2)
    AddTwo = arg1 + arg2
End Function
```

- **VBA manipulates objects.** Excel provides more than 100 objects that you can manipulate. Examples of objects include a workbook, a worksheet, a range on a worksheet, a chart, and a drawn rectangle. You have many, many more objects at your disposal, and you can manipulate them using VBA code.

- **Objects are arranged in a hierarchy.** Objects can act as *containers* for other objects. For example, Excel itself is an object called Application, and it contains other objects such as Workbook objects and Toolbar objects. The Workbook object can contain other objects such as Worksheet objects and Chart objects. A Worksheet object can contain objects such as Range objects and PivotTable objects. The term *object model* refers to the arrangement of these objects.

- **Objects of the same type form a collection.** For example, the Worksheets collection consists of all the worksheets in a particular workbook. The Toolbars collection consists of all Toolbar objects. Collections are themselves objects.

- **You refer to an object by specifying its position in the object hierarchy, using a dot as a separator.** For example, you can refer to the workbook BOOK1.XLS as

```
Application.Workbooks("Book1")
```

This refers to the workbook BOOK1.XLS in the Workbooks collection. The Workbooks collection is contained in the Application object (that is, Excel). Extending this to another level, you can refer to Sheet1 in Book1 as

```
Application.Workbooks("Book1").Worksheets("Sheet1")
```

As shown in the following example, you can take this to still another level and refer to a specific cell:

```
Application.Workbooks("Book1").Worksheets("Sheet1").Range("A1")
```

✔ **If you omit specific references, Excel uses the *active* objects.** If Book1 is the active workbook, you can simplify the previous reference as follows:

```
Worksheets("Sheet1").Range("A1")
```

If you know that Sheet1 is the active sheet, you can simplify the reference even more:

```
Range("A1")
```

✔ **Objects have properties.** You can think of a property as a *setting* for an object. For example, a range object has such properties as Value and Name. A chart object has such properties as HasTitle and Type. You can use VBA to determine object properties and to change them.

✔ **You refer to a property of an object by combining the object's name with the property's name, separated by a period.** For example, you can refer to the value in cell A1 on Sheet1 as follows:

```
Worksheets("Sheet1").Range("A1").Value
```

✔ **You can assign values to variables.** To assign the value in cell A1 on Sheet1 to a variable called *Interest*, use the following VBA statement:

```
Interest = Worksheets("Sheet1").Range("A1").Value
```

✔ **Objects have methods.** A *method* is an action Excel performs with an object. For example, one of the methods for a Range object is ClearContents. This method clears the contents of the range.

✔ **You specify a method by combining the object with the method, separated by a period.** For example, the following statement clears the contents of cell A1:

```
Worksheets("Sheet1").Range("A1").ClearContents
```

✔ **VBA includes all the constructs of modern programming languages, including arrays and looping.**

Believe it or not, the preceding list pretty much describes VBA in a nutshell. Now you just have to learn the details. That's the purpose of the rest of this book.

An Excursion into Versions

If you plan to develop VBA macros, you should have some understanding of Excel's history. I know you weren't expecting a history lesson, but this is important stuff. Among other reasons, a passing knowledge of the various versions of Excel may help you understand why your new macro won't work on someone else's version of Excel.

Here's a list of all the major Excel versions that have seen the light of day, along with a few words about how they handle macros:

- ✔ **Excel 2:** The original version of Excel for Windows was called Version 2 (rather than 1) so that it would correspond to the Macintosh version. Excel 2 first appeared in 1987, and nobody uses it anymore. Although Excel 2 includes the XLM language, you can pretty much forget that it ever existed.

- ✔ **Excel 3:** Released in late 1990, this version features the XLM macro language. A few people live in a time warp and still use this version.

- ✔ **Excel 4:** This version hit the streets in early 1992. It also uses the XLM macro language. A fair number of people still use this version. (They believe that if something ain't broke, don't fix it.)

- ✔ **Excel 5**: This one came out in early 1994. In addition to VBA, this version supports XLM. Many people continue to use this version because they are reluctant to move up to Windows 95.

- ✔ **Excel for Windows 95:** Technically known as Excel 7 (there is no Excel 6), this version began shipping in the summer of 1995. It requires Windows 95 or Windows NT. It has a few enhancements to VBA, and it supports the XLM language.

So, what's the point of this mini history lesson? If you plan to distribute your Excel/VBA files to other users, it's vitally important that you understand which version of Excel they use. For example, if you develop a macro that takes advantage of a new feature found only in Excel for Windows 95, users running Excel 5 may have problems with it. And don't even think about giving an Excel file containing VBA code to someone who still uses a version from the pre-Excel 5 era.

For the most part, you can share your Excel for Windows 95 files with users who are running Excel 5 (or later) for the Macintosh. However, this compatibility goes out the window if your macros use any calls to the Windows Application Programming Interface (API). I discuss this in Chapter 24.

Excel's *other* macro language

VBA made its debut with Excel 5, which Microsoft released in 1994. Previous versions of Excel incorporate a completely different macro language called XLM (which stands for Excel Macro). Most people who know about such things consider VBA to be a giant step forward. However, Microsoft didn't want to abandon its loyal users by making them switch to VBA cold turkey. Therefore, Excel 5 and Excel for Windows 95 both support XLM.

Microsoft keeps XLM around mainly for compatibility purposes. People who wrote macros in earlier versions of Excel can still execute those macros when they run Excel 5 or Excel for Windows 95.

For the most part, you can ignore the fact that another macro language lurks behind the scenes. This book covers VBA exclusively.

Learning More

You're off to a good start (and you have some useless trivia to share at the water cooler). Now, it's time to move on to something a bit more meaty. If you're ready to get your feet wet and do some VBA programming, turn to the next chapter.

Chapter 2
Jumping Right In

• •

In This Chapter

▶ Developing a simple, but useful, macro

▶ Recording your actions using Excel's macro recorder

▶ Examining and testing the recorded macro

▶ Making some changes to the recorded code

• •

I'm not much of a swimmer, but I have learned that the best way to get into a cold body of water is to jump right in — no sense prolonging the agony. By wading through this chapter, you can get your feet wet immediately and start feeling better about this whole programming business. This chapter provides a step-by-step demonstration of how to develop a simple, but useful, VBA macro.

What You'll Be Doing

In this example, you create a useful macro that converts selected formulas to their current values. Sure, you can do this without a macro, but it's a multistep procedure.

To convert a range of formulas to values, you normally complete the following steps:

1. **Select the range that contains the formulas to be converted.**

2. **Copy the range to the Clipboard.**

3. **Choose Edit⇨Paste Special.**

4. **Select the Values option button in the Paste Special dialog box, which is shown in Figure 2-1.**

5. **Click OK.**

6. **Press Esc to clear the cut-copy display indicator (the moving border) in the worksheet.**

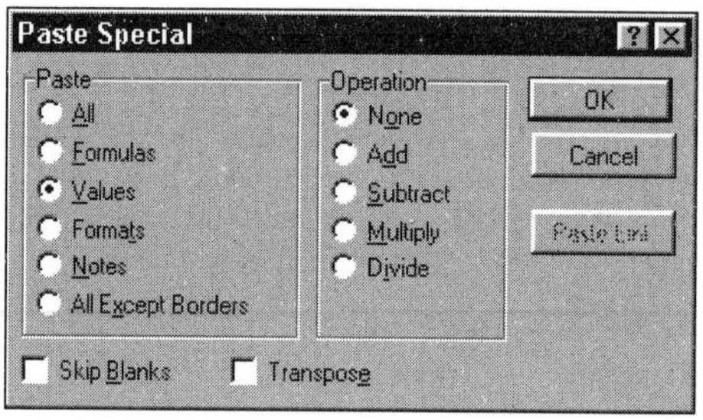

Figure 2-1: The Paste Special dialog box.

The macro you create in this chapter accomplishes all these steps in a single action. As detailed in the following sections, you start by recording your actions as you go through these steps. Then, you test the macro to see if it works. Finally, you edit the macro to add some finishing touches. Ready?

First Steps

To prepare for this lesson, start Excel and open a new workbook. This gives you something to work with — and a place to store the finished macro.

Next, enter some values and formulas into the worksheet. It doesn't matter what you enter. This step simply provides something to work with. Figure 2-2 shows how my workbook looks at this point. The bottom row and the rightmost column contain formulas.

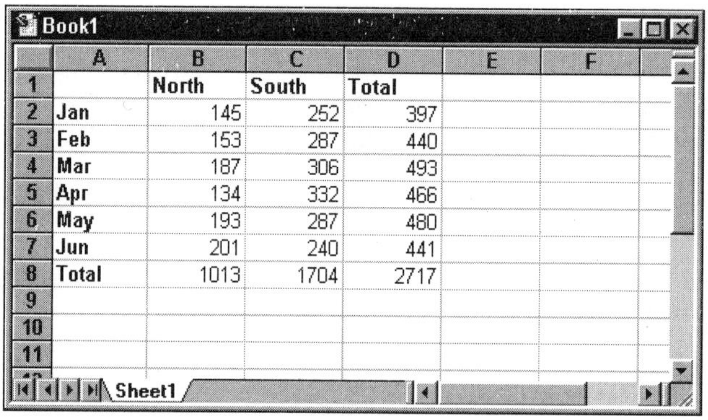

	A	B	C	D	E	F
1		North	South	Total		
2	Jan	145	252	397		
3	Feb	153	287	440		
4	Mar	187	306	493		
5	Apr	134	332	466		
6	May	193	287	480		
7	Jun	201	240	441		
8	Total	1013	1704	2717		
9						
10						
11						

Figure 2-2: Sample values and formulas in a worksheet.

Recording the Macro

Okay, here comes the hands-on part. Follow these instructions carefully:

1. **Choose Tools⇨Record Macro.**

   As shown in Figure 2-3, the menu expands to show more options.

2. **Click the Use Relative References submenu.**

   This tells Excel that you want to record the macro using relative (rather than absolute) references. As I explain more fully in Chapter 6, this makes a more general-purpose macro.

3. **Select the range of cells that contains your formulas.**

   The selection can include both values and formulas. In my case, I chose the range A1:D8.

4. **Choose Tools⇨Record Macro⇨Record New Macro.**

   This displays the Record New Macro dialog box, shown in Figure 2-4.

5. **Click the Options button in the Record New Macro dialog box.**

   This expands the dialog to show additional controls.

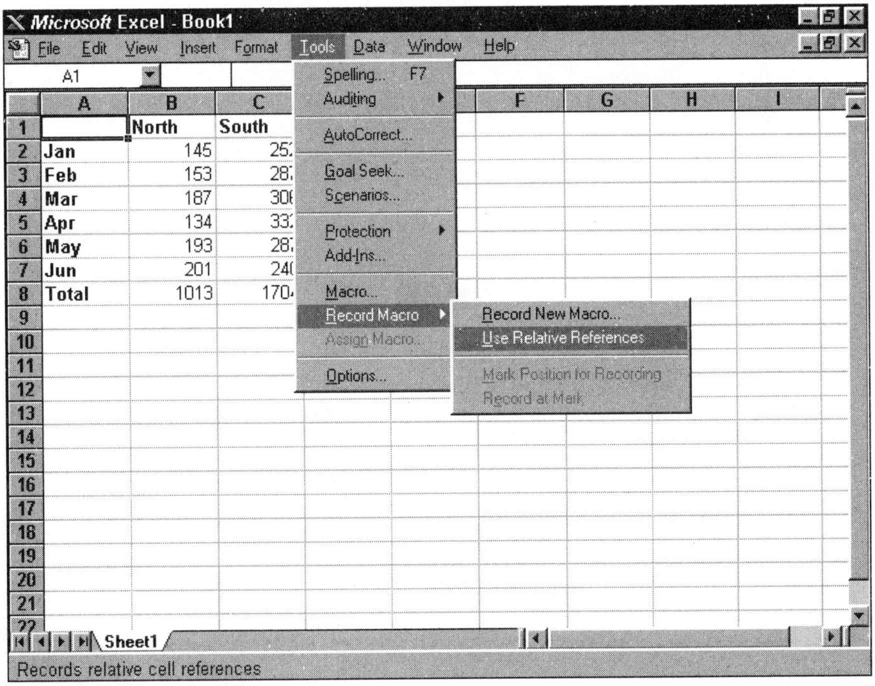

Figure 2-3:
When checked, this option tells Excel to record your actions using relative references.

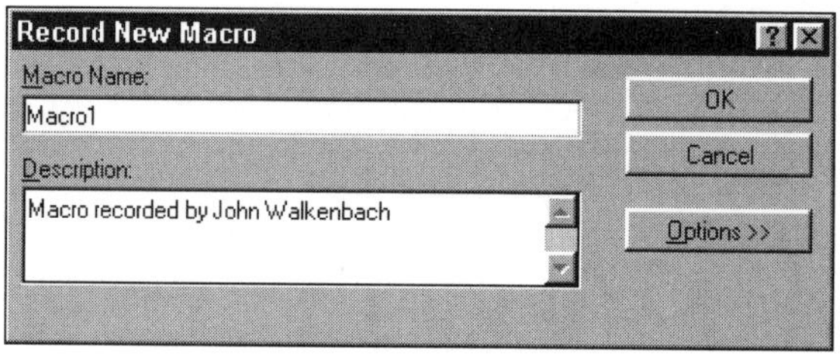

Figure 2-4:
The Record
New Macro
dialog box.

6. **Enter the changes necessary to make the dialog match the example shown in Figure 2-5.**

   Specifically, change the name of the macro to **ConvertFormulas**. Then, click the Menu Item on Tools Menu check box, and enter **Convert Formulas to Values**. Finally, make sure the Visual Basic option is selected.

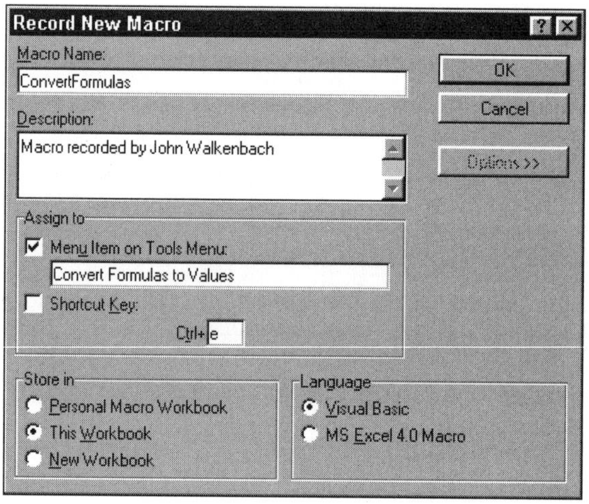

Figure 2-5:
The Record
New Macro
dialog box,
expanded to
show
options.

7. **Click OK.**

   This closes the dialog box and turns on Excel's macro recorder. From this point on, Excel monitors everything you do and converts it into VBA code. Notice that a single-button toolbar appears and the status bar displays *Recording*.

8. **Choose Edit⇨Copy (or, press Ctrl+C) to copy the selected range of cells to the Clipboard.**

9. **Choose Edit⇨Paste Special.**

   Excel displays the Paste Special dialog box.

10. **In the Paste Special dialog, click the Values option.**

11. **Click OK to close the dialog.**

12. **Press Esc to cancel Excel's cut-copy mode display.**

    This removes the moving border from the selection, which is the program's way of telling you that data is ready to be copied.

13. **Choose Tools⇨Record Macro⇨Stop Recording. Or, click the Stop button on the mini-toolbar that's floating on your screen.**

    This turns off the macro recorder.

Congratulations! You just created your first Excel VBA macro. You might want to phone your mother and tell her the good news.

Testing the Macro

Now, you can try out this macro and see if it works properly. To test your macro, you need to add some more formulas to the worksheet (you wiped out the original formulas during the process of recording the macro):

1. **Enter some new formulas in the worksheet. Again, any formulas will do.**

2. **Select the range that contains the formulas.**

3. **Click the Tools menu. Notice that it now has a new menu item: Convert Formulas to Values. Choose this menu item.**

In a flash, Excel executes the macro. The macro converts all the formulas in the selected range to their current values.

If the Tools menu doesn't contain the new Convert Formulas to Values menu item, you forgot to specify this option in the Record New Macro dialog box before you started recording the macro. Although you can easily change this after the fact, I suggest that you simply start over and redo the previous steps.

Examining the Macro

So far, you've recorded a macro and tested it. You're probably wondering what it looks like.

Excel stores the recorded macro in a new sheet (officially known as a *VBA module*) named Module1. A VBA module is unlike a normal worksheet — it's more like a word processing document. A module can hold any number of macros, but in this case it holds only the single macro you recorded.

To see the macro, activate the Module1 sheet by clicking its tab. The new module is the last sheet in the workbook, so you may have to scroll the sheet tabs to find it. The code in Module1 should look like this (with a different date and name, however):

```
'
' ConvertFormula Macro
' Macro recorded 4/1/96 by John Walkenbach
'
Sub ConvertFormulas()
    Selection.Copy
    Selection.PasteSpecial Paste:=xlValues,
            Operation:=xlNone, _
        SkipBlanks:=False, Transpose:=False
    Application.CutCopyMode = False
End Sub
```

At this point, the macro probably looks like Greek to you. Don't fret. Travel a few chapters down the road, and all will be as clear as Evian.

Modifying the Macro

This macro is fairly useful and can actually save you a few seconds every time you need to convert formulas to values. However, it's also a bit dangerous. As you may have noticed, after executing this macro, you can't choose the Edit⇨Undo command. In other words, if you execute this command accidentally, you have no way to convert the values back to the original formulas.

In this section, you make a minor addition to the macro to prompt users to verify their intentions before the formula-to-value conversion takes place. Issuing such a warning isn't completely foolproof, but it's better than nothing.

Actually, you can develop macros that can be undone with the Edit⇨Undo command. However, that's a bit beyond the scope of this chapter.

You need to provide a pop-up message asking the user to confirm the macro by clicking Yes or No. Fortunately, a VBA statement lets you do this quite easily.

Working in a VBA module is much like working in a word processing document (except there's no word wrap). You can press Enter to start a new line, and the familiar editing keys work as expected.

Here's how you modify the macro to include this warning:

1. **Activate the Module1 module.**
2. **Move the cursor directly below the Sub ConvertValues() statement.**
3. **Press Enter to start a new line, then type the following VBA statements:**

```
Answer = MsgBox("Convert formulas to values?", vbYesNo)
If Answer <> vbYes Then Exit Sub
```

These new statements cause Excel to display a message box with two buttons: Yes and No. The user's button click is stored in a variable named Answer. If the Answer is not equal to Yes, Excel exits the subroutine with no further action (<> represents *not equal to*). Figure 2-6 shows this message box in action.

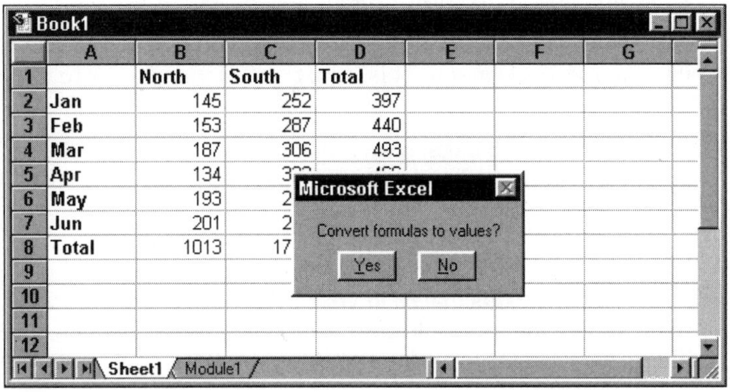

Figure 2-6: The message box displayed by the macro.

Activate a worksheet and try out the revised macro to see how it works. You may need to add some more formulas to your worksheet in order to test your macro. You'll find that clicking the No button cancels the macro, and the formulas in the selection remain intact. When you click the No button, Excel executes the *Exit Sub* part of the macro. If you click Yes, the macro continues its normal course of action.

If you find this macro useful, you should save the workbook file.

More about This Macro

By the time you finish this book, you'll completely understand how ConvertValues works, and you'll be able to develop more sophisticated macros. For now, I'll wrap up the example with a few additional points about this macro:

- ✔ For this macro to work, its workbook must be open. If you close the workbook, the macro doesn't work (and the Tools⇨Convert Formulas to Values command disappears).

- ✔ As long as the workbook containing the macro is open, you can run the macro while any workbook is active. In other words, the macro's own workbook doesn't have to be active.

- ✔ The macro isn't perfect. For example, it generates an error if the selection isn't a range (for example, if you select a drawing object). In Chapter 14, I show you how to fix this problem.

- ✔ Before you started recording the macro, you assigned it to a new menu item on the Tools menu. This is just one of many ways to execute the macro.

- ✔ You could enter this macro manually rather than recording it. To do so, you need a good understanding of VBA (be patient, you'll get there).

- ✔ The two statements you added after the fact are examples of VBA statements that you *cannot* record.

- ✔ You could store this macro in your Personal Macro Workbook. If you were to do so, the macro would be available automatically whenever you start Excel. See Chapter 6 for details about your Personal Macro Workbook.

- ✔ You could also convert the workbook to an add-in file (more about this in Chapter 22).

Learning More

You've now been initiated into the world of Excel programming (sorry, there's no secret handshake). I hope this chapter helps you realize that Excel programming is something you can actually do — and even live to tell about it. Keep reading. Subsequent chapters almost certainly answer any questions you have, and you'll soon understand exactly what you did in this hands-on session.

Part II

How VBA Works
with Excel

"WE SHOULD HAVE THIS FIXED IN VERSION 2."

In this part. . .

The next four chapters provide the necessary foundation for learning the ins and outs of VBA. You learn about modules (the sheets that store your VBA code), and I introduce you to Excel's object model (something you don't want to miss). You also learn the difference between subroutines and functions, and you get a crash course in Excel's macro recorder.

Chapter 3

All about VBA Modules

*A*s an experienced Excel user, you know a good deal about workbooks. For example, you undoubtedly know that a workbook can hold any number of worksheets and chart sheets. Two other types of sheets — both quite important to readers of this book — can also appear in a workbook:

✔ VBA module sheets

✔ Dialog sheets

This chapter deals with VBA module sheets — sheets that hold the VBA code you record or write. I cover dialog sheets in Part IV, so stay tuned.

Of Workbooks and Sheets

When you open a new workbook, it starts out with a set number of worksheets. The exact number depends on the setting in the General tab of the Options dialog box. By the way, I strongly suggest that you set this value to 1 (why Microsoft chose 16 worksheets as the default is a mystery to me).

Adding a new sheet to a workbook

You can add sheets of any type by using the Insert menu. For example, to insert a VBA module sheet before the current sheet, choose Insert⇨Macro⇨Module.

When you begin recording a macro, Excel automatically adds a new module sheet for you, so there's no need to add one manually.

Figure 3-1 shows an empty VBA module just begging for some code. A module sheet looks more like a word processing document than something you'd expect to see in a spreadsheet. Unlike a word processing document, however, a VBA module doesn't have word wrap and it doesn't support any type of formatting. It has a single purpose in life: to hold VBA code.

Figure 3-1:
An empty
VBA module
(looks rather
lonely,
doesn't it?).

You may have noticed another option on the Insert⇨Macro menu: MS Excel 4 Macro Sheet. Don't bother with this. You use these sheets for the obsolete XLM macro system (not covered in this book).

Deleting a sheet

If you determine that you no longer need a sheet (a VBA module, or whatever), you can delete it. Right-click the sheet tab, and then choose Delete from the shortcut menu. Excel asks you to confirm your intentions because you can't undo this action.

Moving or copying a sheet

To move a sheet to a different location in the workbook, click its tab and drag the sheet to its new home. You can even use this technique to move a sheet to a different workbook.

To copy a sheet, press Ctrl and click and drag the sheet's tab to another location (in the same workbook, or in a different workbook). You get an exact copy of the original.

What Goes in a Module Sheet?

In general, a VBA module can hold three types of code:

- ✔ **Subroutine procedures:** A *subroutine* is a set of instructions that performs some action.

- ✔ **Function procedures:** A *function* is a set of instructions that returns a single value (similar in concept to a worksheet function such as SUM).

- ✔ **Declarations:** A *declaration* is a statement of information that you provide to VBA. For example, you can declare the data type for variables you plan to use.

A single VBA module can store any number of subroutines, functions, and declarations. How you organize a VBA module is completely up to you. Some people prefer to keep all their VBA code for an application in a single VBA module; others like to split up the code into several different modules. It's a personal choice.

If you're confused, don't worry. Subsequent chapters clarify all this stuff. For now, just remember that VBA code is broken down into subroutines, functions, and declarations.

Getting Code into a Module

An empty VBA module is like the fake food you see in the windows of some Chinese restaurants; it looks good, but it doesn't really do much for you. Before you can do anything meaningful, you must have some VBA code in the VBA module. You can get VBA code into a VBA module in three ways:

- ✔ By entering the code directly
- ✔ By using Excel's macro recorder to record your actions and convert them to code
- ✔ By copying the code from another module

Entering code directly

Sometimes, the best route is the most direct one. Entering code directly involves . . . well, entering the code directly. In other words, you type the code by using your keyboard. Entering and editing text in a VBA module works pretty much as you might expect. You can select text and copy it or cut it, paste it to another location, and so on.

Pause for a terminology break

I need to digress for a moment to discuss terminology. Throughout this book, I use the terms *subroutine*, *routine*, *procedure*, and *macro*. You may be a bit confused by these terms (I don't blame you). Programming folks usually use the word *procedure* to describe an automated task. Technically, a procedure can be a subroutine or a function — both of which are sometimes called *routines*. I use all these terms pretty much interchangeably. As detailed in the following chapters, however, there is an important difference between subroutines and functions. For now, don't worry about the terminology. Just try to understand the concepts.

You can use the Tab key to indent some of the lines. This isn't really necessary, but it's a good habit to acquire, because it makes your code easier to read. As you study the code I present in this book, you'll understand why this is helpful.

A single line of VBA code can be as long as you like. However, you may want to use the line continuation character to break up lengthy lines of code. To continue a single line of code (also known as a *statement*) from one line to the next, end the first line with a space followed by an underscore (_). Then, continue the statement on the next line. Here's an example of a single VBA statement split into three lines of code:

```
Selection.Sort Key1:=Range("A1"), _
    Order1:=xlAscending, Header:=xlGuess, _
    Orientation:=xlTopToBottom
```

This statement would perform exactly the same way if it were entered in a single line (with no line continuation characters).

Excel limits you to using no more than nine line continuation characters in a single statement. If you try to use more, you'll be rudely interrupted with a message from the big guy.

A VBA module has multiple levels of undo and redo (a completely undocumented feature). Therefore, if you delete a statement that you shouldn't have, you can press Ctrl+Z repeatedly until the statement comes back. After undoing, you can press F4 to redo the changes you've undone. (This feature is more complicated to describe than it is to use. I recommend that you play around with this feature until you understand how it works.)

Ready to enter some real, live code? Try this. Add a new VBA module sheet to your workbook, and then enter the following statements into the module:

```
Sub GuessName()
    Msg = "Is your name " & Application.UserName & "?"
    Ans = MsgBox(Msg, vbYesNo)
    If Ans = vbNo Then MsgBox "Oh, never mind."
    If Ans = vbYes Then MsgBox "I must be clairvoyant!"
End Sub
```

You might notice that Excel makes some adjustments to the text you enter. For example, if you omit the space before or after an equal sign, Excel inserts the space for you. Also, Excel changes the color of some text and capitalizes some words. This is all perfectly normal, so don't be alarmed. It's just the program's way of keeping things neat and readable.

To execute this subroutine, make sure the cursor is located anywhere within the text you typed, and then press F5 (which is a shortcut for the Run⇨Start command). If you entered the code correctly, Excel executes the subroutine, and you can respond to the simple dialog box shown in Figure 3-2.

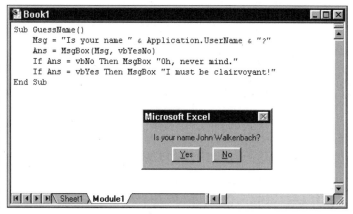

Figure 3-2:
The
message
box
displayed
by the
GuessName
subroutine.

At this point, it's not important that you understand how this code works; that will become clear as you progress through this book.

You've just written a VBA subroutine, also known as a macro. When you press F5, Excel quickly compiles the code and executes it. In other words, Excel evaluates each statement and does what you told it to do (don't let this newfound power go to your head). You can execute this macro any number of times — although it tends to lose its appeal after a few dozen times.

For the record, this simple subroutine uses the following concepts, all of which are covered later in this book:

- Defining a subroutine procedure (the first line)
- Assigning a value to a variable (Msg and Ans)
- Concatenating (joining) a string (using the & operator)
- Using a built-in VBA function (MsgBox)
- Using built-in VBA constants (vbYesNo, vbNo, and vbYes)
- Using an If. . .Then construct (twice)
- Ending a subroutine procedure (the last line)

Not bad for a beginner, eh?

Using the macro recorder

Another way you can get code into a VBA module is by recording your actions using Excel's macro recorder. The example in the preceding chapter introduces you to this technique.

There is absolutely no way you can record the GuessName subroutine shown in the preceding section. You can only record things that you can do directly in Excel. Displaying a message box is not in Excel's normal repertoire (it's a VBA thing). The macro recorder is useful, but for most macros you have to enter at least *some* code manually.

Here's a step-by-step example that shows you how to record a macro that simply turns off the cell gridlines in a worksheet. If you want to try this example, start with a new, blank workbook, and follow these steps:

1. **Activate a worksheet in the workbook (any worksheet will do).**

2. **Choose Tools⇨Record Macro⇨Record New Macro.**

   Excel displays its Record New Macro dialog box.

3. **Just click OK to accept the defaults.**

   Excel automatically inserts a new VBA module named Module1. From this point on, Excel converts your actions into VBA code. While recording, Excel displays the word *Recording* in the status bar. Excel also displays a miniature floating toolbar that contains a single toolbar button, Stop Macro.

4. **Choose Tools⇨Options.**

   Excel displays its Options dialog box.

5. **Click the View tab, remove the check mark from the Gridlines check box, and click OK to close the dialog box.**

6. **Click the Stop Macro button on the miniature toolbar.**

Excel stops recording your actions.

To take a look at the macro, activate the Module1 sheet. Here's the code generated by recording your actions:

```
Sub Macro1()
    ActiveWindow.DisplayGridlines = False
End Sub
```

To try out this macro, activate a worksheet that has gridlines displayed. Then, choose Tools⟹Macro. Excel displays a dialog box that lists all the available macros. Select Macro1 and click the Run button. Excel executes the macro, and the gridlines magically disappear. Are you beginning to see how this macro business can be fun?

Of course, you can execute any number of commands and perform any number of actions while the macro recorder is running. Excel dutifully translates your mouse movements and keystrokes to VBA code. It works similarly to a tape recorder, but Excel never runs out of tape.

The preceding macro isn't really all that useful. To make it useful, change the statement to

```
ActiveWindow.DisplayGridlines = Not
    ActiveWindow.DisplayGridlines
```

This makes the macro serve as a toggle. If gridlines are displayed, the macro turns them off. If gridlines are not displayed, the macro turns them on. Oops, I'm getting ahead of myself — sorry, but I couldn't resist that simple modification.

Copying VBA code

The final method for getting code into a VBA module is to copy it from another module. For example, a subroutine or function you write for one project might also be useful in another project. Rather than waste time reentering the code, you can simply open the workbook, activate the module, and use the normal Clipboard copy and paste procedures to copy it into your current VBA module. After pasting the code into the current VBA module, you can modify the code if necessary.

Customizing the VBA Environment

If you're serious about becoming an Excel programmer, you'll be spending a lot of time with VBA modules on your screen. To help you make things as comfortable as possible (no, please keep your shoes on), Excel provides a few VBA module customization options.

When you choose Tools➪Options, Excel displays the Options dialog box. As you know, this dialog box has 10 sections; you access each one by clicking a tab. As a VBA maven, you need to know about two tabs: Module General and Module Format.

Using the Module General tab

Figure 3-3 shows the options available under the Module General tab. Some of these settings can have a significant effect on what happens when you write or execute VBA code. I discuss these options in the following sections, and you can decide how you want to set them.

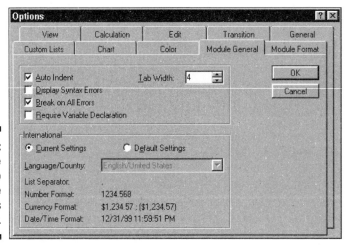

Figure 3-3:
The Module
General tab
of the
Options
dialog box.

Auto Indent

The Auto Indent setting determines whether Excel automatically indents each new line of code by the same amount as the previous line. I'm big on using indentations in my code, so I keep this option on.

To indent your code, use the Tab key, not the spacebar. Also, you can *unindent* a line of code by pressing Shift+Tab.

Display Syntax Errors

The Display Syntax Errors setting determines whether Excel pops up a dialog box if it discovers a syntax error while you're entering your code. The dialog box tells roughly what the problem is. If you don't choose this setting, Excel flags syntax errors by displaying them in a different color from the rest of the code, and you don't have to deal with any dialog boxes popping up on your screen. I usually keep this setting turned off because I find the dialog boxes annoying, and I can usually figure out what's wrong with a statement. But when I was a VBA newbie, I found this assistance quite helpful.

Break on All Errors

If you turn on the Break on All Errors option, your code grinds to a screeching halt when Excel encounters an error. If you write any error-handling code (which I discuss in Chapter 12), make sure you turn off this option; otherwise, Excel ignores the error-handling code.

Require Variable Declaration

If you set the Require Variable Declaration option, Excel inserts the following statement at the beginning of each new VBA module you insert:

```
Option Explicit
```

Changing this setting affects only new modules, not existing modules. If this statement appears in your module, you must explicitly define each variable you use. As I explain in Chapter 7, you should develop this habit.

International

The International option lets you select international settings for procedures (this affects the default formats for numbers, currency, date and time, and list separator characters). Usually, you should stick with the country in which you live.

Using the Module Format tab

Figure 3-4 shows the options you access by clicking the Module Format tab of the Options dialog box. These options deal with the appearance of text in a module. Again, I describe them and let you decide how to proceed.

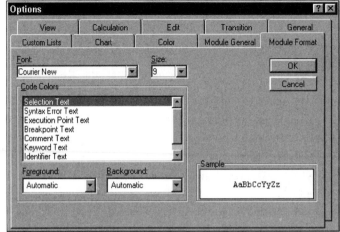

Figure 3-4:
The Module
Format tab
of the
Options
dialog box.

Font

The Font option lets you select the font that's used in your VBA modules. For best results, stick with a fixed-width font such as Courier New. In a fixed-width font, all characters are exactly the same width. This makes your code more readable because the characters align vertically.

Size

The Size setting specifies the size of the font in the VBA modules. Because you can't adjust the zoom factor of a VBA module or format the text itself, this setting is a matter of personal preference determined by your video display resolution and your eyesight.

Code Colors

The Code Colors option lets you set the text color (foreground and background) displayed for various elements of VBA code. Again, this is largely a matter of personal preference. Personally, I find the default colors to be just fine. But for a change of scenery, I occasionally play around with these settings.

Learning More

You don't need to learn a whole lot more about VBA modules. Once you start using them, they seem like old hat (trust me, I've spent far too much time in these things). In Chapter 4, I introduce you to a fundamental concept for mastering VBA: Excel's object model.

Chapter 4

Introducing Excel's Object Model

*E*veryone is familiar with the word *object*. The *American Heritage Dictionary* defines it as follows:

> **ob·ject** (òb′jĭkt, -jèkt´) *noun.* Something perceptible by one or more of the senses, especially by vision or touch; a material thing.

Well folks, forget this definition. In the world of programming, the word *object* has a different meaning. You often see it used as part of the expression *object-oriented programming* (or OOP for short). OOP is based on the idea that software consists of distinct objects, which have attributes (or properties) and can be manipulated. These objects are not material things. Rather, they exist in the form of bits and bytes.

In this chapter, I introduce you to Excel's object model. By the time you finish this chapter, you'll have a reasonably good understanding of what OOP is all about — and why you need to understand this concept in order to become a VBA programmer. After all, Excel programming really boils down to manipulating Excel's objects. It's as simple as that.

The material in this chapter may be a bit overwhelming. But please take my advice and plow through it, even if you don't fully grasp it. This important concept will make lots more sense as you progress through the book.

Excel is an Object?

You've used Excel for quite a while, but you probably never really thought of it as being an object. The more you work with VBA, the more you'll view Excel in those terms. You'll soon understand that Excel is an object, and that it contains other objects. Those objects, in turn, contain still more objects.

In other words, VBA programming involves working with an object hierarchy. At the top of this hierarchy is the Application object — in this case, Excel itself (the mother of all objects).

The Object Hierarchy

An Application object contains other objects. For example, the Excel Application object contains nine other objects:

- AddIn
- AutoCorrect
- Debug
- Dialog
- MenuBar
- Name
- Toolbar
- Window
- Workbook

You won't find the AutoCorrect and Name objects in Excel 5. These new objects are available only in Excel for Windows 95. In other words, the Excel 5 Application object contains only seven other objects.

You might find some of these objects quite strange. For example, how can AutoCorrect be an object? Good question. AutoCorrect isn't much of an object; it's more of a procedure. In some cases, the program's designers had to stretch this object business a bit. You just learn to live with such quirks.

Each object contained in the Application object can contain other objects. For example, a Workbook object can contain the following objects:

- Chart
- DialogSheet
- DocumentProperty
- Module
- Name
- RoutingSlip
- Style
- Window
- Worksheet

In turn, each of these objects can contain still *other* objects. Consider a Worksheet object (which is contained in a Workbook object — which is contained in the Application object). A Worksheet object can contain the following objects:

- DrawingObject
- Outline
- PageSetup
- PivotTable
- Range
- Scenario

Put another way, if you want to do something with a range on a worksheet, you may find it helpful to visualize that range in the following manner:

Range ➪ contained in Worksheet ➪ contained in Workbook ➪ contained in Excel

Is this beginning to make sense?

Visualizing objects

The online help system for Excel for Windows 95 diagrams the complete Excel object model (this diagram isn't available in the Excel 5 help system). To find this diagram, follow these steps:

1. **Choose Help➪Answer Wizard.**

2. **Enter** Excel Objects.

3. **Click the Search button.**

4. **Scroll down the list of topics and double-click Microsoft Excel Objects.**

Excel displays the help window shown in the accompanying figure.

At this point in your introduction to Excel programming, this diagram might add to your confusion. But one day in the not-too-distant future, something will click, and you'll actually find this diagram enlightening.

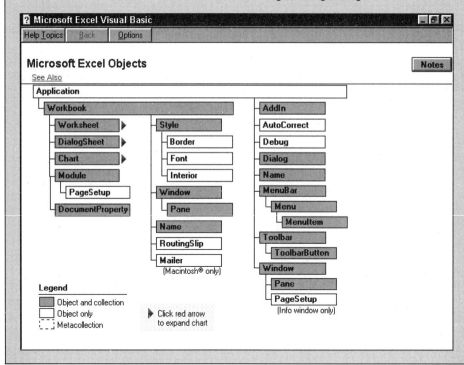

Understanding Collections

Another key concept in VBA programming is *collections*. A collection is a group of objects of the same type. And to add to the confusion, a collection is itself an object.

Here are a few examples of commonly-used collections:

- **Workbooks:** A collection of all currently open Workbook objects
- **Worksheets:** A collection of all Worksheet objects contained in a particular Workbook object
- **Charts:** A collection of all Chart objects contained in a particular Workbook object
- **Sheets:** A collection of all sheets (regardless of their type) contained in a particular Workbook object

You might notice that the names of collections are all plural — which makes sense (at least to me).

Referring to Objects

I presented the information in the preceding sections to prepare you for the next concept: how to refer to objects in your VBA code.

You can work with an entire collection of objects in one fell swoop. More often, you need to work with a specific object in a collection (such as a particular worksheet in a workbook). To reference a single object from a collection, you put the object's name or index number in parentheses after the name of the collection, like this:

```
Worksheets("Sheet1")
```

If Sheet1 is the first (or only) worksheet in the collection, you can also use the following reference:

```
Worksheets(1)
```

Another collection, called Sheets, contains all the sheets (regardless of their type) in a workbook. If Sheet1 is the first sheet in the workbook, you can reference it as:

```
Sheets(1)
```

Avoiding ambiguity

When you refer to an object that's contained in another object, you often must qualify the reference to the object by connecting object names with the dot (.) operator. Consider this example: What if you have two workbooks open and they both contain worksheets named Sheet1? To eliminate this potential ambiguity, you need to qualify the reference by adding the object's *container*, like this:

```
Workbooks("Book1").Worksheets("Sheet1")
```

To refer to a specific range (such as cell A1) on a worksheet named Sheet1 in a workbook named Book1, you can use the following expression:

```
Workbooks("Book1").Worksheets("Sheet1").Range("A1")
```

Simplifying object references

The fully-qualified reference for the previous example also includes the Application object, as follows:

```
Application.Workbooks("Book1").Worksheets("Sheet1").Range("A1")
```

However, you can omit the Application object in your references (it is assumed). If the Book1 object is the active workbook, you can even omit that object and use the following reference:

```
Worksheets("Sheet1").Range("A1")
```

And (I think you know where I'm going with this), if Sheet1 is the active worksheet, you can use an even simpler expression:

```
Range("A1")
```

Contrary to what some people may think, Excel does not have a Cell object. A cell is simply a Range object that consists of just one element.

Object Properties and Methods

You can't do anything useful by simply referring to objects (as in the examples in the preceding sections). To accomplish anything meaningful, you must do one of two things:

- ✔ Read or modify an object's *properties*.
- ✔ Specify a *method* of action to be used with an object.

With literally thousands of properties and methods available, you can easily be overwhelmed. (This book is just filled with insights, right?)

Object properties

Every object has properties. These properties are similar to attributes that describe the object. An object's properties determine how it looks, how it behaves, and whether it is visible. You can do two things with an object's properties:

- ✔ Examine the current setting for a property.
- ✔ Change the property's setting.

For example, a single-cell Range object has a property called Value. You can write VBA code to display the Value property, or you might write VBA code to set the Value property to a specific value. The following subroutine uses the built-in MsgBox function to pop up a box that displays the value in cell A1 on Sheet1:

```
Sub ShowValue()
    Contents = Worksheets("Sheet1").Range("A1").Value
    MsgBox Contents
End Sub
```

MsgBox is a useful function; you'll often use it to display results while Excel executes your VBA code. I tell you more about this function in Chapter 15.

The code in the preceding example displays the current setting of a cell's Value property. What if you want to change the setting for that property? The following subroutine changes the value displayed in cell A1 by changing the cell's Value property:

```
Sub ChangeValue()
    Worksheets("Sheet1").Range("A1").Value = 123
End Sub
```

Another slant on McObjects, McProperties, and McMethods

Here's an analogy that may help you understand the relationships between objects, properties, and methods in VBA. In this analogy, I compare Excel with a fast-food restaurant chain.

The basic unit in Excel is a workbook object. In a fast-food chain, the basic unit is an individual restaurant. In Excel, you can add workbooks and close workbooks, and all the open workbooks are part of Workbooks, the collection of workbook objects. Similarly, the management of a fast-food chain can add restaurants and close restaurants; you can view all the restaurants in the chain as a collection of Restaurant objects.

An Excel workbook is an object, but it also contains other objects such as worksheets, charts, and VBA modules. Furthermore, each object in a workbook can contain its own objects. For example, a worksheet can contain Range objects, PivotTable objects, Drawing objects, and so on.

Continuing with the analogy, a fast-food restaurant contains objects such as Kitchen, DiningArea, and ParkingLot. Furthermore, management can add or remove objects from the Restaurant object. For example, they may add a DriveupWindow object. Each of these objects can contain other objects. For example, the Kitchen object has a Stove object, a VentilationFan object, a Chef object, a Sink object, and so on.

Excel objects have properties. For example, a Range object has properties such as Value and Name, and a Rectangle object has properties such as Width and Height. Not surprisingly, objects in a fast-food restaurant also have properties. For example, the Stove object has properties such as Temperature and NumberofBurners. The VentilationFan has its own set of properties (TurnedOn, RPM, and so on).

In addition to properties, Excel objects have methods, each of which performs an operation on an object. For example, the ClearContents method erases the contents of a Range object. An object in a fast-food restaurant also has methods. You can easily envision a ChangeThermostat method for a Stove object, or a SwitchOn method for a VentilationFan object.

In Excel, methods sometimes change an object's properties. A Range object's ClearContents method changes the Range's Value property. Similarly, the ChangeThermostat method affects a Stove object's Temperature property.

With VBA, you can write or record subroutine procedures to manipulate Excel's objects. In a fast-food restaurant, the management can give orders to manipulate the objects in the restaurants ("Turn on the stove and switch the ventilation fan to high.").

I don't know about you, but I'm suddenly very hungry.

After Excel executes this subroutine, cell A1 on Sheet1 has the value 123.

Each object has its own set of properties, although some properties are common to many objects. For example, many (but not all) objects have a Visible property. Most objects also have a Name property.

Some object properties are read-only, which means you can find out the property's value, but you can't change it.

As I mentioned earlier in this chapter, collections are also objects. This means collections also have properties. For example, you can determine how many workbooks are open by accessing the Count property of the Worksheets collection. The following VBA routine pops up a message box that tells you how many workbooks are open:

```
Sub CountBooks()
    MsgBox Workbooks.Count
End Sub
```

Object methods

In addition to properties, objects have methods. A *method* is an action you perform with an object. A method can change an object's properties, or make the object do something.

This simple example uses the Calculate method on a Range object to calculate the formula in cell A1 on Sheet1:

```
Sub CalcCell()
    Worksheets("Sheet1").Range("A1").Calculate
End Sub
```

Most methods also take one or more *arguments* that further specify the action to perform. You place the arguments for a method in parentheses.

The following example activates Sheet1, and then copies cell A1 to cell B1 using the C``opy method of the Range object. In this example, the Copy method has one argument — the destination of the copy:

```
Sub CopyOne()
    Worksheets("Sheet1").Activate
    Range("A1").Copy (Range("B1"))
End Sub
```

Notice that I omit the worksheet reference in this example. I can do this because the preceding statement activates Sheet1 (using the Activate method).

As I mentioned earlier in this chapter, collections are also objects. This means collections have methods. The following statement uses the Add method for the Workbooks collection:

```
Workbooks.Add
```

As you might expect, this statement opens a new workbook. In other words, it adds a new workbook to the Workbooks collection.

Learning More

You learn more about objects, properties, and methods in the following chapters. You might also be interested in two other excellent learning tools:

- ✔ VBA's online help
- ✔ The Object Browser

Using online help

VBA's online help system describes every object, property, and method. This is an excellent resource for learning VBA.

If you're working in a VBA module and you want information about a particular object, method, or procedure, just move the cursor to the word you're interested in, and then press F1. In a few seconds, Excel displays the appropriate help topic, complete with cross-references and perhaps even an example or two.

Figure 4-1 shows a screen from the online help system — in this case, for a Rectangle object. You can click Properties to get a complete list of this object's properties, or click Methods to get a listing of its methods.

Using the Object Browser

Excel includes another tool, known as the Object Browser. As the name implies, this tool lets you browse through the objects available in Excel and VBA. (Yes, VBA has its own objects — but you can just forget about that for now.) This tool may not be of much value now, but you'll probably find it more useful as you gain experience with VBA.

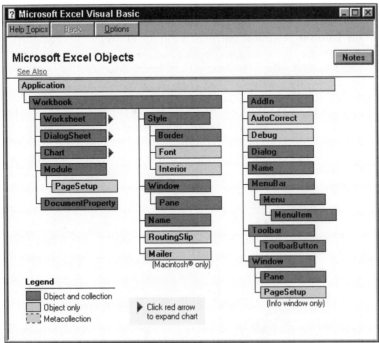

Figure 4-1:
An example
of VBA's
online help.

To access the Object Browser, press F2 when a VBA module is active (or choose
View⇨Object Browser). Excel displays a dialog box like the one shown in
Figure 4-2.

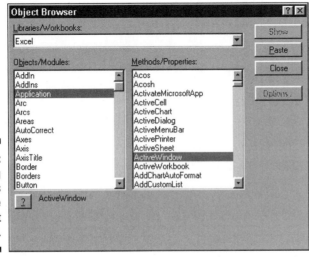

Figure 4-2:
Browsing
for objects
with the
Object
Browser.

The pull-down list labeled Libraries/Workbooks includes a list of all open workbooks, plus at least two other entries: Excel and VBA. Your selection in this list determines what Excel displays in the Objects/Modules portion of the dialog box (you'll usually choose Excel, because you're interested in Excel's objects). And, your selection in the Objects/Modules list determines what Excel displays in the Methods/Properties section.

Choosing Excel in the Libraries/Workbooks list displays a list of the program's objects and constants on the left, and the properties and methods for the selected object on the right. Unfortunately, properties and methods are intermixed, so you can't really tell what's what. The question mark button is a direct link to online help; clicking it brings up the help topic for the selected object or property.

Chapter 5

VBA Subroutines and Functions

In This Chapter

▶ Understanding the difference between subroutines and functions

▶ Executing subroutines (many ways)

▶ Executing functions (two ways)

S everal times in previous chapters, I mention the term *subroutine*, and I allude to that fact that *functions* also play a role in VBA. In this chapter, I clear up any confusion you may have about the use of subroutines and functions in VBA.

Subroutines versus Functions

The VBA code you write is known as a *procedure*. You can actually write two types of procedures:

> ✔ **A subroutine procedure:** This is a group of VBA statements that perform an action (or actions) with Excel.
>
> ✔ **A function procedure:** This is a group of VBA statements that perform a calculation and return a single value.

Most macros you write in VBA are subroutine procedures. You can think of a subroutine as being like a command: execute the subroutine and something happens (of course, exactly *what* happens depends on the subroutine's code).

A function is also a procedure, but it's quite different from a subroutine. Actually, you're already familiar with the concept of a function. Excel includes many *worksheet* functions that you use every day (well, at least every weekday). Examples include SUM, PMT, and VLOOKUP. Each of these worksheet functions takes one or more arguments, does some behind-the-scenes calculations, and returns a single value in the cell. The same goes for functions that you develop with VBA.

Looking at subroutines

Every subroutine procedure starts with the keyword Sub and ends with an End Sub statement. Here's an example:

```
Sub UpdateSalesSummary()
    [VBA code goes here]
End Sub
```

This example shows a subroutine named UpdateSalesSummary. A set of parentheses follows the subroutine name. In most cases, these parentheses are empty. However, you can pass arguments to subroutines — in which case, you list the arguments between the parentheses.

When you record a macro with Excel's macro recorder, the result is a subroutine procedure.

There are quite a few ways to execute a subroutine. More about this later.

Looking at functions

Every function procedure starts with the keyword Function, and ends with an End Function statement. Here's an example:

```
Function CubeRoot(number)
    [VBA code goes here]
End Function
```

This function, named CubeRoot, takes one argument (named *number*), which is enclosed in parentheses. In most cases, function procedures have at least one argument. When you execute the function, it returns a single value.

A few words about arguments

You're probably well aware of the normal definition of *argument* — but this term has a different meaning in the world of programming. An argument is a value that is passed to a subroutine or a function procedure. The procedure then uses that argument to do its thing.

To better understand the concept, think of the work-sheet functions you use regularly. Most take one or more arguments. For example, Excel's SQRT function takes one argument — which it uses in the calculation. The function then returns the square root of the argument. Some of Excel's worksheet functions don't take any arguments (for example, RAND and NOW). Arguments passed to VBA subroutines and functions work exactly the same way. Some procedures require arguments, and others do not.

There are only two ways to execute a function. You can execute it from another procedure, or you can use it in a worksheet formula.

You cannot use the macro recorder to record a function. You must manually enter every function.

Executing Subroutines

Although you may not know much about *developing* subroutines at this point, I'm going to jump ahead a bit and discuss how to *execute* subroutines. This is important, because a subroutine is absolutely worthless unless you know how to execute it.

By the way, *executing* a subroutine means the same thing as *running* a subroutine, or *calling* a subroutine. You can use whatever terminology you like.

You can execute a VBA subroutine in many ways — that's one reason why you can do so many useful things with subroutines. Here's an exhaustive list of the ways in which you can execute a subroutine (well, at least all the ways I could think of):

- ✔ With the Run⇨Start command (in a VBA module). Or, you can press the F5 shortcut key. Excel executes the subroutine at the cursor position

- ✔ From the Macro dialog box (which you open by choosing Tools⇨Macro). Just select the subroutine you want, and click Run

- ✔ Using the Ctrl-key shortcut assigned to the subroutine (assuming you assigned one)

- ✔ From a menu item on the Tools menu (if you assigned the subroutine to such a menu item)

- ✔ By clicking a button, or any other drawing object on a worksheet (assuming you assigned it)

- ✔ From another subroutine you write

- ✔ From a Toolbar button (see Chapter 20)

- ✔ From a custom menu you develop (see Chapter 19)

- ✔ Automatically, when you open or close a workbook (see Chapter 11)

- ✔ When an *event* occurs. As detailed in Chapter 11, these include saving the workbook and activating a sheet

- ✔ From the Debug window, which is a special window that helps you track down errors (see Chapter 13)

Naming subroutines and functions

Like humans and pets, every subroutine and function procedure must have a name. When naming subroutines and functions, you must follow a few rules:

✔ You can use letters, numbers, and some punctuation characters, but the first character must be a letter.

✔ The name cannot look like a cell reference. For example, if you try to name a subroutine AC45, Excel complains because that name resembles a cell address.

✔ You cannot use any spaces or periods in the name.

✔ VBA does not distinguish between upper- and lowercase letters.

✔ You cannot embed any of the following characters in a name: #, $, %, &, or !.

✔ Names can be no longer than 254 characters. (Of course, you would never make a procedure name this long.)

✔ You can't use any of VBA's numerous reserved words. If you use a reserved word, Excel displays the following cryptic error message: `Expected: Identifier without type suffix`.

Ideally, a procedure's name should describe the routine's purpose. A good rule of thumb is to create a name by combining a verb and a noun — for example: ProcessData, PrintReport, Sort_Array, or CheckFilename.

Some programmers prefer using sentence-like names that provide a complete description of the subroutine. Examples include WriteReportToTextFile or something like Get_Print_Options_and_Print_Report. The use of such lengthy names has its pros and cons. On the one hand, such names are descriptive and unambiguous. On the other hand, they are difficult to type.

Everyone develops a naming style, but the main objectives should be to make the names descriptive and to avoid meaningless names such as DoIt, Update, and Fix.

I demonstrate some of these techniques in the following sections. Before I can do that, you need to enter the following subroutine into a VBA module:

```
Sub ShowSquareRoot()
    Num = InputBox("Enter a positive number")
    MsgBox Num ^ 0.5 & " is the square root."
End Sub
```

This simple subroutine asks the user for a number, and then displays the square root of that number in a message box. Figures 5-1 and 5-2 show what happens when you execute this subroutine.

By the way, ShowSquareRoot is not an example of a *good* macro. It doesn't check for errors, so you can easily make it fail (try clicking the Cancel button to see what I mean).

Figure 5-1:
Using VBA's
built-in
InputBox
function to
get a
number.

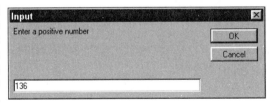

Figure 5-2:
Displaying
the square
root of a
number by
using the
MsgBox
function.

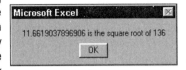

Executing the subroutine directly

The quickest way you can execute this subroutine is to do so directly from the VBA module in which you defined it. Move the cursor anywhere within the subroutine, and press F5 (or choose Run⇨Start). Respond to the subroutine's request, and click OK. The subroutine displays the square root of the number you entered.

You can't use this technique with a subroutine that uses any arguments because you have no way to pass the arguments to the subroutine.

Executing the subroutine from the Macro dialog box

Next, choose Tools⇨Macro. Excel displays the dialog box shown in Figure 5-3. Select the macro and click Run (or just double-click the macro's name in the list box).

The advantage of using the Macro dialog box is that you can execute the macro regardless of which sheet is active (the Tools⇨Macro command appears on all the menu bars).

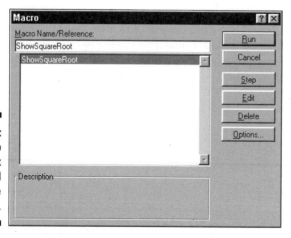

Figure 5-3:
The Macro
dialog box
lists all
available
subroutines.

Assigning a shortcut key

Before you can execute this macro by pressing a key combination, you have to
set up the shortcut. Specifically, you must assign a shortcut key to the macro.

Choose Tools⇨Macro and select the macro name in the list box. Then, click the
Options button. Excel displays the dialog box shown in Figure 5-4.

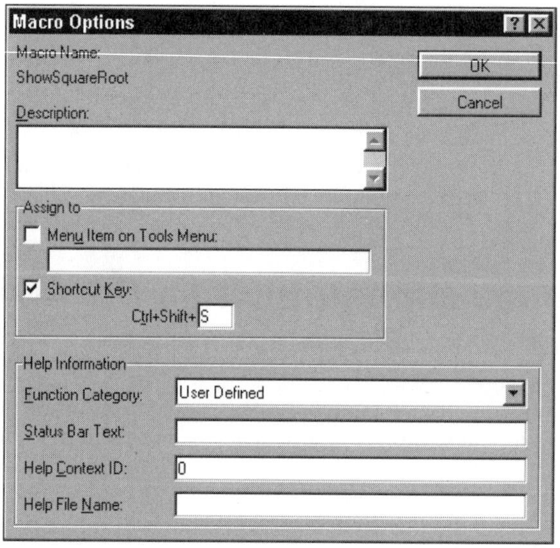

Figure 5-4:
The Macro
Options
dialog box
lets you
choose
options for
your
macros.

Click the check box labeled Shortcut Key and enter a letter in the box labeled Ctrl. This corresponds to the key combination you want to use for executing the macro. For example, if you enter the letter *s*, you can then execute the macro by pressing Ctrl+S. If you enter an uppercase letter, you need to add the Shift key to the key combination. For example, if you enter *S* (uppercase), you can execute the macro by pressing Ctrl+Shift+S. Click OK and then click Close to close the Macro dialog box.

The shortcut keys you assign to macros override the program's built-in shortcut keys. For example, if you assign Ctrl+S to a macro, you can't use this shortcut key to save your workbook.

Assigning a macro to a Tools menu item

You can create another means for executing a macro by adding the macro to the Tools menu as a new menu item. To do this, choose Tools⇨Macro, and select the macro name in the list box. Then, click the Options button. Excel displays the Macro Options dialog box.

Click the check box labeled Menu Item on Tools Menu and enter the text you want to appear in the menu. For this example, enter **Calculate Square Root** as the name of the new menu item. Click OK and then click Close to dismiss the Macro dialog.

After adding the new menu item, click the Tools menu. The new menu item appears at the bottom of the menu. Click the menu item, and the macro does its thing.

To underline one of the letters in the menu item, (just like an official Excel menu item), precede the letter with an ampersand. For example, if you want the menu item to read Calculate Square Root (with the *C* underlined), enter **&Calculate Square Root**. After doing so, you can execute the macro by pressing Alt+T and then C.

If you *really* want it to look like an official Excel menu item, add a description of the macro in the text box labeled Status Bar Text. Then, when you move the mouse pointer over the menu item, Excel displays the descriptive text in the status bar.

Executing the macro from a button

You can create still another means for executing the macro by assigning the macro to a button (or any other drawing object, for that matter). To try this, activate a worksheet, and then add a button from the Drawing toolbar (click the toolbar button named Create Button).

If the Drawing toolbar is not visible, display it by choosing View⇨Toolbars.

After you add the button, Excel jumps right in and displays the Assign Macro dialog box shown in Figure 5-5. Select the macro you want to assign to the button, and then click OK.

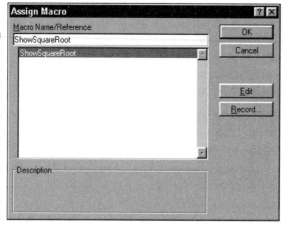

Figure 5-5:
When you add a button to a worksheet, Excel automatically displays the Assign Macro dialog box.

You can also assign a macro to any other drawing object — however, Excel doesn't display the Assign Macro dialog for you. Instead, you need to right-click the object, and then choose Assign Macro from its shortcut menu.

Executing the macro from another subroutine

As I mentioned earlier in this chapter, you can also execute a subroutine from another subroutine. If you want to give this a try, activate the VBA module that holds the ShowSquareRoot routine, and then enter this new subroutine (either above or below ShowSquareRoot — it makes no difference):

```
Sub NewSub()
    Call ShowSquareRoot
End Sub
```

Now, execute the NewSub macro. Notice that this subroutine simply executes the ShowSquareRoot subroutine.

By the way, the keyword *Call* is optional. The statement could consist of only the subroutine's name. However, I find that using the Call keyword makes things clearer.

Executing Functions

Functions, unlike subroutines, can be executed in only two ways:

✔ By calling the function from another subroutine or function

✔ By using the function in a worksheet formula

Here's a simple function you can try. Enter this function into a VBA module:

```
Function Squared(number)
    Squared = number * number
End Function
```

This function is pretty wimpy — it merely squares the number passed to it as its argument.

Calling the function from a subroutine

Because you can't execute this function directly, you must call it from another procedure. Enter the following simple procedure:

```
Sub CallerSub()
    MsgBox Squared(25)
End Sub
```

When you execute this procedure (using any of the methods I describe earlier in this chapter), Excel displays a message box like the one shown in Figure 5-6. It's pretty easy to see what's going on. The MsgBox statement refers to a custom function (Squared), and passes an argument (the number in parentheses) to this function. The Squared function computes the answer and returns it to the MsgBox statement. The MsgBox statement then displays the result. Try changing the argument that's passed, and run the CallerSub macro again. You'll see that it works just like it should.

Calling a function from a worksheet formula

Now, it's time to call this custom VBA function from a worksheet formula. Activate a worksheet in the same workbook that holds the Squared function definition. Then, enter the following formula into any cell:

```
=Squared(45)
```

The cell displays 2025, which is indeed 45 squared.

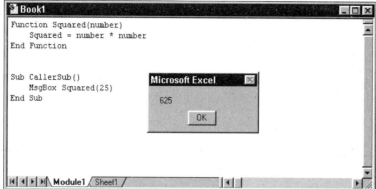

Figure 5-6:
This message box displays the result obtained by calling a custom function.

As you might expect, you can use a cell reference as the argument for the Squared function. For example, if cell A1 contains a value, you can enter **=Squared(A1)**. In this case, the function returns the number obtained by squaring the value in A1.

You can use this function any number of times in the worksheet. And, this function even appears in the Function Wizard. Click the Function Wizard toolbar button, and scroll down to the User Defined category. As shown in Figure 5-7, the Function Wizard lists your very own function.

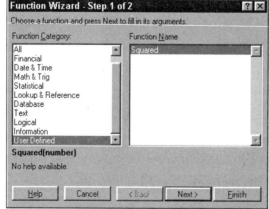

Figure 5-7:
The Squared function appears in the Function Wizard.

If you want the Function Wizard to display a description of the function, choose Tools⇨Macro. Excel displays the Macro dialog box, but Squared doesn't appear in the list. That's because Squared is a function, and this list shows only subroutines. Don't fret. Simply type the word **Squared**, and then click the Options button. Enter a description of the function in the box labeled Description. Close the Options dialog, and then close the Macro dialog. This descriptive text now appears in the Function Wizard dialog box.

Because custom worksheet functions are so useful, I devote an entire chapter to this topic (see Chapter 21).

Learning More

By now, things may be starting to come together for you. (I wish I had this book when *I* was starting out). You've learned lots about subroutines and functions. You still have a lot to learn, but the finer points come later.

In the next chapter, you start creating macros. Chapter 6 discusses the ins and outs of developing macros using Excel's macro recorder.

Chapter 6
Using the Excel Macro Recorder

In This Chapter

▶ Recording your actions by using the built-in Excel macro recorder

▶ Understanding the types of macros you can record

▶ Setting the appropriate options for macro recording

*Y*ou now know that you can use two methods for developing a subroutine macro:

  ✔ Recording it, using Excel's macro recorder

  ✔ Writing it (knowledge of VBA required)

This chapter deals with the ins and outs of using the Excel macro recorder. Although recording a macro isn't always the best approach, it *is* an excellent learning tool.

Is It Live, or Is It VBA?

Recording a macro is sort of like using a tape recorder. Turn it on, do your thing, and then turn if off when you're finished. However, this analogy only goes so far. Table 6-1 compares tape recording with macro recording.

Recording Basics

You take the following basic steps when you record a macro (I describe these steps in more detail later in this chapter):

1. **Think about what you want the macro to do.**

2. **Get things set up properly.**

   This step determines how well your macro works.

Table 6-1	Tape Recording versus Macro Recording	
	Tape Recorder	*The Excel Macro Recorder*
What equipment is required?	A tape recorder and a microphone	A computer and a copy of Excel
What is recorded?	Sounds	Actions taken in Excel
Where is the recording stored?	On magnetic tape	In a VBA module
How do you play it back?	Rewind the tape and press Play	Choose Tools⇨Macro (or any of various other methods)
Can you edit the recording?	Yes, if you have the proper equipment	Yes, if you know what you're doing
Can you copy the recording?	Yes, if you have a second tape recorder	Yes (no additional equipment required)
Is the recording accurate?	Depends on the situation and the quality of the equipment	Depends on how you set things up
What if you make a mistake?	Rerecord the tape (or, edit it if possible)	Rerecord the macro (or, edit it if possible)
Can you view the recording?	No, it's just a bunch of magnetic impulses	Yes, by activating a VBA module
Can you make money with the recording?	Yes, if it's good (editing usually required)	Yes, but you need to do a lot of editing first

3. **Determine whether you want the recording to be relative or absolute.**

4. **Choose Tools⇨Record Macro⇨Record New Macro.**

   Excel displays its Record New Macro dialog box.

5. **Click the Options button, and enter the settings for the macro.**

   This step is optional.

6. **Click OK in the Record New Macro dialog box.**

   If the workbook doesn't have a module, Excel automatically inserts one named Module1. From this point on, Excel converts your actions into VBA code. Excel also displays a miniature floating toolbar which contains a single toolbar button: Stop Macro.

7. **Perform the actions you want to record, using the mouse or the keyboard.**

8. **When you're finished, click the Stop Macro button on the miniature toolbar (or, you can choose Tools⇨Record Macro⇨Stop Recording).**

   Excel stops recording your actions.

9. Test the macro to make sure it works correctly.

The Visual Basic toolbar contains several useful buttons. At this point, you may find the Record Macro, Stop Macro, and Run Macro buttons useful.

Types of Macros Appropriate For Recording

You should only use macro recording for simple, straightforward macros. For example, you may want to record a macro that applies certain formatting to a selected range. Or, you can record a macro that sets up row and column headings for a new worksheet.

As I mention in the preceding chapter, you cannot use the macro recorder to create function procedures.

However, you may also find the macro recorder helpful for developing more complex macros. Often, I record some actions and then copy the recorded code into another, more complex macro. In most cases, you need to edit the recorded code and add some new VBA statements.

The macro recorder cannot generate code for any of the following tasks:

- ✔ Performing any type of repetitive looping
- ✔ Assigning values to variables
- ✔ Specifying data types
- ✔ Displaying pop-up messages
- ✔ Displaying custom dialog boxes

I describe these concepts later in the book. But for now, just understand that the macro recorder isn't the ultimate answer for programming Excel.

The limited capability of the macro recorder certainly doesn't diminish the importance of this tool. I make this point throughout the book: *Recording your actions is perhaps the **best** way to learn VBA*. When in doubt, try recording. Although the result may not be exactly what you want, it will probably steer you in the right direction.

Preparing to Record

Before you take the big step and turn on the macro recorder, take a minute or two to think about what you're going to do. Remember, you record a macro so that Excel can automatically repeat the actions you record.

Ultimately, the success of a recorded macro depends on five factors:

✔ How the workbook is set up while you record the macro

✔ The location of the cell pointer when you start recording

✔ Whether you use absolute or relative recording mode

✔ The accuracy of your recorded actions

✔ The context in which you play back the recorded macro

The importance of these factors becomes crystal clear in the next section, where I walk you through an example.

Relative or Absolute?

When recording your actions, Excel normally records absolute references to cells, which is the default recording mode. Very often, this is the *wrong* recording mode.

In the following sections, I demonstrate the difference between absolute and relative recording mode.

Recording in absolute mode

Follow these steps to record a simple macro in absolute mode:

1. **Choose Tools⇨Record Macro, and make sure the Use Relative References menu item does not have a check mark next to it, as shown in Figure 6-1.**

   In other words, you want to record this macro in the default, absolute mode.

2. **Start the macro recorder.**

3. **Enter** Absolute **as the name for this macro.**

4. **Activate cell B1, and enter** Jan **in that cell.**

5. **Move to cell C1, and enter** Feb.

6. **Move to cell D1, and enter** Mar.

7. **Click cell B1 to activate it again.**

8. **Stop the macro recorder.**

Excel generates the following code:

```
Sub Absolute()
    Range("B1").Select
    ActiveCell.FormulaR1C1 = "Jan"
    Range("C1").Select
    ActiveCell.FormulaR1C1 = "Feb"
    Range("D1").Select
    ActiveCell.FormulaR1C1 = "Mar"
    Range("B1").Select
End Sub
```

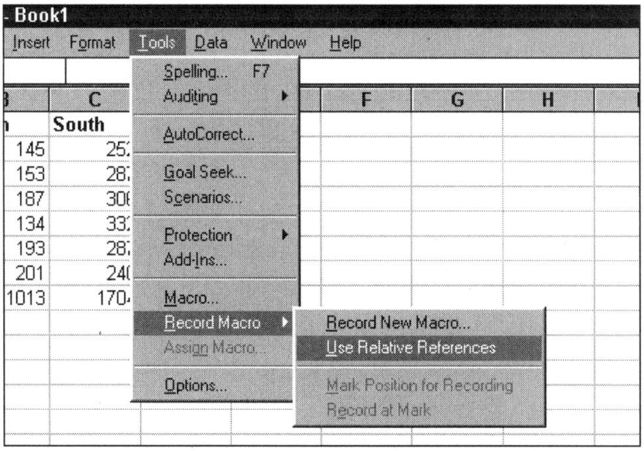

Figure 6-1:
You can set the recording mode to either absolute or relative.

When executed, this macro selects cell B1 and inserts the month names in the range B1:D1. Then the macro reactivates cell B1.

These same actions occur regardless of which cell is active when you execute the macro. A macro recorded using absolute references always produces the exact same results. In this case, the macro always enters the first three months into the range B1:D1.

Recording in relative mode

In some cases, however, you may want your recorded macro to work with cell locations in a *relative* manner. In the preceding example, you may want the macro to start entering the month names in the current cell. In this case, you need to use relative recording.

You can change the manner in which Excel records your actions by choosing Tools⇨Record Macro⇨Use Relative References. This command is a toggle — when Excel displays a check mark next to the command, your macro is recorded using relative references.

You can change the recording method at any time, even in the middle of recording.

To see how this works, perform the following steps:

1. **Choose Tools⇨Record Macro, and make sure that Excel displays a check mark next to the Use Relative References menu item.**

    In other words, Excel will record this macro in relative mode.

2. **Name this macro** Relative.

3. **Activate cell B1.**

4. **Start the macro recorder.**

5. **Enter the first three month names in B1:D1, as in the previous example.**

6. **Select cell B1.**

7. **Stop the macro recorder.**

Notice that this procedure differs slightly from the previous example. In this example, you activate the beginning cell *before* you start recording. This step is important when you record macros that use the active cell as a base.

Unlike the previous macro (which you recorded in absolute mode), this one always starts entering text in the active cell. Try it.

With the recording mode set to relative, the code Excel generates is quite different from the previous example:

```
Sub Relative()
    ActiveCell.FormulaR1C1 = "Jan"
    ActiveCell.Offset(0, 1).Range("A1").Select
    ActiveCell.FormulaR1C1 = "Feb"
    ActiveCell.Offset(0, 1).Range("A1").Select
    ActiveCell.FormulaR1C1 = "Mar"
    ActiveCell.Offset(0, -2).Range("A1").Select
End Sub
```

Notice that the code generated by this macro refers to cell A1, which may seem strange because you never used cell A1 during the recording of the macro. This unusual configuration is simply a by-product of the way the macro recorder works. (I discuss the Offset method in Chapter 8.) At this point, all you need to know is that the macro works like it should.

The important point here is that the macro recorder has two distinct modes, and you need to be aware of which mode you're using. Otherwise, you might not get the results you expected.

What Gets Recorded?

The Excel macro recorder translates your mouse and keyboard actions into valid VBA code. I could probably write several pages describing how Excel does this, but the best way to understand the process is by watching the macro recorder in action. Follow these steps:

1. **Start with a blank worksheet.**

2. **Start the macro recorder.**

   Excel inserts a new module and starts recording on that sheet.

3. **Choose Window⇨New Window.**

   Excel opens a second window for your workbook.

4. **Choose Window⇨Arrange and then select the Horizontal option.**

5. **In the top window, activate a worksheet. In the bottom window, activate the VBA module that Excel creates (Module1).**

Your screen should look something like the example in Figure 6-2.

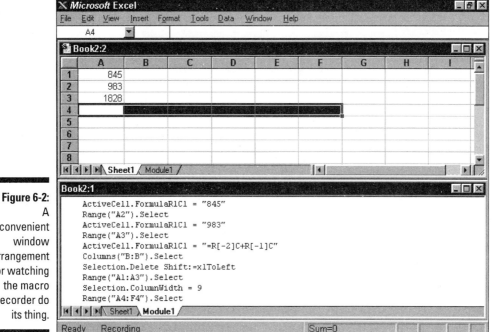

Figure 6-2:
A
convenient
window
arrangement
for watching
the macro
recorder do
its thing.

```
ActiveCell.FormulaR1C1 = "845"
Range("A2").Select
ActiveCell.FormulaR1C1 = "983"
Range("A3").Select
ActiveCell.FormulaR1C1 = "=R[-2]C+R[-1]C"
Columns("B:B").Select
Selection.Delete Shift:=xlToLeft
Range("A1:A3").Select
Selection.ColumnWidth = 9
Range("A4:F4").Select
```

Now, play around for a while: select various Excel commands, and watch the code being generated in the window that displays the VBA module. Select cells, enter data, format cells, use the menus and toolbars, create a chart, manipulate graphic objects, and so on — go crazy! I guarantee you'll be enlightened as you watch Excel spit out the code before your very eyes.

Recording Options

When recording your actions to create VBA code, you have several options. Remember that the Tools⇨Record Macro⇨Record New Macro command displays the Record New Macro dialog box before recording begins. If you click the Options button, the dialog box expands as shown in Figure 6-3.

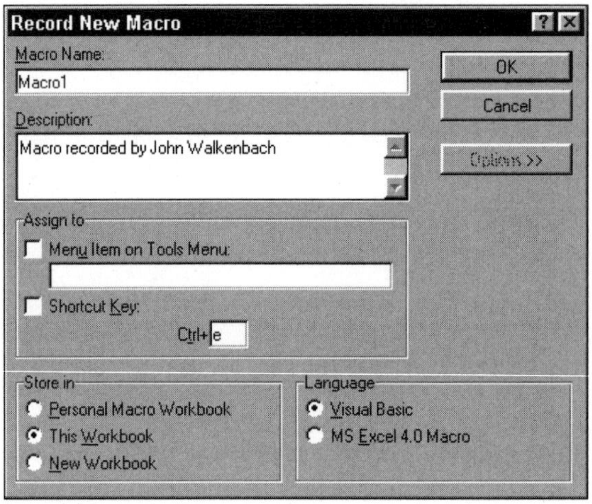

Record New Macro	? X
Macro Name:	OK
Macro1	Cancel
Description:	Options >>
Macro recorded by John Walkenbach	

Assign to
☐ Menu Item on Tools Menu:

☐ Shortcut Key:
     Ctrl+ e

Store in
○ Personal Macro Workbook
● This Workbook
○ New Workbook

Language
● Visual Basic
○ MS Excel 4.0 Macro

Figure 6-3:
The Record
New Macro
dialog box,
expanded to
display
some
recording
options.

This dialog box gives you quite a bit of control over your macro. In the following sections, I describe your options.

Macro Name

You can enter a name for the macro subroutine. By default, Excel uses the names Macro1, Macro2, and so on, for each macro you record. I usually just accept the default name and change the name of the subroutine later on.

Description

By default, Excel inserts five lines of comments (three of them blank) that list the macro name, the user's name, and the date. You can put any information you like on these lines, or nothing at all. As far as I'm concerned, the Description option is a waste of time because I always end up deleting these lines in the module.

Assign to

The Assign to option lets you assign the macro to a command on the Tools menu. For example, if you define a macro that changes the printer orientation to landscape, you can assign the macro to a command named Landscape Orientation. After you assign this macro, the Tools menu contains the new command.

Use an ampersand (&) to specify a letter to be underlined in the menu. For example, if you want to underline the *L* in Landscape Orientation, enter the menu item as **&Landscape Orientation**.

You can also assign a shortcut key to the macro. For example, you can assign Ctrl+L to run your landscape macro.

You can add or change either of these items — the Tools menu command and the shortcut key — at any time, so you don't need to set these options when recording a macro.

Store in

The Store in option tells Excel where to store the macro. By default, Excel puts the recorded macro in a module in the active workbook. If you prefer, you can record it in a new workbook (Excel opens a blank workbook) or in your Personal Macro Workbook.

Your Personal Macro Workbook

If you create some VBA macros that you find particularly useful, you may want to store these routines in your Personal Macro Workbook. Excel stores this workbook (PERSONAL.XLS) in the EXCEL\STARTUP directory. Whenever you start Excel, this workbook is loaded. It's a hidden workbook, so it's out of your way. When you record a macro, one of your options is to record it to your Personal Macro Workbook.

To examine or add macros to your Personal Macro Workbook, choose Window⇨Unhide.

Language

You can choose either VBA or XLM. If you choose XLM, this book won't do you any good.

Recording at a Particular Location

Normally, you use the Tools⇨Record Macro⇨Record New Macro command to create a brand new subroutine. But the macro recorder is also useful for adding new VBA code to an existing subroutine.

Excel lets you specify the exact position at which you want to start recording. Here's how you do it:

1. **In a VBA module, move the insertion point to the location in your code at which you want to begin recording.**

2. **Choose Tools⇨Record Macro⇨Mark Position for Recording.**

3. **Choose Tools⇨Record Macro⇨Record at Mark.**

4. **Perform the actions you want to record.**

5. **Stop the macro recorder.**

Excel inserts the generated code at the insertion point you specified.

You can also insert recorded code into an existing macro by recording your actions into a new subroutine and then cutting and pasting the results to the appropriate position in your existing subroutine. Personally, I find this technique much easier than marking the position at which you want to record.

Is This Thing Efficient?

You may think that recording a macro would generate some award-winning VBA code — better than you could write manually. Think again. In many cases, the recorder spits out lots of extraneous garbage — and it often generates code that's less than efficient.

Don't get me wrong. I said it before, and I'll say it again: The macro recorder is a great tool for helping you learn VBA. However, except for very simple macros, I've never actually used a recorded macro without fixing it up a bit.

To demonstrate just how inefficient the macro recorder's code can be, try this:

1. **Turn on the macro recorder.**

2. **Choose File⇨Page Setup.**

3. **Click the Page Tab in the Page Setup dialog box.**

4. **Change the page orientation to Landscape, and click OK.**

5. **Turn off the macro recorder.**

To take a look at the macro, activate the Module1 sheet. This single — and very simple — command generates the following code:

```
Sub Macro1()
    With ActiveSheet.PageSetup
        .PrintTitleRows = ""
        .PrintTitleColumns = ""
    End With
    ActiveSheet.PageSetup.PrintArea = ""
    With ActiveSheet.PageSetup
        .LeftHeader = ""
        .CenterHeader = "&A"
        .RightHeader = ""
        .LeftFooter = ""
        .CenterFooter = "Page &P"
        .RightFooter = ""
        .LeftMargin = Application.InchesToPoints(0.75)
        .RightMargin = Application.InchesToPoints(0.75)
        .TopMargin = Application.InchesToPoints(1)
        .BottomMargin = Application.InchesToPoints(1)
        .HeaderMargin = Application.InchesToPoints(0.5)
        .FooterMargin = Application.InchesToPoints(0.5)
        .PrintHeadings = False
        .PrintGridlines = False
        .PrintNotes = False
        .PrintQuality = 300

        .CenterHorizontally = False
        .CenterVertically = False
        .Orientation = xlLandscape
        .Draft = False
        .PaperSize = xlPaperLetter
        .FirstPageNumber = xlAutomatic
        .Order = xlDownThenOver
        .BlackAndWhite = False
        .Zoom = 100
    End With
End Sub
```

You may be surprised by the amount of code generated by this single command (I know I was the first time I tried something like this). Although you only changed one setting in the Page Setup dialog box, Excel generated code that reproduces *all* of the dialog's settings.

This is a good example of macro recording overkill. If you just want a macro that switches the page setup to landscape mode, you can simplify this macro considerably by deleting the extraneous code. This makes the macro easier to read. The macro also runs faster because it doesn't perform any unnecessary tasks. You can simplify this macro as follows:

```
Sub Macro1()
    With ActiveSheet.PageSetup
        .Orientation = xlLandscape
    End With
End Sub
```

I deleted all the code except the line that sets the Orientation property. Actually, you can simplify this macro even more, because you don't really need the With. . .End With construct:

```
Sub Macro1()
    ActiveSheet.PageSetup.Orientation = xlLandscape
End Sub
```

In this case, the macro changes the Orientation property of the PageSetup object on the active sheet. By the way, xlLandscape is a built-in constant which VBA provides to make things easier for you. I discuss built-in constants in Chapter 7.

Rather than record it, you could enter this macro directly into a VBA module. To do so, you have to know which objects, properties, and methods to use. Although the recorded macro isn't all that great, by recording it you learned that the PageSetup object has an Orientation property. This example shows how the macro recorder can help you learn VBA.

Learning More

This chapter pretty much sums it up when it comes to using the macro recorder. The only thing missing is experience. The more you work with the macro recorder, the more you realize that it's a great tool.

This chapter concludes Part II. In Part III, you learn everything you've always wanted to know about programming — and probably more.

Part III
Programming Concepts

The 5th Wave — By Rich Tennant

Re·al Pro·gram·mers

Real Programmers curse a lot, but only at inanimate objects.

In this part . . .

This is the part of the book that you've been waiting for all along. In the next eight chapters, you learn all the essential elements of Excel programming. And in the process, you see some illuminating examples that you can adapt to your own needs.

Chapter 7

Some Essential VBA Language Elements

● ●

In This Chapter

▶ Learning when, why, and how to use comments in your code

▶ Using variables and constants

▶ Telling VBA which type of data you're using

▶ Scoping variables

▶ Assigning information to variables

▶ Learning all about arrays

▶ Understanding why you might need to use labels in your procedures

● ●

*V*BA is a real-live programming language, and it uses elements that other programming languages use. In this chapter, I cue you in to several of these elements: comments, variables, constants, data types, arrays, and a few other goodies.

Using Comments in Your Code

A comment is the simplest type of VBA statement. VBA completely ignores comments, so they can consist of anything you want. Comments are, of course, for your own use. You can insert a comment to remind yourself why you did something, or to clarify some particularly elegant code. You should use comments liberally throughout your code to describe what the code does (which isn't always obvious by reading the code itself). Often, code that makes perfect sense today completely mystifies you tomorrow.

Mark a line of code as a comment by beginning the line with an apostrophe ('). VBA ignores any text that follows an apostrophe in a line of code. You can use a complete line for your comment or insert your comment at the end of a line of code.

The following example shows a VBA subroutine with three comments (not necessarily *good* comments):

```
Sub Comments()
'   This subroutine does nothing of value
    x = 0    'x represents nothingness
    'Display the result
    MsgBox x
End Sub
```

The *apostrophe-indicates-a-comment* rule has one exception. VBA doesn't interpret an apostrophe contained within a set of quotation marks as a comment indicator. For example, the following statement doesn't contain a comment, even though it has an apostrophe:

```
Msg = "Can't continue"
```

You can also use the Rem keyword to mark a line of code as a comment. Here's an example:

```
Rem — The next statement prompts the user for a workbook name
```

The Rem keyword is a holdover from previous versions of BASIC; VBA includes it for the sake of compatibility. Rem works only for complete lines of code. The apostrophe is the preferred method for inserting comments.

Often, you want to test a procedure without a particular statement or group of statements. Rather than delete the statements, simply turn them into comments by inserting apostrophes. VBA ignores these statements when it executes the routine. Then simply remove the apostrophes to convert the comments back to statements.

Although comments can be helpful, not all comments are created equal. For example, the following procedure uses lots of comments, but they really add nothing of value:

```
Sub BadComments()
'   Declare variables
    Dim x As Integer
    Dim y As Integer
    Dim z As Integer
'   Start the routine
    x = 100 ' Assign 100 to x
    y = 200 ' Assign 200 to y
'   Add x and y and store in z
    z = x + y
'   Show the result
    MsgBox z
End Sub
```

Everyone develops his or her own style of commenting. To be useful, however, comments must convey information that's not immediately obvious from reading the code. Otherwise, your comments just chew up bytes.

The following tips can help you make effective use of comments:

- ✔ Briefly describe the purpose of each subroutine or function you write.
- ✔ Use comments to keep track of changes you make to a procedure.
- ✔ Use a comment to indicate that you're using a function or a construct in an unusual or nonstandard manner.
- ✔ Be sure to describe the variables you use, especially if you don't use meaningful names.
- ✔ Use a comment to describe any workarounds you develop to overcome bugs in Excel.
- ✔ Get into the habit of writing comments as you develop code, rather than saving this task for a final step.

Using Variables, Constants, and Data Types

VBA's main purpose in life is to manipulate data. VBA stores the data in your computer's memory; it may or may not end up on disk. Some data resides in objects, such as worksheet ranges. Other data is stored in *variables* that you create.

Understanding variables

A variable is simply a named storage location in your computer's memory. You have lots of flexibility in naming your variables, so you should make the variable names as descriptive as possible. You can assign a value to a variable by using the equal sign operator (more about this later in the "Assignment Statements" section of this chapter).

Here are some examples of statements that use variables (the variable names are on the left side of the equal signs):

```
x = 1
InterestRate = 0.075
LoanPayoffAmount = 243089
DataEntered = False
x = x + 1
MyNum = YourNum * 1.25
UserName = "Bob Johnson"
DateStarted = #3/14/94#
```

VBA enforces a few rules regarding variable names:

- ✔ You can use letters, numbers, and some punctuation characters, but the first character must be alphabetic.
- ✔ You cannot use any spaces or periods in a variable name.
- ✔ VBA does not distinguish between upper- and lowercase letters.
- ✔ You cannot use the following characters in a variable name: #, $, %, &, or ! (see the sidebar, "Another way of data-typing variables," later in this chapter).
- ✔ Variable names can be no longer than 254 characters. Of course, you're only asking for trouble by using names as long as this.

To make variable names more readable, programmers often use mixed case (for example, InterestRate) or the underscore character (Interest_Rate).

VBA has many reserved words that you cannot use for variable names or procedure names. If you attempt to use one of these names as a variable, you get an error message. Table 7-1 lists these taboo names.

Table 7-1		VBA Reserved Words	
Abs	DefSng	LBound	ReDim
And	DefStr	Len	Rem
Any	DefVar	LenB	Resume
As	Dim	Let	Return
Boolean	Dir	Like	RSet
ByRef	Do	Line	Scale
ByVal	Double	Load	Seek
Call	Each	Local	Select
Case	Else	Lock	Set
CBool	ElseIf	Long	Sgn
CCur	Empty	Loop	Shared
CDate	End	LSet	Single
CDbl	EndIf	Me	Spc
CDecl	Eqv	Mid	Static
CInt	Erase	MidB	Stop
Circle	Error	Mod	StrComp
CLng	Exit	Name	String

Close	Fix	New	Sub
Const	For	Next	Tab
CSng	Format	Not	Then
CStr	FreeFile	Nothing	To
CurDir	Function	Null	Type
Currency	Get	Object	TypeOf
CVar	Global	On	UBound
CVDate	GoSub	Open	Unload
CVErr	GoTo	Option	Unlock
Date	If	Optional	Until
Debug	Imp	Or	Variant
Declare	In	Point	Wend
DefBool	Input	Preserve	While
DefCur	InputB	Print	Width
DefDate	Instr	Private	With
DefDbl	InstrB	Property	Write
DefInt	Int	PSet	Xor
DefLng	Integer	Public	False
DefObj	Is	Put	True

Some of these reserved words would make good variable names, but you get an error if you try to use any of them. For example, the reserved word *Name* would often make a very descriptive variable name. However, the following statements generate syntax errors:

```
Dim Name as String
Name = "Sally Jones"
```

Unfortunately, VBA doesn't provide very descriptive error messages. The first line in this example generates the following error message:

```
Expected: Shared or Identifier
```

The second statement produces the following error message:

```
Expected: Expression
```

So, if a statement produces a strange error message, check the list of reserved words.

Often, you can get around this reserved word business by using a variation on a reserved word. For example, you can use TheName or UserName as your variable name.

Learning about VBA's data types

The term *data type* refers to the manner in which a program stores data in memory — for example, as integers, real numbers, or strings. VBA makes life very easy for programmers, because it can automatically handle all the details involved in dealing with data. Not all programming languages make this task so easy. For example, some languages are *strictly typed*, which means the programmer must explicitly define the data type for every variable used.

Although VBA can take care of these details automatically, it does so at a cost (there's no free lunch). Letting VBA handle your data typing results in slower execution and inefficient use of memory. For small applications, this usually doesn't present much of a problem. But for large or complex applications, which may be slow or need to conserve every last byte of memory, you need to be on familiar terms with data types.

VBA has a wide variety of built-in data types (you can also define custom data types). Table 7-2 lists the types of data that VBA can handle.

Table 7-2	VBA's Built-in Data Types		
Data Type	*Bytes Used*	*Range of Values*	*Significant Digits*
Boolean	2	True or False	1
Integer	2	-32,768 to 32,767	5
Long	4	-2,147,483,648 to 2,147,483,647	10
Single	4	-3.402823E38 to 1.401298E45	7
Double (negative)	8	-1.79769313486232E308 to -4.94065645841247E-324	15
Double (positive)	8	4.94065645841247E-324 to 1.79769313486232E308	15
Currency	8	-922,337,203,685,477.5808 to 922,337,203,685,477.5807	19
Date	8	1/1/100 to 12/31/9999	NA
String	1/char	Varies	NA
Object	16 + 1/char	Any defined object	NA
Variant	Varies	Any data type	NA
User-defined	Varies	Varies	NA

In general, you should choose the data type that uses the smallest number of bytes, yet can still handle all the data the program assigns to it.

When VBA is working with data, execution speed depends on the number of bytes VBA must handle. The fewer bytes used by the data, the faster VBA can access and manipulate the data.

Declaring and scoping variables

You now know about variables and data types. In this section, you learn how to declare a variable as a certain data type.

If you don't declare the data type for a variable you use in a VBA routine, VBA uses the default data type: variant. Data stored as a variant acts like a chameleon; it changes type depending on what you do with it. For example, if a variable is a variant data type and contains a text string that looks like a number (such as *143*), you can use this variable for string manipulations as well as for numeric calculations. VBA automatically handles the conversion. This may seem like an easy way out, but remember that you sacrifice speed and memory when VBA handles the conversion.

Before you use variables in a procedure, you should *declare* your variables — that is, tell VBA each variable's name and data type. Declaring your variables makes your program run faster and use memory more efficiently. The default data type, variant, causes VBA to repeatedly perform time-consuming checks and reserve more memory than necessary. If VBA knows a variable's data type, it doesn't have to investigate. VBA can reserve just enough memory to store the data.

To force yourself to declare all the variables you use, include the following as the first statement in your VBA module:

```
Option Explicit
```

This statement causes your program to stop whenever VBA encounters a variable name that has not been declared. VBA displays an error message, and you must declare the variable before you can proceed.

Say that you use an undeclared variable (a variant) named CurrentRate. At some point in your routine, you insert the statement `CurentRate = .075`. This misspelled variable, which is very difficult to spot, will likely cause your routine to give incorrect results. Using the Option Explicit statement (and declaring CurrentRate as a variable) would cause Excel to generate an error message if it encountered a misspelled variation of that variable name.

To ensure that the Option Explicit statement is inserted automatically whenever you insert a new VBA module, enable the Require Variable Declaration option in the Module General tab of the Options dialog box. I highly recommend doing so.

You can see the advantages of declaring variables, but *how* do you do this? Before getting into the mechanics, I need to discuss one other topic: a variable's scope.

Remember that a workbook can have any number of VBA modules. A VBA module can also have any number of procedures (that is, subroutines and functions). A variable's *scope* determines which modules and procedures can use the variable. A variable's scope can be any of the following:

Scope	How the Scope is Declared
Procedure only	By using a Dim or a Static statement within the procedure that uses the variable
Modulewide	By using a Dim or a Static statement before the first Sub statement in a module
All procedures in all modules	By using a Public statement before the first Sub statement in a module

If you're completely confused at this point, don't despair. I discuss each of these in the following sections.

Procedure-only variables

The lowest level of scope for a variable is at the procedure level. Variables declared with this scope can be used only in the procedure in which they are declared. When the procedure ends, the variable no longer exists and Excel frees up its memory. If you execute the procedure again, the variable comes back to life, but its previous value is lost.

The most common way to declare a procedure-only variable is with a Dim statement placed between a Sub statement and an End Sub statement. You usually place Dim statements immediately after the Sub statement, before the procedure's code.

The keyword Dim is an abbreviation for Dimension — which is relevant to arrays (a topic I discuss later in this chapter). In older versions of BASIC, Dim was used to declare the size of an array. In VBA, Dim is used to declare any type of variable.

A note about the examples in this chapter

This chapter contains many examples of VBA code, usually presented in the form of simple subroutine procedures. I provide these examples to demonstrate various concepts as simply as possible. Most of these examples do not perform any particularly useful task; in fact, you can often perform the task using a different method. In other words, don't use these examples in your own work. Subsequent chapters provide many more useful code examples.

The following examples show some procedure-only variables declared by using Dim statements:

```
Sub MySub()
    Dim x As Integer
    Dim First As Long
    Dim InterestRate As Single
    Dim TodaysDate As Date
    Dim UserName As String * 20
    Dim MyValue
'    ... [The procedure's code goes here] ...
End Sub
```

Notice that the last Dim statement in the preceding example doesn't actually declare a data type; it just declares the variable itself. The result is that the variable MyValue is a variant.

By the way, you can also declare several variables with a single Dim statement, as in the following example:

```
Dim x as Integer, y as Integer, z as Integer
Dim First as Long, Last as Double
```

Unlike some languages, VBA doesn't allow you to declare a group of variables to be a particular data type by separating the variables with commas. For example, the following statement, though valid, does *not* declare all the variables as integers:

```
Dim i, j, k as Integer
```

In this example, only k is declared to be an integer; the other variables are declared variants.

If you declare a variable with procedure-only scope, other procedures in the same module can use the same variable name, but each instance of the variable is unique to its own procedure. In general, variables declared at the procedure level are the most efficient because VBA frees up the memory the variables use when the procedure ends.

Modulewide variables

Sometimes, you want a variable to be available to all procedures in a module. To make the variable available to all procedures in a module, just declare the variable *before* the module's first Sub or Function statement — that is, outside any subroutines.

Another way of data-typing variables

Like most other dialects of BASIC, VBA lets you append a character to a variable's name to indicate the data type. For example, you can declare the MyVar variable as an integer by tacking % onto its name:

```
MyVar% = 189
```

Most VBA data types have type-declaration characters. The following table shows the type-declaration characters for VBA's data types (data types not listed don't have type-declaration characters).

Data Type	Type-Declaration Character
Integer	%
Long	&
Single	!
Double	#
Currency	@
String	$

This method of data-typing variables is essentially a holdover from older versions of BASIC.

In general, it's better to declare your variables using the procedures described in this chapter.

In the following example, the Dim statement is the first statement in the module:

```
Dim CurrentValue as Integer

Sub MySub()
'    ... [Code goes here] ...
End Sub

Sub YourSub()
'    ... [Code goes here] ...
End Sub
```

Both MySub and YourSub have access to the CurrentValue variable, the value of which does not change when a procedure ends.

Public variables

If you need to make a variable available to all the procedures in all your VBA modules, declare the variable at the module level by using the Public keyword rather than the Dim keyword.

Here's an example:

```
Public CurrentRate as Long
```

The Public keyword makes the CurrentRate variable available to any procedure in the workbook, even those in other VBA modules. You must insert this statement before the first Sub or Function statement in a module.

Static variables

Static variables are a special case. Although you declare these variables at the procedure level, they retain their value even when the procedure ends. This fact may be useful if you need to keep track of the number of times you execute a subroutine. You can declare a static variable and increment it each time you run the subroutine.

As shown in the following example, you declare static variables by using the Static keyword:

```
Sub MySub()
    Static Counter as Integer
    ... [Code goes here] ...
End Sub
```

Working with constants

A variable's value may — and usually does — change while your procedure is executing (that's why they call it a variable). Sometimes, you need to refer to values or strings that never change — these values or strings are called *constants*. In such cases, you can define a constant. A constant is a named element (like a variable) but its value doesn't change.

As shown in the following examples, you declare constants by using the Const statement:

```
Const NumQuarters as Integer = 4
Const Rate = .0725, Period = 12
Private Const ModName as String = "Budget Macros"
Public Const AppName as String = "Budget Application"
```

Like variables, constants have a scope. If you want a constant to be available only within a single procedure, declare the constant after the procedure's Sub or Function statement. To make a constant available to all procedures in a module, use the Private keyword and declare the constant before the first Sub or Function statement in the module (as in the third line of the preceding example). To make a constant available to all modules in the workbook, use the Public keyword and declare the constant before the first Sub or Function statement in a module (as in the fourth line of the preceding example).

If you attempt to change the value of a constant in a VBA routine, you get an error message — not surprising because a constant is a constant.

Using constants in place of hard-coded values or strings is an excellent programming practice. For example, if your procedure needs to refer to a specific value (such as an interest rate) several times, it's better to declare the value as a constant and refer to the constant's name rather than the value. This procedure makes your code more readable and easier to change; should the need for changes arise, you have only to change one statement rather than several.

Excel and VBA contain many predefined constants, which you can use without declaring. In general, you don't need to know the value of these constants to use them. The macro recorder always uses constants rather than actual values.

The following simple procedure uses a built-in constant (xlManual) to change the Calculation property of the Application object. In other words, this procedure changes Excel's recalculation mode to manual:

```
Sub CalcManual()
    Application.Calculation = xlManual
End Sub
```

I discovered the xlManual constant by recording a macro that changed the calculation mode. I also could have looked in the online help under Calculation Property. As shown in Figure 7-1, the online help screen lists all the relevant constants for this property.

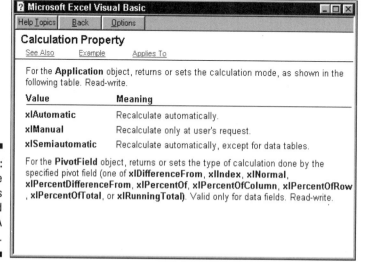

Figure 7-1: The online help lists Excel and VBA constants.

The actual value of the built-in xlManual constant is –4135. Obviously, it's easier to use the constant's name than look up the value (even if you know where to look). By the way, the constant for changing to automatic calculation mode is xlAutomatic; its value is –4105.

Working with strings

Excel can manipulate both numbers and text, so it should come as no surprise that VBA has this same power. Actually, you can work with two types of strings in VBA:

- ✓ **Fixed-length strings** are declared with a specified number of characters. The maximum length is 56,529 characters.

- ✓ **Variable-length strings** can theoretically hold as many as 2 billion characters.

Each character in a string takes one byte of storage.

When you declare a string variable with a Dim statement, you can specify the maximum length if you know it (that is, a fixed-length string), or let VBA handle it dynamically (a variable-length string). The following example declares the MyString variable as a string with a maximum length of 50 characters (use an asterisk to specify the number of characters). YourString is also declared as a string, but its length is unspecified:

```
Dim MyString as String * 50
Dim YourString as String
```

Working with dates

Another data type you may find useful is the date. Of course, you can use a string variable to store dates, but you can't perform date calculations on strings. Using the date data type gives your routines greater flexibility. For example, you may need to calculate the number of days between two dates, which would be impossible if you use strings to hold your dates.

A variable defined as a date uses 8 bytes of storage and can hold dates ranging from January 1, 0100, to December 31, 9999. That's a span of nearly 10,000 years, which is more than enough for even the most aggressive financial forecast. You can also use the date data type to work with time data, accurate to whole seconds only.

Here are some examples of declaring variables and constants as a date data type:

```
Dim Today As Date
Dim StartTime As Date
Const FirstDay As Date = #1/1/95#
Const Noon = #12:00:00#
```

In VBA, you specify dates and times by placing them between pound signs (#), as shown in these examples.

Date variables display dates according to your system's short date format, and times display according to your system's time format (either 12- or 24-hour). These system settings are stored in the Windows Registry, and you can modify them by using the Regional Settings dialog box in the Windows Control Panel. Displaying a date or time using VBA may vary depending on the settings for the system on which the application is running.

Assignment Statements

An *assignment statement* is a VBA statement that assigns the result of an expression to a variable or an object. The Excel online help screen defines the term *expression* as

> "... a combination of keywords, operators, variables, and constants that yields a string, number, or object. An expression can perform a calculation, manipulate characters, or test data."

I couldn't have said it better myself.

Much of your work in VBA involves developing (and debugging) expressions. If you know how to create formulas in Excel, you'll have no trouble creating expressions. The only difference is that an expression must have its result assigned to a variable. With a formula, Excel displays the result in a cell.

Here are a few examples of assignment statements (the expressions are to the right of the equal sign):

```
x = 1
x = x + 1
x = (y * 2) / (z * 2)
FileOpen = True
FileOpen = Not FileOpen
Range("TheYear").Value = 1996
```

Expressions can be as complex as you need; use the line continuation character (a space followed by an underscore) to make lengthy expressions easier to read.

Operators play a major role in VBA. Operators describe mathematical operations such as addition (+), multiplication (*), division (/), subtraction (–), exponentiation (^), and string concatenation (&). VBA uses a few other less-familiar operators, including the backslash operator (\) for integer division, and the Mod operator for modulo arithmetic (this operator returns the remainder of a division operation).

As shown in Table 7-3, VBA also provides a full set of logical operators. Consult the online help for complete details.

Table 7-3	VBA's Logical Operators
Operator	*What It Does*
Not	Performs a logical negation on an expression
And	Performs a logical conjunction on two expressions
Or	Performs a logical disjunction on two expressions
XoR	Performs a logical exclusion on two expressions
Eqv	Performs a logical equivalence on two expressions
Imp	Performs a logical implication on two expressions

The order of precedence for operators in VBA is exactly the same as in Excel formulas. Of course, you can use parentheses to change the natural order of precedence.

Arrays

All programming languages support *arrays*. An array is a group of variables that have a common name; you refer to a specific variable in the array by using the array name and an index number. For example, you might define an array of 12 string variables to hold the names of the months of the year. If you name the array *MonthNames*, you can refer to the first element of the array as MonthNames(1), the second element as MonthNames(2), and so on.

Declaring arrays

You declare an array with a Dim or a Public statement, just like you declare a
regular variable. However, you also need to specify the number of elements in
the array. Designate the number of elements in an array by specifying the first
index number, the keyword *to*, and the last index number — all inside parentheses. The following example shows how to declare an array of 100 integers:

```
Dim MyArray(1 to 100) as Integer
```

When you declare an array, you can specify only the upper index. VBA assumes
that 0 is the lower index. Therefore, the following statements both declare
exactly the same array:

```
Dim MyArray(0 to 100) as Integer
Dim MyArray(100) as Integer
```

If you want VBA to assume that 1 is the lower index for your arrays, simply include
the following statement before any Sub or Function statements in your module:

```
Option Base 1
```

The preceding statement forces VBA to use 1 as the first index number for
arrays that declare only the upper index. If this statement is present, the
following statements are identical:

```
Dim MyArray(1 to 100) as Integer
Dim MyArray(100) as Integer
```

Multidimensional arrays

The arrays created in the preceding examples are all one-dimensional arrays.
Arrays you create in VBA can have as many as 60 dimensions — although you
rarely need more than three dimensions in an array. The following example
declares a 100-integer array with two dimensions:

```
Dim MyArray(1 to 10, 1 to 10) as Integer
```

You can think of this array as occupying a 10-x-10 matrix. To refer to a specific
element in this array, you need to specify two index numbers. The following
example shows how you can assign a value to an element in this array:

```
MyArray(3, 4) = 125
```

This statement assigns a value to a single element in the array. If you're thinking of the array in terms of a 10-x-10 matrix, this assigns 125 to the element located in the third row and fourth column of the matrix.

You can think of a three-dimensional array as a cube. However, I can't tell you how to visualize the data layout of an array of more than three dimensions.

You can also create *dynamic* arrays. A dynamic array doesn't have a preset number of elements. You declare a dynamic array with a blank set of parentheses:

```
Dim MyArray() as Integer
```

Before you can actually use this array, you must use the ReDim statement to tell VBA how many elements the array has. You can use the ReDim statement any number of times, changing the array's size as often as you need.

When you redimension an array by using ReDim, you wipe out the values stored in the array elements. You can avoid this data loss by using the Preserve keyword. The following example shows how you can preserve an array's values when you redimension the array:

```
ReDim Preserve MyArray(200)
```

The topic of arrays comes up again in Chapter 10, where I discuss looping.

Using Labels

In early versions of BASIC, every line of code requires a label. For example, if you were writing a BASIC program in the '70s (dressed, of course, in your bellbottoms) it might look something like this:

```
010: LET X=5
020: LET Y=3
030: LET Z=X*Y
040: PRINT Z
050: END
```

VBA permits the use of such line numbers, or labels. You don't typically use a label for each line, but you might occasionally need to use a label. For example, if you use a GoTo statement (which I discuss in Chapter 10), you need to insert a label. A label must begin with the first nonblank character in a line and end with a colon.

Here's an example of code with one label. This useful VBA function determines whether a particular path exists:

```
Private Function PathExists(PathName As String) As Boolean
'    Returns True if PathName is a valid path
    On Error GoTo NoPath
    x = Dir(PathName & "\*.*")
    If x = "" Then GoTo NoPath
    PathExists = True
    Exit Function
NoPath:
    PathExists = False
End Function
```

In this example, NoPath is a label. If the path does not exist, execution jumps to this label. Otherwise, execution ends before it gets to the label.

Learning More

The information in this chapter definitely becomes clearer as you progress through subsequent chapters. If you want to find out more about VBA language elements, I refer you to the online help. You'll find as much detail as you need, or care to know.

In the next chapter, I return to the ever-popular topic of Range objects.

Chapter 8

Working with Range Objects

*I*n Chapter 4, I run the risk of overwhelming you with an introduction to Excel's object model. In that chapter, I also cover the basics of properties and methods. Now you get to dig a bit deeper and take a close look at Range objects. Why do you need to know so much about Range objects? Because much of the programming work you do in Excel focuses on Range objects. You'll thank me later.

A Quick Review

I start this chapter with a brief review. Recall that a Range object is a range contained in a worksheet. A Range object can be as small as a single cell or as large as every cell on a worksheet (A1:IV16384).

You can refer to a Range object like this:

```
Range("A1:C5")
```

Or, if the range has a name, you can use an expression like this:

```
Range("PriceList")
```

Unless you tell it otherwise, Excel assumes you're referring to a range on the active sheet. If anything other than a worksheet is active (such as a VBA module), the range reference fails.

As shown in the following example, you can refer to a range that is not on the active sheet by qualifying the range reference with a worksheet name from the active workbook:

```
Worksheets("Sheet1").Range("A1:C5")
```

And, if you need to refer to a range in a different workbook (that is, any workbook other than the active one), you can use a statement like this:

```
Workbooks("Budget").Worksheets("Sheet1").Range("A1:C5")
```

A Range object can consist of one or more entire rows or columns. You can refer to an entire row (in this case, row 3) by using syntax like this:

```
Range("3:3")
```

And you can refer to an entire column (column 4 in this example) like this:

```
Range("D:D")
```

To further confuse matters, you can even work with noncontiguous ranges. (You select noncontiguous ranges by holding down the Ctrl key while you select various ranges in a worksheet.) The following expression refers to a two-area noncontiguous range. Notice that a comma separates the two areas.

```
Range("A1:B8,D9:G16")
```

Finally, recall that Range objects (like all other objects) have properties (which you can examine and change) and methods (which perform actions on the object).

Other Ways to Refer to a Range

The more you work with VBA, the more you realize that it's a well-conceived language. Often, it provides multiple ways of performing an action. When faced with performing an action, you can choose the most appropriate method for your problem.

The Cells method

Instead of using the Range keyword, you can refer to a range by using the Cells method.

Notice that I wrote Cells *method* — not Cells *object*. Although Cells certainly might seem like an object, it's really not. Rather, it's a method that is evaluated and then returns an object (specifically, a Range object).

The Cells method takes two arguments: the row and the column. For example, the following expression refers to cell C2 on Sheet1:

```
Worksheets("Sheet1").Cells(2,3)
```

You can also use the Cells method to refer to a larger range — that is, a range containing more than a single cell. The following example demonstrates the syntax you use:

```
Range(Cells(1, 1), Cells(10, 10))
```

This syntax refers to a range that extends from cell A1 (row 1, column 1) to cell J10 (row 10, column 10).

The following statements both produce exactly the same result; they enter a value of 100 into a 10-by-10 range of cells:

```
Range("A1:J10").Value = 100
Range(Cells(1, 1), Cells(10, 10)).Value = 100
```

The advantage of using the Cells method to refer to ranges becomes apparent when you use variables as the Cells arguments rather than actual numbers. Things with the cells method really start to click when you understand looping, which I cover in Chapter 10.

The Offset method

The Offset method provides another handy means for referring to ranges. This method, which operates on a Range object and returns another Range object, lets you refer to a cell that is a particular number of rows and columns away from another cell.

Like the Cells method, the Offset method takes two arguments. The first argument represents the number of rows to offset; the second represents the number of columns to offset.

The following expression refers to a cell that is one row below cell A1, and two columns to the right of cell A1 — in other words, this refers to the cell commonly known as C2:

```
Range("A1").Offset(1, 2)
```

The Offset method can also use negative arguments. The following example refers to cell A1:

```
Range("C2").Offset(-1, -2)
```

And, as you might expect, you can use zero as one or both of the arguments for Offset. The following expression refers to cell A1:

```
Range("A1").Offset(0, 0)
```

The Offset method is most useful when you use variables instead of actual values for the arguments. In Chapter 10, I present some examples that demonstrate this.

Some Useful Range Object Properties

A Range object has 59 properties. You can write Excel programs nonstop for the next century, and I guarantee that you will never need to use all 59 properties. In this section, I briefly describe some commonly-used Range properties. For details on Range properties, consult the program's online help (search for *range object*, and then click *Properties*).

Range properties (like other object properties) are either read-write or read-only. You can't change a read-only property. For example, every Range object has an Address property. You can access this read-only property, but you can't change it.

The following examples are typically statements rather than complete subroutines. If you'd like to try any of these (which you should), you need to create a subroutine. Also, many of these statements work properly only if a worksheet is the active sheet.

The Value property

The Value property represents the value contained in a cell. It's a read-write property; your VBA code can either read the value or change it. For an empty cell, the Value property contains Empty.

The following statement displays a message box that contains the value in cell A1 on Sheet1:

```
MsgBox Worksheets("Sheet1").Range("A1").Value
```

It stands to reason that you would only read the Value property for a single-cell Range object. For example, the following statement generates an error:

```
MsgBox Worksheets("Sheet1").Range("A1:C3").Value
```

However, you can change the Value property for a range of any size. The following statement enters 123 into a range of cells:

```
Worksheets("Sheet1").Range("A1:C3").Value = 123
```

The Count property

The Count property returns the number of cells in a range (it's a read-only property). The following statement accesses the Count property of a range and displays the result (9) in a message box:

```
MsgBox Range("A1:C3").Count
```

The Column and Row properties

The Column property returns the column number of a single-cell range, and the Row property returns the row number of a single-cell range. For example, the following expression returns 5, because the cell is in the fifth column:

```
Sheets("Sheet1").Range("F3").Column
```

The Address property

The Address property (a read-only property) displays the cell address for a Range object. The following statement displays the message box shown in Figure 8-1:

```
MsgBox Range(Cells(1, 1), Cells(5, 5)).Address
```

The HasFormula property

The HasFormula property returns True if the single-cell Range contains a formula. If the range consists of more than one cell, accessing this property results in an error unless all the cells in the range have a formula, or all the cells in the range don't have a formula.

Figure 8-1:
This
message
box displays
the Address
property of a
1-x-5 range.

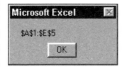

The Font property

The Font property returns a Font object, which is contained within the Range object. The Font object, as you might expect, has many properties that you can access. To change some aspect of a range's font, you must first access the range's Font object, and then you must manipulate the properties of that Font object. This might be confusing at first, but it eventually makes sense.

The following expression returns a Font object for a range:

```
Range("A1").Font
```

The following statement sets the Bold property of the Font object contained in the Range object to True. In plain English, this makes the cell display in boldface:

```
Range("A1").Font.Bold = True
```

To see other examples of manipulating Font objects, record your actions while you modify some of the font attributes of a range.

The Interior property

The Interior property returns an Interior object, which is contained within the Range object. This works the same way as the Font property.

For example, the following statement sets the ColorIndex property of the Interior object to True:

```
Range("A1").Interior.ColorIndex = 3
```

In other words, this changes the cell's background to red.

The ColorIndex values correspond to the colors shown in the Color tool on the Formatting toolbar. Black is 1, white is 2, red is 3, and so on.

The Formula property

The Formula property represents the formula in a cell. This is a read-write property, and so you can access this property to insert a formula into a cell. For example, the following statement enters a SUM formula into cell A13:

```
Range("A13").Formula = "=SUM(A1:A12)"
```

The NumberFormat property

The NumberFormat property represents the number format (expressed as a string) of the Range object. This is a read-write property, and so your VBA code can change the number format. The following statement changes the number format of column A to percent, with two decimal places:

```
Columns("A:A").NumberFormat = "0.00%"
```

VBA uses the same number format codes as Excel. To see a list of those formats, open the Format Cells dialog box (press Ctrl+1), click the Number tab, and then select the Custom category.

Some Useful Range Object Methods

As you know, a VBA method performs an action. You can use 78 methods to do things with a Range object. But again, you may never need most of these. In this section, I point out some of the more commonly-used Range object methods.

The Select method

You use the Select method to select a range of cells. The following statement selects a range on the active worksheet:

```
Range("A1:C12").Select
```

Before you select a range, make sure you activate the range's worksheet; otherwise, you get an error. For example, if Sheet1 contains the range you want to select, you can use the following statements to select the range:

```
Sheets("Sheet1").Activate
Range("A1:C12").Select
```

Contrary to what you might expect, the following statement generates an error if Sheet1 is not the active sheet:

```
Sheets("Sheet1").Range("A1:C12").Select
```

When you record a macro that manipulates a range, the recorded code selects the range and performs the actions with it. However, you don't have to select a range before you do something with it. In fact, it's usually more efficient *not* to select the range first.

The Copy and Paste methods

You can perform copy and paste operations in VBA by using the Copy method and the Paste method. This short subroutine copies range A1:A12 and pastes it to the range beginning at cell C1:

```
Sub CopyRange()
    Range("A1:A12").Select
    Selection.Copy
    Range("C1").Select
    ActiveSheet.Paste
End Sub
```

Notice that the preceding example — which the macro recorder generated — selects the range before copying it. As I note in the previous section, you don't have to select a range before doing something with it. In fact, the following subroutine accomplishes the same task as the preceding example by using a single statement:

```
Sub CopyRange2()
    Range("A1:A12").Copy Range("C1")
End Sub
```

This routine takes advantage of the fact that the Copy method can use an argument which corresponds to the destination range for the copying operation.

The Clear method

The Clear method simply deletes the contents of a range. For example, if you want to zap everything in column D, the following statement does the trick:

```
Range("D:D").Clear
```

 You should be aware of two other related methods: the ClearContents method deletes the contents of the range but leaves the formatting intact; the ClearFormats method deletes the formatting in the range but not the cell contents.

The Delete method

As you know, clearing a range differs from deleting a range. When you delete a range, Excel shifts the remaining cells around to fill up the range you deleted.

The following example uses the Delete method to delete the entire row 6:

```
Range("6:6").Delete
```

When you delete a range that's not a complete row or column, Excel needs to know how to shift the cells (to see how this works, experiment with the Edit⇨Delete command).

The following statement deletes a range and then fills the resulting gap by shifting the other cells to the left:

```
Range("C6:C10").Delete xlToLeft
```

The Delete method uses an argument that indicates how Excel should shift the remaining cells. In this case, I use a named constant (xlToLeft) for the argument. I could also use xlUp, another named constant.

Learning More

This chapter probably gave you greater insight into Excel's object model. You now know about the Range object, as well as some of the more useful properties and methods for this object. However, this chapter barely scratches the surface. As you work with VBA, you'll probably need to access other properties and methods. The program's online help is the best place to learn about additional properties and methods, but it's also helpful to simply record your actions and examine the code that Excel generates.

In the next chapter, I shift gears a bit and discuss functions — both those provided by VBA and those provided by Excel.

Chapter 9

Using VBA Functions and Excel Functions

*I*n a previous chapter, I allude to the fact that you can use functions in your VBA expressions. In this chapter, I explain myself. As this chapter describes, functions can make your VBA code perform some powerful feats, with little or no programming effort required.

What Is a Function?

All Excel users beyond rank beginners use worksheet functions in their formulas. The most common worksheet function is SUM, and you have hundreds of others at your disposal.

A function essentially performs a calculation and returns a single value. The same holds true for functions used in your VBA expressions.

The functions you use in VBA come from three sources:

✔ Special functions provided by VBA

✔ Worksheet functions provided by Excel

✔ Custom functions that you (or someone else) writes in VBA

The rest of this chapter clarifies the differences, and — I hope — convinces you of the value of using functions in your VBA code.

Using VBA Functions

VBA provides numerous built-in functions. Some of them take arguments, and some do not.

VBA function examples

In this section, I present a few examples of using VBA functions in code. You can enter these short subroutines and try them out. In many of these examples, I use the MsgBox function to display a value in a message box.

Yes, MsgBox is a VBA function — a rather unusual one, but a function nonetheless. This useful function displays a message in a pop-up dialog box. For more details about the MsgBox function, see Chapter 15.

Displaying the system date

The first example uses VBA's Date function to display the current system date in a message box:

```
Sub ShowDate()
    MsgBox Date
End Sub
```

Notice that the Date function doesn't use an argument. Unlike worksheet functions, a VBA function with no argument doesn't require an empty set of parentheses.

To get the system date and time, use the Now function instead of the Date function. Or, to get only the time, use the Time function.

Finding the length of a string

The following subroutine uses the Len function, which returns the length of a string (it takes one argument). When you execute this subroutine, the message box displays 11:

```
Sub GetLength()
    MyString = "Hello World"
    StringLen = Len(MyString)
    MsgBox StringLen
End Sub
```

Excel also has a LEN function, which you can use in your formulas. The Excel version and the VBA function work exactly the same.

Displaying the integer part of a number

The following subroutine uses the Fix function, which returns the integer part of a value:

```
Sub GetIntegerPart()
    MyValue = 123.456
    IntValue = Fix(MyValue)
    MsgBox IntValue
End Sub
```

In this case, the message box displays 123.

Determining the size of a file

The following subroutine displays the size, in bytes, of the Excel executable file. It finds this value by using the FileLen function.

```
Sub GetFileSize()
    TheFile = "C:\MSOFFICE\EXCEL\EXCEL.EXE"
    MsgBox FileLen(TheFile)
End Sub
```

Notice that this routine *hard codes* the filename, which isn't a good idea because the file might not be on the C drive, or the Excel folder might have a different name. The following statement shows a better approach:

```
TheFile = Application.Path & "\EXCEL.EXE"
```

Path is a property of the Application object. It simply returns the folder in which the application is installed (without a trailing backslash).

Identifying the type of a selected object

The following subroutine uses the TypeName function, which returns the type of the selected object:

```
Sub ShowSelectionType()
    SelType = TypeName(Selection)
    MsgBox SelType
End Sub
```

This could be a Range, a Button, a TextBox, or any other type of object that can be selected.

VBA functions that do more than return a value

A few VBA functions go above and beyond the call of duty. Rather than simply return a value, the following functions have some useful side effects:

Function	What It Does
MsgBox	Displays a handy dialog box containing a message and buttons. The function returns a code that identifies which button the user clicks. See Chapter 15 for details.
InputBox	Displays a simple dialog box that asks the user for some input. The function returns whatever the user enters into the dialog box. I discuss this in Chapter 15.
Shell	Executes another program. The function returns the *task ID* of the other program (or an error if the function can't start the other program). I show an example of this in Chapter 26.

Discovering VBA functions

So, how do you find out which functions VBA provides? Good question. I dove into the online help looking for a comprehensive list of functions, and I came up empty-handed. To save you some time, I compiled a complete list, which I share with you in the form of Table 9-1. Although this table lists some obscure functions, others are quite useful. Their usefulness depends on your uses for VBA.

Table 9-1	VBA's Built-in Functions
Function	What It Does
Abs	Returns the absolute value of a number
Array	Returns a variant containing an array
Asc	Converts the first character of a string to its ASCII value
Atn	Returns the arctangent of a number
CBool	Converts an expression to Boolean data type
CCur	Converts an expression to currency data type
CDate	Converts an expression to date data type
CDbl	Converts an expression to double data type
Chr	Converts an ANSI value to a string
CInt	Converts an expression to integer data type
CLng	Converts an expression to long data type

Function	What It Does
Cos	Returns the cosine of a number
CreateObject	Creates an OLE Automation object
CSng	Converts an expression to single data type
CStr	Converts an expression to string data type
CurDir	Returns the current path
CVar	Converts an expression to variant data type
CVErr	Returns a user-defined error number
Date	Returns the current system date
DateSerial	Converts a date to a serial number
DateValue	Converts a string to a date
Day	Returns the day of the month from a date value
Dir	Returns the name of a file or directory that matches a pattern
EOF	Returns True if the end of a text file has been reached
Erl	Returns the line number that caused an error
Err	Returns the error number of an error condition
Error	Returns the error message that corresponds to an error number
Exp	Returns the base of the natural logarithm (*e*) raised to a power
FileAttr	Returns the file mode for a text file
FileDateTime	Returns the date and time when a file was last modified
FileLen	Returns the number of bytes in a file
Fix	Returns the integer portion of a number
Format	Displays an expression in a particular format
FreeFile	Returns the next available file number when working with text files
GetAttr	Returns a code representing a file attribute
GetObject	Retrieves an OLE Automation object from a file
Hex	Converts from decimal to hexadecimal
Hour	Returns the hours portion of a time
Input	Returns characters from a sequential text file
InputBox	Displays a box to prompt a user for input
InStr	Returns the position of a string within another string

(continued)

Table 9-1 *(continued)*

Function	What It Does
Int	Returns the integer portion of a number
IsArray	Returns True if a variable is an array
IsDate	Returns True if a variable is a date
IsEmpty	Returns True if a variable has been initialized
IsError	Returns True if an expression is an error value
IsMissing	Returns True if an optional argument was not passed to a procedure
IsNull	Returns True if an expression contains no valid data
IsNumeric	Returns True if an expression can be evaluated as a number
IsObject	Returns True if an expression references an OLE Automation object
LBound	Returns the smallest subscript for a dimension of an array
LCase	Returns a string converted to lowercase
Left	Returns a specified number of characters from the left of a string
Len	Returns the number of characters in a string
Loc	Returns the current read or write position of a text file
LOF	Returns the number of bytes in an open text file
Log	Returns the natural logarithm of a number to base *e*
LTrim	Returns a copy of a string, with any leading spaces removed
Mid	Returns a specified number of characters from a string
Minute	Returns the minutes portion of a time
Month	Returns the month from a date value
MsgBox	Displays a modal message box
Now	Returns the current system date and time
Oct	Converts from decimal to octal
RGB	Returns a numeric RGB value representing a color
Right	Returns a specified number of characters from the right of a string
Rnd	Returns a random number between 0 and 1
RTrim	Returns a copy of a string with any trailing spaces removed
Second	Returns the seconds portion of a time
Seek	Returns the current position in a text file

Function	What It Does
Sgn	Returns an integer that indicates the sign of a number
Shell	Runs an executable program
Sin	Returns the sine of a number
Space	Returns a string with a specified number of spaces
Spc	Positions output when printing to a file
Sqr	Returns the square root of a number
Str	Returns a string representation of a number
StrComp	Returns a value indicating the result of a string comparison
String	Returns a repeating character or string
Tab	Positions output when printing to a file
Tan	Returns the tangent of a number
Time	Returns the current system time
Timer	Returns the number of seconds since midnight
TimeSerial	Returns the time for a specified hour, minute, and second
TimeValue	Converts a string to a time serial number
TypeName	Returns a string that describes the data type of a variable
UBound	Returns the largest available subscript for a dimension of an array
UCase	Converts a string to uppercase
Val	Returns the numbers contained in a string
VarType	Returns a value indicating the subtype of a variable
Weekday	Returns a number representing a day of the week
Year	Returns the year from a date value

Using Worksheet Functions in VBA

Although VBA offers a decent assortment of built-in functions, you may not always find exactly what you need. Fortunately, you can also use the Excel worksheet functions in your VBA procedures.

VBA makes the Excel worksheet functions available through the Application object (remember, the Application object is Excel). Therefore, any statement that uses a worksheet function must use the Application qualifier. In other words, you must precede the function name with **Application** (with a dot separating the two).

Worksheet function examples

In this section, I demonstrate how to use worksheet functions in your VBA expressions.

Finding the maximum value in a range

Here's an example showing how to use the MAX worksheet function in a VBA procedure. This subroutine displays the maximum value in the range named NumberList on the active worksheet:

```
Sub ShowMax()
    TheMax = Application.Max(Range("NumberList"))
    MsgBox TheMax
End Sub
```

You can use the MIN function to get the smallest value in a range. And, as you might expect, you can use other worksheet functions in a similar manner. For example, you can use the LARGE function to determine the kth-largest value in a range. The following expression demonstrates this:

```
SecondHighest = Application.Large(Range("NumberList"),2)
```

Notice that the LARGE function uses two arguments; the second argument represents the kth part — in this case, 2 (the second-largest value).

Calculating a mortgage payment

The next example uses the PMT worksheet function to calculate a mortgage payment. In this example, I use three variables to store the data that's passed to the PMT function as arguments. A message box displays the calculated payment.

```
Sub PmtCalc()
    IntRate = 0.0825
    Periods = 30 * 12
    LoanAmt = 150000
    MsgBox Application.Pmt(IntRate / 12, Periods, -LoanAmt)
End Sub
```

As the following statement shows, you can also insert the values directly as the function arguments:

```
MsgBox Application.Pmt(.0825 / 12, 360, -150000)
```

However, using variables to store the parameters makes the code easier to read.

Using a lookup function

The following example uses the simple lookup table shown in Figure 9-1. Range A1:B15 is named PriceList.

```
Sub GetPrice()
    PartNum = InputBox("Enter the Part Number")
    PartNum = Val(PartNum)
    Sheets("Prices").Activate
    Price = Application.VLookup(PartNum, _
    Range("PriceList"), 2, False)
    MsgBox PartNum & " costs " & Price
End Sub
End Sub
```

	A	B	C	D	E	F	
1	Part	Price					
2	A-145	39.95					
3	A-147	45.00					
4	C-091	129.50					
5	D-231	16.95					
6	D-244	29.49					
7	E-001	0.79					
8	F-972	4.79					
9	G-172	11.99					
10	G-190	12.99					
11	G-293	14.99					
12	M-045	9.99					
13	M-145	59.95					
14	N-092	40.00					
15	W-222	12.95					

Figure 9-1: This range, named PriceList, contains prices for parts.

The subroutine starts by using VBA's InputBox function to ask the user for a part number. (Figure 9-2 shows the dialog box displayed when this statement is executed.) The statement containing the InputBox function assigns the part number the user enters to the PartNum variable. Then I use VBA's Val function in the code to convert PartNum to a value (the InputBox function always returns a string). The next statement simply activates the Prices worksheet — just in case it's not already the active sheet.

Next, the subroutine uses the VLOOKUP function to find the part number in the table. Notice that this statement uses the same arguments as if you were using the function in a worksheet formula. This statement assigns the result of the function to the Price variable.

Finally, the subroutine displays the price for the part by using the MsgBox function.

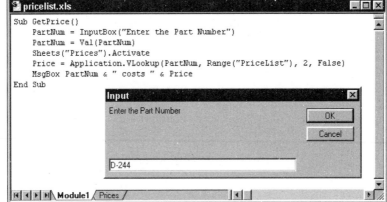

Figure 9-2:
Using the
InputBox to
get input
from the
user.

This subroutine fails if you enter a nonexistent part number. Just try it and see what happens. For a more robust subroutine, you need to add some error-handling statements. I discuss error handling in Chapter 12.

Entering worksheet functions

You can't use the Function Wizard to insert a worksheet function into a VBA module. Instead, you enter worksheet functions the old-fashioned way: by hand. However, you *can* use the Function Wizard to identify the function you want to use and learn about its arguments. Just activate a worksheet and use the Function Wizard as you normally would. Then when you figure out how the function works, you can enter it into your module.

More about Using Worksheet Functions

Newcomers to VBA often confuse VBA's built-in functions with Excel workbook functions. A good rule of thumb is that VBA doesn't try to reinvent the wheel. For the most part, VBA doesn't duplicate Excel worksheet functions.

However, this is not a hard-and-fast rule. In some cases, VBA *does* duplicate worksheet functions (for example, the Len function, which you used in this chapter). And to confuse the issue even more, a VBA function may have the same name as a worksheet function, but work differently. For example, Excel's LOG function and VBA's Log function return different values! The VBA version of Log returns the natural logarithm to the base *e*. The worksheet version returns the logarithm of a number to the base you specify as the second, optional argument. If you omit the second argument, it uses 10. If you use 2.718282 as the second argument, the worksheet function returns the same value as the VBA version.

Bottom line? If you need to use a function, first determine whether VBA has something that meets your needs. If not, check out the worksheet functions. If all else fails, you might be able to write your own custom function by using VBA.

For most worksheet functions that are not available as methods of the Application object, you can use an equivalent VBA built-in operator or function. For example, the Mod() worksheet function is not available as a method of the Application object because VBA has an equivalent, built-in Mod operator. This is by design — a VBA operator works faster than a Microsoft Excel function in a VBA module.

To display a list of all the worksheet functions that are available as methods of the Application object in VBA, do the following:

1. Click the Answer Wizard tab in Microsoft Excel Help.

2. Enter **using worksheet functions in VBA**, and then click Search.

3. In the list of topics, click List of Worksheet Functions Available to Visual Basic, and then click Display.

Table 9-2 lists VBA's equivalent functions for the worksheet functions you can't use in your VBA code.

Table 9-2   VBA Equivalents for Worksheet Functions

Worksheet Function	VBA Equivalent Function
CHAR	Chr
CODE	Asc
DATE	DateSerial
ERROR.TYPE	Err
EXACT	StrComp
INDIRECT	No direct equivalent. Use Range, Cells, Offset, or any other way of referencing cells.
INFO	No direct equivalent. Use Curdir function, or the following Application properties: MemoryTotal, MemoryUsed, MemoryFree, Version, OperatingSystem, Calculation, and Count.
ISBLANK	IsEmpty
ISREF	TypeName
LOWER	Lcase
NA	No equivalent. Use ActiveCell.Value = "#N/A"

(continued)

Table 9-2 (continued)	
Worksheet Function	**VBA Equivalent Function**
RAND	Rnd
SIGN	Sgn
SQRT	Sqr
TODAY	Date
TRUNC	Fix
TYPE	Typename
UPPER	UCase
VALUE	Val

Using Custom Functions

The third category of functions you can use in your VBA procedures is custom functions, a function you develop yourself using (what else?) VBA. To use a custom function, you must define it in the workbook in which you use it.

Here's an example of defining a simple custom function, and then using it in a VBA subroutine:

```
Function MultiplyTwo(firstnum, secondnum)
    MultiplyTwo = firstnum * secondnum
End Function

Sub ShowResult()
    ValOne = 123
    ValTwo = 544
    Result = MultiplyTwo(ValOne, ValTwo)
    MsgBox Result
End Sub
```

The custom function MultiplyTwo has two arguments. The ShowResult subroutine uses this custom function by passing two arguments to it (in parentheses). The ShowResult subroutine then displays a message box showing the value returned by the MultiplyTwo function.

You can also use custom functions in your worksheet formulas. I devote an entire chapter to this important — and useful — topic (see Chapter 21).

Learning More

My goal in this chapter is to let you know about functions — VBA functions and Excel worksheet functions — that you can use in your code to construct more powerful expressions. The best source of information about these functions is the online help system available in Excel where you can find the complete syntax for each function, a description of its arguments, and usually an example or two. Throughout the rest of this book, you can see many more examples of functions at work.

In the next chapter, you learn how to control the flow of your VBA programs.

Chapter 10

Controlling Program Flow and Making Decisions

● ●

In This Chapter

▶ Understanding the available methods for controlling the flow of your VBA routines and making decisions

▶ Learning about the dreaded GoTo statement

▶ Using If. . . Then and Select Case structures

▶ Performing looping in your procedures

● ●

Some VBA procedures start at the beginning and progress line by line to the end, never deviating from this top-to-bottom program flow. Macros you record always work like this. In many cases, however, you need to control the flow of your routines by skipping over some statements, executing some statements multiple times, and testing conditions to determine what the routine does next. Ready or not, you learn how to do all that stuff in this chapter.

Go with the Flow, Dude

Some programming newbies can't understand how a dumb computer can make intelligent decisions. The secret lies in several programming constructs that most programming languages support. Table 10-1 provides a quick summary of these constructs (I explain all of these in this chapter).

The GoTo Statement

A GoTo statement offers the most straightforward means for changing the flow of a program. The GoTo statement simply transfers program control to another statement, which is preceded by a label.

Table 10-1   Programming Constructs for Making Decisions

Construct	How It Works
The GoTo statement	Jumps to a particular statement
The If. . . Then structure	Does something if something else is true
The Select Case structure	Does any of several things, depending on the value of something
The For. . . Next loop	Executes a series of statements a specified number of times
The Do. . . While loop	Does something as long as something else remains true
The Do. . . Until loop	Does something until something else becomes true

Your VBA routines can contain as many labels you like. A label is just a text string followed by a colon.

The following subroutine shows how a GoTo statement works:

```
Sub GoToDemo()
    UserName = InputBox("Enter Your Name: ")
    If UserName <> "Bill Gates" Then GoTo WrongName
    MsgBox ("Welcome Bill. . . ")
'    . . . [More code here] . . .
    Exit Sub
WrongName:
    MsgBox "Sorry. Only Bill Gates can run this."
End Sub
```

This subroutine uses a label called WrongName. The subroutine uses the InputBox function to get the user's name. If the user enters a name other than Bill Gates, the program flow jumps to the WrongName label, a MsgBox function displays an apologetic message, and the subroutine ends. On the other hand, if Mr. Gates signs on, the procedure displays a welcome message and then executes some additional code. Then, the Exit Sub statement ends the routine before the MsgBox function has a chance to work.

This simple routine works, but VBA provides several better alternatives than using GoTo. In general, you should use the GoTo statement only when you have no other way to perform an action. In VBA, you only need to use a GoTo statement for trapping errors (I cover this in Chapter 12).

Many hard-core programming types have a deep-seated dislike for GoTo statements. Therefore, you should avoid this subject when talking with other programmers.

Decisions, Decisions

In this section, I discuss two programming structures that can empower your VBA procedures with some impressive decision-making capabilities: If. . . Then, and Select Case.

The If. . . Then structure

Okay, I'll say it: If. . . Then is VBA's most important control structure. You'll probably use this command on a daily basis (at least *I* do). As in other aspects of life, effective decision making is the key to success in writing programs. If this book has the effect I intend, you'll soon share my philosophy that a successful Excel application boils down to making decisions and acting upon them.

The If. . . Then structure has this basic syntax:

```
If condition Then statements [Else elsestatements]
```

You use the If. . . Then structure when you want to execute one or more statements conditionally. If included, the optional Else clause lets you execute one or more statements if the condition you're testing is not true. Sound confusing? Don't worry, a few examples will make this crystal clear.

If. . . Then examples

The following routine demonstrates the use of the If. . . Then structure without the optional Else clause:

```
Sub GreetMe()
    If Time < 0.5 Then MsgBox "Good Morning"
End Sub
```

This uses VBA's Time function to get the system time. If the current system time is less than .5 (in other words, before noon), the routine displays a message. If Time is greater than or equal to .5, the routine ends and nothing happens.

To display a different greeting if Time is greater than or equal to .5, add another If. . . Then statement after the first one, like this:

```
Sub GreetMe()
    If Time < 0.5 Then MsgBox "Good Morning"
    If Time >= 0.5 Then MsgBox "Good Afternoon"
End Sub
```

Notice that I use >= (greater than or equal to) for the second If. . . Then statement. This covers the remote chance that the time is exactly noon.

An If. . . Then. . . Else example

Another approach to the preceding problem uses the Else clause. Here's the same routine recoded to use the If. . . Then. . . Else structure:

```
Sub GreetMe()
    If Time < 0.5 Then MsgBox "Good Morning" else _
    MsgBox "Good Afternoon"
End Sub
```

Notice that I use the line continuation character in the preceding example. The If. . . Then. . . Else statement is actually a single statement.

What if you need to expand this routine to handle three conditions: morning, afternoon, and evening? You have two options: use three If. . . Then statements, or use a *nested* If. . . Then. . . Else structure. The first approach is the simplest:

```
Sub GreetMe()
    If Time < 0.5 Then MsgBox "Good Morning"
    If Time >= 0.5 And Time < 0.75 Then MsgBox "Good Afternoon"
    If Time >= 0.75 Then MsgBox "Good Evening"
End Sub
```

The following routine performs the same action, but uses a nested If. . . Then. . . Else structure:

```
Sub GreetMe()
    If Time < 0.5 Then MsgBox "Good Morning" Else
        If Time >= 0.5 And Time < 0.75 Then MsgBox "Good _
        Afternoon" Else
            If Time >= 0.75 Then MsgBox "Good Evening"
End Sub
```

The preceding example works fine, but you can simplify it a bit by omitting the last If. . . Then part. Because the routine has already tested for two conditions (morning and afternoon), the only remaining condition is evening. Here's the modified subroutine:

```
Sub GreetMe()
  If Time < 0.5 Then MsgBox "Good Morning" Else
    If Time >= 0.5 And Time < 0.75 Then MsgBox "Good _
        Afternoon" Else _
        MsgBox "Good Evening"
End Sub
```

Using ElseIf

In both of the preceding examples, every statement in the routine gets executed — even in the morning. A more efficient structure would exit the routine as soon as a condition is found to be true. In the morning, for example, the procedure should display the "Good Morning" message and then exit without evaluating the other superfluous conditions.

With a tiny routine like this, you don't have to worry about execution speed. But for larger applications that you must optimize for speed, you should know about another syntax for the If. . . Then structure, the ElseIf syntax:

```
If condition Then
    [statements]
[ElseIf condition-n Then
    [elseifstatements]] . . .
[Else
    [elsestatements]]
End If
```

Here's how you can rewrite the GreetMe routine by using this syntax:

```
Sub GreetMe()
    If Time < 0.5 Then
        MsgBox "Good Morning"
        ElseIf Time >= 0.5 And Time < 0.75 Then
            MsgBox "Good Afternoon"
            Else MsgBox "Good Evening"
    End If
End Sub
```

When a condition is true, VBA executes the conditional statements, and the If structure ends. In other words, VBA doesn't waste time evaluating the extraneous conditions, which makes this routine a bit more efficient than the previous examples. The trade-off (there are always trade-offs) is that the code is more difficult to understand (of course, you already knew that).

Another If. . . Then example

Here's another example that uses the simple form of the If. . . Then structure. This routine prompts the user for a Quantity, and then displays the appropriate discount, based on the quantity the user enters:

```
Sub Discount1()
    Quantity = InputBox("Enter Quantity: ")
    If Quantity >= 0 Then Discount = 0.1
    If Quantity >= 25 Then Discount = 0.15
    If Quantity >= 50 Then Discount = 0.2
    If Quantity >= 75 Then Discount = 0.25
    MsgBox "Discount: " & Discount
End Sub
```

NOTE

I was tempted to name this subroutine Discount. But that wouldn't work, because VBA doesn't allow you to use a variable name that's the same as a procedure name.

Notice that each If. . . Then statement in this routine is executed, and the value for Discount can change as the statements are executed. However, the routine ultimately displays the correct value for Discount.

The following routine performs the same tasks by using the alternative ElseIf syntax. In this case, the routine ends immediately after executing the statements for a true condition.

```
Sub Discount2()
    Quantity = InputBox("Enter Quantity: ")
    If Quantity >= 0 And Quantity < 25 Then
        Discount = 0.1
            ElseIf Quantity >= 25 And Quantity < 50 Then
                Discount = 0.15
                    ElseIf Quantity >= 50 And Quantity < 75 _
        Then
                        Discount = 0.2
                            ElseIf Quantity > 75 Then
                                Discount = 0.25
        End If
    MsgBox "Discount: " & Discount
End Sub
```

Personally, I find nested If. . . Then structures rather cumbersome. I generally use the If. . . Then structure only for simple binary decisions. When a decision involves three or more choices, the Select Case structure offers a simpler, more efficient approach than using nested If. . . Then structures.

The Select Case structure

The Select Case structure is useful for decisions involving three or more options (although it also works with two options, providing a good alternative to the If. . . Then. . . Else structure).

The syntax for the Select Case structure is

```
Select Case testexpression
[Case expressionlist-n
    [statements-n]] . . .
[Case Else
    [elsestatements]]
End Select
```

Don't be scared off by this official syntax. As the following example shows you, using the Select Case structure is actually quite easy.

A Select Case example

The following example shows how you use the Select Case structure. This also shows another way to code the examples presented in the previous section:

```
Sub Discount3()
    Quantity = InputBox("Enter Quantity: ")
    Select Case Quantity
        Case 0 To 24
            Discount = 0.1
        Case 25 To 49
            Discount = 0.15
        Case 50 To 74
            Discount = 0.2
        Case Is >= 75
            Discount = 0.25
    End Select
    MsgBox "Discount: " & Discount
End Sub
```

In this example, the routine evaluates the Quantity variable. The routine checks for four different cases (0 to 24, 25 to 49, 50 to 74, and 75 or greater).

Any number of statements can follow each Case statement, and they all get executed if the case is true. If you use only one statement, as in this example, you can put the statement on the same line as the Case keyword, preceded by a colon — VBA's statement separator character. In my opinion, this makes the code more compact and a bit clearer. Here's how the routine looks using this format:

```
Sub Discount3()
    Quantity = InputBox("Enter Quantity: ")
    Select Case Quantity
        Case  0 To 24: Discount = 0.1
        Case 25 To 49: Discount = 0.15
        Case 50 To 74: Discount = 0.2
        Case Is >= 75: Discount = 0.25
    End Select
    MsgBox "Discount: " & Discount
End Sub
```

When VBA executes a Select Case structure, the structure is exited as soon as VBA finds a true case.

A nested Select Case example

As demonstrated in the following example, you can nest Select Case structures. This routine examines cell A1 on Sheet1, and displays a message describing the cell's contents. Notice that the subroutine has three Select Case structures, and each has its own End Select statement.

```
Sub CheckCell()
   Select Case Sheets("Sheet1").Range("A1").Value
      Case Empty:  Msg = "Cell A1 is blank."
      Case Else
         Select Case Sheets("Sheet1").Range("A1").HasFormula
            Case True:  Msg = "Cell A1 has a formula"
            Case False
               Select Case _
            IsNumeric(Sheets("Sheet1").Range("A1"))
                  Case True: Msg = "Cell A1 has a number"
                  Case Else: Msg = "Cell A1 has text"
               End Select
         End Select
   End Select
   MsgBox Msg
End Sub
```

The logic goes something like this:

1. Find out whether the cell is empty.

2. If it's not empty, see if it contains a formula.

3. If not, find out whether it contains a numeric value.

When the routine ends, the Msg variable contains a string that describes the cell's contents, which is displayed by the MsgBox function.

You can nest Select Case structures as deeply as you need, but make sure that each Select Case statement has a corresponding End Select statement.

As you can see, indenting makes this potentially confusing code much more understandable. If you don't believe me, take a look at the same procedure without any indentation:

```
Sub CheckCell()
Select Case Sheets("Sheet1").Range("A1").Value
Case Empty:  Msg = "Cell A1 is blank."
Case Else
Select Case Sheets("Sheet1").Range("A1").HasFormula
Case True:  Msg = "Cell A1 has a formula"
Case False
```

```
Select Case IsNumeric(Sheets("Sheet1").Range("A1"))
Case True: Msg = "Cell A1 has a number"
Case Else: Msg = "Cell A1 has text"
End Select
End Select
End Select
MsgBox Msg
End Sub
```

Fairly incomprehensible, eh?

Knocking Your Code for a Loop

The term *looping* refers to the process of repeating a block of commands numerous times. You might know how many times your program needs to loop, or this might be determined by the current values of variables in your program.

There are two types of loops: good loops and bad loops. The following code demonstrates a bad loop. The procedure simply enters consecutive numbers into a range. It starts by prompting the user for two values: a starting value and the total number of cells to fill. (Because InputBox returns a string, I convert the strings to integers by using the Cint function). This loop uses the GoTo statement to control the flow. The CellCount variable keeps track of how many cells are filled. If this value is less than the number requested by the user, program control loops back to DoAnother.

```
Sub BadLoop()
    StartVal = Cint(InputBox("Enter the starting value: "))
    NumToFill = Cint(InputBox("How many cells? "))
    ActiveCell.Value = StartVal
    CellCount = 1
DoAnother:
    ActiveCell.Offset(CellCount, 0).Value = StartVal
        CellCount
    CellCount = CellCount + 1
    If CellCount < NumToFill Then GoTo DoAnother Else Exit Sub
End Sub
```

This routine works as intended, so why is it an example of bad looping? As I mentioned earlier in this chapter, you should avoid using a GoTo statement unless it's absolutely necessary. Using GoTo statements to perform looping:

✔ Is contrary to the concept of structured programming (see the sidebar, "What is structured programming?")

✔ Makes the code more difficult to read

✔ Is more prone to errors than using structured looping procedures

VBA has enough structured looping commands that you almost never have to rely on GoTo statements for your decision making. The exception, as I mentioned earlier, is for error handling.

Now, you can move on to a discussion of the good looping structures.

For. . . Next loops

The simplest type of loop is a For. . . Next loop. Here's the syntax for this structure:

```
For counter = start To end [Step stepval]
    [statements]
    [Exit For]
    [statements]
Next [counter]
```

What is structured programming? Does it matter?

If you hang around with programmers, sooner or later you'll hear the term *structured programming*. This term has been around for decades, and programmers generally agree that structured programs are superior to unstructured programs. So, what is structured programming? And can you write structured programs by using VBA?

The basic premise of structured programming is that a routine or a code segment should have only one entry point and only one exit point. In other words, a block of code should be a stand-alone unit, and program control cannot jump into the middle of this unit, nor can it exit at any point except the single exit point. When you write structured code, your program progresses in an orderly manner and is easy to follow — unlike a program that jumps around in a haphazard fashion. This pretty much rules out the GoTo statement.

In general, a structured program is easier to read and understand. More important, it's also easier to modify.

VBA is indeed a structured language. It offers standard structured constructs such as If. . . Then. . . Else, For. . . Next loops, Do. . . Until loops, Do. . . While loops, and Select Case structures. Furthermore, it fully supports modular code construction. If you're new to programming, you should try to develop good, structured programming habits early on. End of lecture.

The looping is controlled by a counter, which starts at one value and stops at another value. The statements between the For statement and the Next statement are the statements in the loop. To see how this works, keep reading.

A For. . . Next example

The following example shows a For. . . Next loop that doesn't use the optional Step value or the optional Exit For statement. This routine loops 100 times and uses VBA's Rnd function to enter a random number into 100 cells:

```
Sub FillRange()
    For Count = 1 To 100
        ActiveCell.Offset(Count - 1, 0) = Rnd
    Next Count
End Sub
```

In this example, Count (the loop counter variable) starts with a value of 1, and increases by 1 each time through the loop. Because no Step value is specified, VBA uses the default value (1). The Offset method uses the value of Count as an argument. The first time through the loop, the procedure enters a number into the active cell offset by zero rows. The second time through (Count = 2), the procedure enters a number into the active cell offset by one row, and so on.

Because the loop counter is a normal variable, you can change its value within the block of code between the For and the Next statements. However, this is a *bad* practice. You should avoid changing the counter within the loop because this can have unpredictable results. In fact, you should take special precautions to ensure that your code does not change the value of the loop counter.

A For. . . Next example with a Step

You can use a Step value to skip some values in a For. . . Next loop. Here's the same procedure as in the preceding section, but rewritten to insert random numbers into every *other* cell:

```
Sub FillRange()
    For Count = 1 To 100 Step 2
        ActiveCell.Offset(Count - 1, 0) = Rnd
    Next Count
End Sub
```

This time, Count starts out as 1, and then takes on a value of 3, 5, 7, and so on. Its final value is 99.

Earlier in this chapter, the introduction to looping presents the BadLoop example, which uses a GoTo statement. Here's the same example, but I convert a bad loop into a good loop by using the For. . . Next structure:

```
Sub FillRange()
    StartVal = CInt(InputBox("Enter the starting value: "))
    NumToFill = CInt(InputBox("How many cells? "))
    For CellCount = 1 To NumToFill
      ActiveCell.Offset(CellCount - 1, 0) = StartVal + _
          CellCount - 1
    Next CellCount
End Sub
```

A For. . . Next example with an Exit For statement

A For. . . Next loop can also include one or more Exit For statements within the loop. When VBA encounters this statement, the loop terminates immediately and doesn't finish.

The following example demonstrates the Exit For statement. This routine identifies which cell in column A of the active worksheet has the largest value:

Sub ExitForDemo()

```
    MaxVal = Application.Max(Range("A:A"))
    For Row = 1 To 16384
        If Range("A1").Offset(Row - 1, 0).Value = MaxVal Then
            Range("A1").Offset(Row - 1, 0).Activate
            MsgBox "Max value is in Row " & Row
             Exit For
        End If
    Next Row
End Sub
```

The routine calculates the maximum value in the column by using the program's MAX function, and assigns the result to the MaxVal variable. Then, the For. . . Next loop checks each cell in the column. If the cell being checked is equal to MaxVal, the routine doesn't need to continue looping (its job is done), so the Exit For statement terminates the loop. Before terminating the loop, the procedure activates the cell with the maximum value and informs the user of its location.

A nested For. . . Next example

So far, all the examples in this chapter use relatively simple loops. However, you can have any number of statements in the loop, and you can nest For. . . Next loops inside of other For. . . Next loops.

The following example uses a nested For. . . Next loop to insert random numbers into a 12-row by 5-column range of cells. Notice that the routine executes the inner loop (the loop with the Row counter) once for each iteration of the outer loop (the loop with the Col counter). In other words, the routine executes the Cells(Row, Col) = Rnd statement 60 times.

```
Sub FillRange()
    For Col = 1 To 5
        For Row = 1 To 12
            Cells(Row, Col) = Rnd
        Next Row
    Next Col
End Sub
```

The next example uses nested For. . . Next loops to initialize a three-dimensional array with all zeros. This routine executes the statement in the middle of all the loops (the assignment statement) 1,000 times, each time with a different combination of values for i, j, and k:

```
Sub NestedLoops()
    Dim MyArray(10, 10, 10)
    For i = 1 To 10
        For j = 1 To 10
            For k = 1 To 10
                MyArray(i, j, k) = 0
            Next k
        Next j
    Next i
End Sub
```

Do. . . While loops

VBA supports another type of looping structure known as a Do. . . While loop. Unlike a For. . . Next loop, a Do. . . While loop continues until a specified condition is met. Here's the Do. . . While loop syntax:

```
Do [While condition]
    [statements]
    [Exit Do]
    [statements]
Loop
```

The following example uses a Do. . . While loop. This routine uses the active cell as a starting point, and then travels down the column, multiplying each cell's value by 2. The loop continues until the routine encounters an empty cell.

```
Sub DoWhileDemo()
    Do While ActiveCell.Value <> Empty
        ActiveCell.Value = ActiveCell.Value * 2
        ActiveCell.Offset(1, 0).Select
    Loop
End Sub
```

Do... Until loops

The Do... Until loop structure is similar to the Do... While structure. The two structures differ in their handling of the tested condition. A program continues to execute a Do... While loop *while* the condition remains true. In a Do... Until loop, the program executes the loop *until* the condition is true.

Here's the Do... Until syntax:

```
Do [Until condition]
    statements]
    [Exit Do]
    [statements]
Loop
```

The following example is the same one presented for the Do... While loop, but recoded to use a Do... Until loop:

```
Sub DoUntilDemo()
    Do Until ActiveCell.Value = Empty
        ActiveCell.Value = ActiveCell.Value * 2
        ActiveCell.Offset(1, 0).Select
    Loop
End Sub
```

Learning More

This chapter introduces you to two key concepts that every programmer must understand: program flow and decision making. These concepts come into play frequently throughout the book, and you can read more about them in the online help.

The next chapter moves on to a completely different topic: using automatic events and procedures.

Chapter 11
Automatic Procedures and Events

● ●

In This Chapter

▶ Learning about the types of events that can trigger the execution of a subroutine (no, this chapter is *not* about capital punishment)

▶ Using specially-named subroutines such as Auto_Open and Auto_Close

▶ Executing a subroutine automatically when you activate a particular workbook, sheet, or window

▶ Executing a subroutine at a particular time of day

▶ Learning about still more events, including double-clicking a cell, entering data into a cell, saving a file, calculating a worksheet, or pressing a key or a key combination

● ●

*W*ay back in Chapter 5, I mention that subroutines can be executed automatically. In this chapter, I cover the ins and outs of this potentially useful feature. I explain how to set things up so a subroutine is executed automatically when a particular event occurs.

Preparing for the Big Event

Okay, what types of events am I talking about here? Good question. Excel can recognize many events, but it can't recognize quite a few others.

Excel can recognize the following events:

> ✔ A workbook is opened.
>
> ✔ A workbook is closed.
>
> ✔ A window is activated.
>
> ✔ A worksheet is activated.
>
> ✔ A worksheet is deactivated.
>
> ✔ A workbook is saved.
>
> ✔ A worksheet is calculated.

✔ An object is clicked.

✔ A particular key or key combination is pressed.

✔ A cell is double-clicked.

✔ A particular time of day occurs.

✔ Data is entered into a cell, or the cell is edited.

✔ An error occurs.

✔ DDE- or OLE-linked data arrives into Excel.

✔ A link is updated.

Most Excel programmers never need to worry about most of the events in this list. However, you should at least know that these events exist. You never know when that may come in handy. In this chapter, I discuss the most commonly used events.

Is this stuff useful?

You might wonder how this event business can be useful. Here's a quick example.

Suppose you have a worksheet that other people use for data entry. Any values entered into this worksheet must be greater than 1,000. You can write a simple macro that is executed whenever someone enters data into a cell. If the user enters a value less than 1,000, the macro displays a dialog box reprimanding the user.

That's just one example of how you can take advantage of an event. Keep reading for some more examples.

More about programming automatic events

Programming these events is relatively straightforward once you understand how it works. It all boils down to a few steps:

1. **Write a subroutine that you want Excel to execute whenever a particular event occurs.**

2. **Tell Excel which event you want to associate with that subroutine.**

   You can do this by assigning a property, by executing a method, or by executing a specially-named subroutine.

3. **Turn off the automatic calling of the subroutine when you no longer need it (optional).**

These steps become clearer as you progress through the chapter. Trust me.

Specially-Named Subroutines

In VBA, two subroutine names have special significance:

- ✔ **Auto_Open:** This subroutine is executed automatically whenever its workbook is opened.
- ✔ **Auto_Close:** This subroutine is executed automatically whenever its workbook is closed.

Two other subroutine names have special significance in VBA: Auto_Activate and Auto_Deactivate. As you might expect, Excel automatically executes these subroutines when a worksheet is activated or deactivated, respectively. VBA provides these subroutines primarily for backward compatibility with older versions of Excel. As you learn later in this chapter, VBA offers better ways to handle these events.

If you press the Shift key while opening a workbook, Excel ignores the workbook's Auto_Open subroutine (if it has one).

An Auto_Open example

Here's an example of an Auto_Open macro:

```
Sub Auto_Open()
   If WeekDay(Now) = 6 Then
       Msg = "Today is Friday. Make sure that you"
       Msg = Msg & "do your weekly backup!"
       MsgBox Msg
   End If
End Sub
```

This subroutine is executed automatically whenever the workbook is opened. It uses VBA's Weekday function to determine the day of the week. If it's Friday, a message box appears reminding the user to perform a weekly file backup. If it's not Friday, nothing happens.

An Auto_Open subroutine can do almost anything. These subroutines are often used for:

- ✔ Displaying welcome messages
- ✔ Opening other workbooks
- ✔ Setting up custom menus
- ✔ Displaying (or hiding) toolbars
- ✔ Setting up other automatic event procedures

An Auto_Close example

Here's an example of an Auto_Close macro, which is executed automatically whenever the workbook is closed:

```
Sub Auto_Close()
    Msg = "Would you like to make a backup of this file?"
    Ans = MsgBox(Msg, vbYesNo)
    If Ans = vbYes Then
        FName = "F:\BACKUP\" & ThisWorkbook.Name
        ThisWorkbook.SaveCopyAs FName
    End If
End Sub
```

This routine uses a message box to ask whether the user would like to make a backup copy of the workbook. If the user clicks Yes, the routine uses the SaveCopyAs method to save a backup copy of the file on drive F.

Excel programmers often use Auto_Close subroutines to clean up after themselves. If you use an Auto_Open subroutine to change some settings when a workbook is opened (hiding the status bar, for example), it's only appropriate that you return the settings to their original state when the workbook is closed. You can perform this electronic housekeeping by using an Auto_Close subroutine.

Activation Events

Another category of events consists of activating or deactivating objects — specifically, activating or deactivating sheets or windows.

Sheet activation or deactivation events

Excel can detect when a sheet is activated or deactivated, and the program can execute a macro whenever either of these events occurs. To do this, you set the OnSheetActivate or OnSheetDeactivate properties to a subroutine name.

The following listing shows two small subroutines that demonstrate how this works:

```
Sub SetupSheetEvent()
    Application.OnSheetActivate = "EventSub"
End Sub

Sub EventSub()
    MsgBox "You just activated " & ActiveSheet.Name
End Sub
```

When Auto_Open and Auto_Close don't work

VBA programmer (that's you), take note! When a VBA macro opens a workbook, the workbook's Auto_Open subroutine (if it has one) is not executed automatically. Similarly, if a VBA macro closes a workbook, the workbook's Auto_Close subroutine (if it has one) is not executed automatically.

This doesn't mean a VBA macro can't execute Auto_Open or Auto_Close subroutines. It just means you must program an additional step. Here's a simple example of opening a workbook from a VBA macro:

```
Sub OpenBudget()
    Workbooks.Open "My _
    Budget.xls"
End Sub
```

If the My Budget workbook has an Auto_Open macro, it will *not* be executed. To force execution of the Auto_Open macro, simply add another line that uses the RunAutoMacros method, like this:

```
Sub OpenBudget()
    Workbooks.Open "My
Budget.xls"

    ActiveWorkbook.RunAuto _
Macros (xlAutoOpen)
End Sub
```

In this case, xlAutoOpen is the argument for the RunAutoMacros method.

Similarly, to close a workbook in a VBA subroutine and execute its Auto_Close subroutine, you must use two statements. Here's an example:

```
Sub CloseBudget()
    Workbooks("My
Budget.xls").RunAutoMacros _
(xlAutoClose)

    Workbooks("My
Budget.xls").Close
End Sub
```

Notice that the RunAutoMacros method is executed before the workbook is actually closed — which makes perfect sense.

The SetupSheetEvent subroutine consists of a single statement that tells Excel to execute the EventSub subroutine. The EventSub subroutine simply pops up a message box that displays the name of the active sheet.

After executing SetupSheetEvent, every time you activate a new sheet, Excel displays a message like the one in Figure 11-1.

To cancel this event, execute the following routine:

```
Sub CancelSheetEvent()
    Application.OnSheetDeactivate = ""
End Sub
```

After this subroutine is executed, nothing happens when you activate a sheet. That is, Excel stops monitoring this event, and things go back to normal (whatever *that* is).

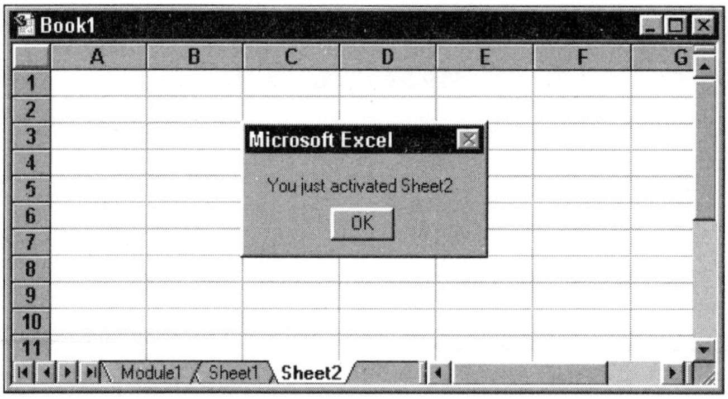

Figure 11-1:
This
message
appears
whenever
you activate
a sheet.

The code in this EventSub example is about as simple as it gets. However, the subroutine that Excel executes when the event occurs can be as complex as you like.

In most cases, you don't want the event to be so general. In the preceding example, the triggering event is the activation of *any* sheet in *any* workbook. If you want Excel to execute a subroutine when a sheet in only one particular workbook (say, Book2) is activated, use a statement like this:

```
Workbooks("Book2").OnSheetActivate = "EventSub"
```

As shown in the following example, you can get even more specific by designating a particular sheet:

```
Worksheets("Sheet3").OnSheetActivate = "EventSub"
```

The OnSheetDeactivate property works exactly the same as the OnSheetActivate property. The only difference is that Excel executes the event subroutine when you deactivate any sheet (or a particular sheet).

Window activation events

You can also trigger the execution of a subroutine with the activation of a particular window. After executing the following statement, Excel executes the EventSub subroutine whenever you switch to a new window:

```
Application.OnWindow = "EventSub"
```

To cancel this event, assign an empty string to the OnWindow property, like this:

```
Application.OnWindow = ""
```

If you want to execute a subroutine when only a particular window is activated (such as My Budget.xls), use a statement like this:

```
Application.Windows("My Budget.xls").OnWindow = _ "EventSub"
```

You cannot program a subroutine to be executed when a window is deactivated. Don't ask me why; you just can't.

The OnTime Event

Another useful event is time. For example, you can set up a subroutine to be executed at a particular time of day. The following example demonstrates how to program Excel so that it beeps and then displays a message at 3:00 p.m.:

```
Sub SetAlarm()
    Application.OnTime 0.625, "DisplayAlarm"
End Sub

Sub DisplayAlarm()
    Beep
    MsgBox "Wake up. It's time for your afternoon break!"
End Sub
```

In this example, I use the OnTime method of the Application object. This method takes two arguments: the time (0.625, or 3:00 p.m.) and the subroutine to execute when the time occurs (DisplayAlarm).

This subroutine is quite useful if you tend to get so wrapped up in your work that you forget about meetings and appointments. Just set an OnTime event to remind yourself.

Most people (this author included) find it difficult to think of time in terms of Excel's numbering system. Therefore, you might want to use VBA's TimeValue function to represent the time. TimeValue converts a string that looks like a time into a value that Excel can handle. The following statement shows an easier way to program an event for 3:00 p.m.:

```
Application.OnTime TimeValue("3:00:00 pm"), _ "DisplayAlarm"
```

If you want to schedule an event relative to the current time — for example, 20 minutes from now — you can use a statement like this:

```
Application.OnTime Now + TimeValue("00:20:00"), _
            "DisplayAlarm"
```

You can also use the OnTime method to schedule a subroutine on a particular day. Of course, you must make sure your computer keeps running and the workbook with the procedure is open. The following statement runs the DisplayAlarm procedure at 5:00 a.m. on July 4, 1996:

```
Application.OnTime DateValue("7/4/96 5:00 am"), DisplayAlarm
```

The OnTime method has two additional arguments. If you plan to use this method, you should refer to the program's online help for complete details.

Worksheet-Related Events

In this section, I discuss four events that occur in worksheets: double-clicking a cell, entering data into a cell, calculating formulas, and saving the workbook.

The OnDoubleClick event

You can set up a subroutine to be executed when the user double-clicks a cell. In the following example, the Setup_OnClick subroutine assigns the ToggleBold subroutine to the OnDoubleClick event. The ToggleBold subroutine makes the cell bold (if it's not bold) or not bold (if it is bold).

```
Sub Setup_OnClick()
    Sheets("Sheet1").OnDoubleClick = "ToggleBold"
End Sub

Sub ToggleBold()
    ActiveCell.Font.Bold = Not ActiveCell.Font.Bold
End Sub
```

The following statement cancels the OnDoubleClick event:

```
Sheets("Sheet1").OnDoubleClick = ""
```

By programming a double-click event, you override the normal double-click behavior in Excel which usually activates in-place editing of the cell.

The OnEntry event

You can trigger execution of a subroutine whenever a user enters data into a cell. In the following example, the Setup_OnEntry procedure assigns the VerifyEntry subroutine to the OnEntry event:

```
Sub Setup_OnEntry()
    Sheets("Sheet1").OnEntry = "VerifyEntry"
End Sub

Sub VerifyEntry()
    If IsNumeric(ActiveCell.Value) Then
        If ActiveCell.Value < 0 Then
            MsgBox "Negative values not allowed you dolt!"
            ActiveCell.Value = ""
        End If
    End If
End Sub
```

After executing the Setup_OnEntry subroutine, Excel executes VerifyEntry whenever the user enters a new value (or edits an existing value) on Sheet1.

The VerifyEntry routine is designed to prevent the user from entering negative values into the worksheet. The routine uses a nested If. . .Then structure. First, it determines whether the entry is numeric. If so, the subroutine determines whether the entry is less than zero. If it's less than zero, the procedure displays a message box with a disparaging remark, as shown in Figure 11-2. It then erases the value entered so that the dolt (oops, the user) can enter a new value.

To cancel this event, just assign an empty string, like this:

```
Sheets("Sheet1").OnEntry = ""
```

The OnCalculate event

The OnCalculate event is triggered whenever the worksheet is calculated. Personally, I've never used this particular event, and I can't really think of a reason to do so. But if you ever need it, it's there.

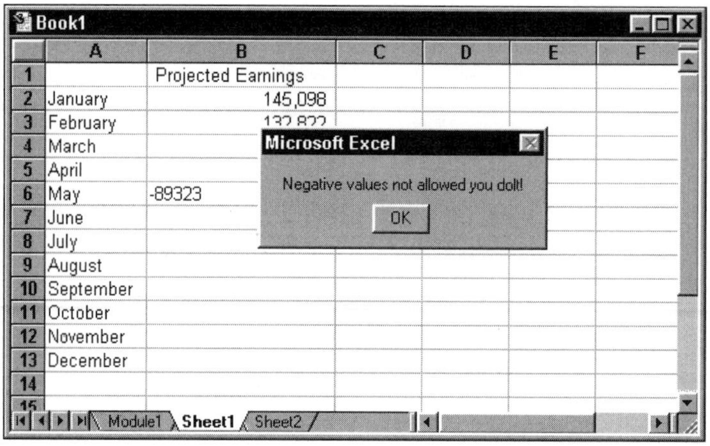

	A	B	C	D	E	F
1		Projected Earnings				
2	January	145,098				
3	February	132,822				
4	March					
5	April					
6	May	-89323				
7	June					
8	July					
9	August					
10	September					
11	October					
12	November					
13	December					
14						
15						

Book1

Microsoft Excel

Negative values not allowed you dolt!

OK

Module1 \ **Sheet1** / Sheet2 /

Figure 11-2:
If the user enters a negative value, this message appears.

The OnSave event

You can also set up an OnSave event, which executes a subroutine whenever the user saves the workbook. Excel executes the assigned subroutine after the user invokes either the Save or the Save As command — but before Excel actually saves the workbook.

The OnSave event is new in Excel for Windows 95. Therefore, don't program this event if your workbook is used by someone who still uses Excel 5.

Keypress Events

While you work, Excel constantly monitors what you type. Because of this, you can set up a keystroke or a key combination to execute a subroutine.

Here's an example that reassigns the PgDn and PgUp keys:

```
Sub Setup_OnKey()
    Application.OnKey "{PgDn}", "PgDn_Sub"
    Application.OnKey "{PgUp}", "PgUp_Sub"
End Sub

Sub PgDn_Sub()
    On Error Resume Next
    If TypeName(ActiveSheet) = "Worksheet" _
      Then ActiveCell.Offset(1, 0).Activate
End Sub

Sub PgUp_Sub()
```

```
     On Error Resume Next
     If TypeName(ActiveSheet) = "Worksheet" _
        Then ActiveCell.Offset(-1, 0).Activate
End Sub
```

After setting up the OnKey events in the Setup_OnKey procedure, pressing PgDn moves down one row. Pressing PgUp moves up one row.

Notice that the key codes are enclosed in brackets, not parentheses. For a complete list of the keyboard codes, consult the program's online help. Search for *OnKey*.

In this example, I use On Error Resume Next to ignore any errors that are generated. For example, if the active cell is in the first row, trying to move up one row causes an error. Also, notice that the subroutines check to see which type of sheet is active. The routine only reassigns the PgUp and PgDn keys when a worksheet is the active sheet.

By executing the following routine, you cancel the OnKey events:

```
Sub Cancel_OnKey()
     Application.OnKey "{PgDn}"
     Application.OnKey "{PgUp}"
End Sub
```

Using an empty string as the second argument for the OnKey method does *not* cancel the OnKey event. Rather, it causes Excel to simply ignore the keystroke and do nothing at all. For example, the following statement tells Excel to ignore Alt+F4 (the percent sign represents the Alt key):

```
Application.OnKey "%{F4}", ""
```

Although you can use the OnKey method to assign a shortcut key for executing a macro, you should use the Macro Options dialog box for this task. For more details, see "Assigning a Shortcut Key" in Chapter 5.

Learning More

Most of the events described in this chapter have additional options that I don't cover. Check the online help for all the ugly details.

The next chapter covers yet another type of event (one that's all too common): an error event. You learn how to trap errors in your code and handle them gracefully.

Chapter 12
Error-Handling Techniques

• •

In This Chapter

▶ Understanding the difference between programming errors and run-time errors

▶ Trapping and handling run-time errors

▶ Using VBA's On Error and Resume statements

▶ Using an error to your advantage

• •

*W*hen working with VBA, you should be aware of two broad classes of errors: programming errors (which I cover in the next chapter), and *run-time* errors (which I cover in this chapter). A well-written program handles errors with ease. Fortunately, VBA includes several tools to help you identify and handle errors gracefully.

Types of Errors

If you've tried any of the examples in this book, you have probably encountered one or more error messages. Some of these errors result from bad VBA code. For example, you may misspell a keyword or type a statement with the wrong syntax. If you commit such an error, your procedure grinds to a halt, and you must fix the mistake.

This chapter does not deal with programming errors. Instead, I discuss run-time errors — the errors that occur while Excel executes your macro.

The ultimate goal of error handling is to write code that avoids Excel's error messages as much as possible. In other words, you want to anticipate potential errors and deal with them before Excel has a chance to rear its ugly head with a (usually) less-than-informative error message.

An Erroneous Example

To see how errors happen and how they can be handled, take a look at the following short subroutine:

```
Sub EnterSquareRoot()
'    Prompt for a value
     Num = InputBox("Enter a value")

'    Insert the square root
     ActiveCell.Value = Sqr(Num)
End Sub
```

As shown in Figure 12-1, this subroutine asks the user for a value. It then enters the square root of that value into the active cell.

Figure 12-1:
The
InputBox
function
dialog box
asks the
user for a
value.

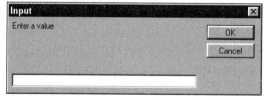

You can add a button to a worksheet (use the Drawing toolbar to do this), and then attach the macro to the button (Excel prompts you for the macro to attach). Then you can run the procedure by simply clicking the button.

Not quite perfect

After entering this subroutine, try it out. It works pretty well, doesn't it? Now, try entering a negative number. Oops. Trying to calculate the square root of a negative number is illegal on this planet. Excel responds with the message shown in Figure 12-2, indicating that your procedure generated a run-time error.

Most folks don't find this error message very helpful. To improve the subroutine, you need to anticipate this error and handle it more gracefully.

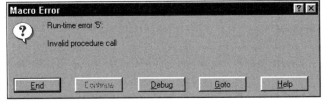

Figure 12-2:
Trying to calculate the square root of a negative number generates this message.

Here's a modified version of EnterSquareRoot:

```
Sub EnterSquareRoot()
'    Prompt for a value
    Num = InputBox("Enter a value")

'    Make sure the number is nonnegative
    If Num < 0 Then
        MsgBox "You must enter a positive number."
        Exit Sub
    End If

'    Insert the square root
    ActiveCell.Value = Sqr(Num)
End Sub
```

An If. . .Then structure checks the value contained in the Num variable. If Num is less than zero, the subroutine displays a message box containing a message that humans can actually understand. Then the subroutine ends with the Exit Sub statement so that the error never has a chance to occur.

Still not perfect

So, the modified EnterSquareRoot subroutine is perfect, right? Not really. Try entering text instead of a value. Or try clicking the Cancel button. Both of these actions generate errors.

The following modified code uses the IsNumeric function to make sure that Num contains a numeric value. If the user doesn't enter a number, the subroutine displays a message and then stops:

```
Sub EnterSquareRoot()
'    Prompt for a value
    Num = InputBox("Enter a value")

'    Make sure Num is a number
    If Not IsNumeric(Num) Then
        MsgBox "You must enter a number."
        Exit Sub
    End If

'    Make sure the number is nonnegative
    If Num < 0 Then
        MsgBox "You must enter a positive number."
        Exit Sub
    End If

'    Insert the square root
    ActiveCell.Value = Sqr(Num)
End Sub
```

Is it perfect yet?

Now it's absolutely perfect, right? Not quite. Try running the subroutine while the active sheet is something other than a worksheet (for example, a VBA module or a Chart sheet). As shown in Figure 12-3, Excel displays another message that's almost as illuminating as the other error messages you see in this chapter. This error message is displayed because there is no active cell, but you wouldn't know that from just reading the following error message.

Figure 12-3:
Running the Enter-SquareRoot procedure when a worksheet is not active generates this error message.

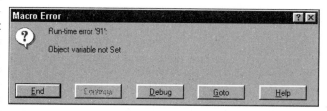

The following listing uses the TypeName function to make sure the active sheet is a worksheet. If the active sheet is anything other than a worksheet, this subroutine displays a helpful, descriptive message and then exits:

```
Sub EnterSquareRoot()
'   Make sure a worksheet is active
    If TypeName(ActiveSheet) <> "Worksheet" Then
        MsgBox "A worksheet must be active."
        Exit Sub
    End If
'   Prompt for a value
    Num = InputBox("Enter a value")

'   Make sure Num is a number
    If Not IsNumeric(Num) Then
        MsgBox "You must enter a number."
        Exit Sub
    End If

'   Make sure the number is nonnegative
    If Num < 0 Then
        MsgBox "You must enter a positive number."
        Exit Sub
    End If

'   Insert the square root
    ActiveCell.Value = Sqr(Num)
End Sub
```

Ready to give up on perfection?

By now, this subroutine simply *must* be perfect. Think again, pal. Protect the worksheet and then run the subroutine and see what happens. Yep, a protected worksheet generates yet another error. And that's just one more example — it's next to impossible to think of all the errors that can occur. Keep reading for another way to deal with errors — even those you can't anticipate.

Another Way to Handle Errors

From the previous examples, you have a better idea of the types of errors that can occur. The question is: *How can you identify and handle every possible error?* The answer is: Often, you can't. Fortunately, VBA doesn't expect you to be a fortune teller; it provides another way to deal with errors.

The EnterSquareRoot subroutine, revisited

Examine the following subroutine. I modified the routine from the previous section by adding an On Error statement to trap all errors:

```
Sub EnterSquareRoot()

'   Set up error handling
    On Error GoTo BadEntry

'   Prompt for a value
    Num = InputBox("Enter a value")

'   Insert the square root
    ActiveCell.Value = Sqr(Num)

    Exit sub
BadEntry:
    Msg = "An error occurred." & Chr(13)
    Msg = Msg & "Make sure that a worksheet is active "
    Msg = Msg & "and you enter a nonnegative value."
    MsgBox Msg
End Sub
```

This routine traps any type of run-time error. After trapping a run-time error, the revised EnterSquareRoot subroutine displays the message box shown in Figure 12-4.

Figure 12-4:
Any error in the Enter-SquareRoot subroutine generates this error message.

Microsoft Excel

An error occurred.
Make sure that a worksheet is active and you enter a non-negative value.

OK

The code builds the error message and assigns it to a variable, Msg. The code builds the error message by using the concatenation operator (&). Chr(13) causes the text to skip to the next line.

If an On Error statement doesn't seem to be working as advertised, one of your settings may be blocking it. Choose the Tools⇨Options command, and click the Module General tab of the Options dialog box. Make sure the Break on All Errors setting is *not* checked. If this setting is checked, Excel essentially ignores any On Error statements.

More about the On Error statement

Using an On Error statement in your VBA code causes Excel to bypass its built-in error handling. In the previous example, a run-time error causes macro execution to jump to the statement labeled BadEntry. As a result, you avoid Excel's unfriendly error messages, and you can display your own (hopefully, friendly) message to the user.

 Notice that the example uses an Exit Sub statement right before the BadEntry label. This statement is necessary because you don't want to execute the error-handling code if an error does *not* occur.

Handling Errors: The Details

You can use the On Error statement in three ways:

Syntax	What It Does
On Error GoTo *line*	After executing this statement, Excel resumes macro execution at the specified line. The value you enter in place of *line* can be a label or a line number. In either case, you must include a colon so Excel recognizes this as a label.
On Error Resume Next	After executing this statement, Excel simply ignores all errors and resumes execution with the next statement. I present an example of how this works in the next section.
On Error GoTo 0	After executing this statement, Excel resumes its normal error-checking behavior. Use this statement after you use one of the other On Error statements.

Resuming after an error

In some cases, you simply want your routine to end gracefully when an error occurs. For example, you might display a message describing the error and then exit the subroutine. In other cases, you want to recover from the error, if possible.

To recover from an error, you must use a Resume statement. This clears the error condition and lets you continue execution at some location. You can use the Resume statement in three ways:

Syntax	*What It Does*
Resume [0]	Execution resumes with the statement that caused the error. Use this if your error-handling code fixes the problem.
Resume Next	Execution resumes with the statement immediately following the statement that caused the error. This essentially ignores the error.
Resume line	Execution resumes at the line you specify (which must be a line label or a line number).

The following example uses a Resume statement after an error occurs:

```
Sub EnterSquareRoot()
TryAgain:
'    Set up error handling
     On Error GoTo BadEntry

'    Prompt for a value
     Num = InputBox("Enter a value")

'    Insert the square root
     ActiveCell.Value = Sqr(Num)

     Exit Sub
BadEntry:
     Msg = "An error occurred. Try again?"
     Ans = MsgBox(Msg, vbYesNo)
     If Ans = vbYes Then Resume TryAgain
End Sub
```

If an error occurs, execution continues at the BadEntry label, and the subroutine displays the message shown in Figure 12-5. If the user responds by clicking Yes, the Resume statement kicks in, and execution jumps back to the TryAgain label. If the user clicks No, the subroutine ends.

Figure 12-5:
If an error occurs, you can try again.

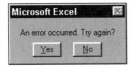

Remember that the Resume statement clears the error condition before continuing. To see what I mean, try substituting the following statement for the last statement in the preceding example:

```
If Ans = vbYes Then GoTo TryAgain
```

If you use GoTo instead of Resume, the subroutine doesn't work correctly. Execution is transferred to the proper location, but the error condition is not cleared.

Knowing when to ignore errors

In some cases, it's perfectly okay to ignore errors. That's when the On Error Resume Next statement comes into play.

The following example loops through each cell in the selection and converts the value to its square root. This procedure generates an error message if any cell in the selection contains a negative number:

```
Sub SelectionSqrt()
    For Each cell In Selection
        cell.Value = Sqr(cell.Value)
    Next cell
End Sub
```

In this case, you may want to simply skip any cell that contains a value you can't convert to a square root. You *could* create all sorts of error-checking capabilities by using If statements. You could also devise a better (and simpler) solution by simply ignoring the errors.

The following routine accomplishes this by using the On Error Resume Next statement:

```
Sub SelectionSqrt()
    On Error Resume Next
    For Each cell In Selection
        cell.Value = Sqr(cell.Value)
    Next cell
End Sub
```

In general, you can use an On Error Resume Next statement if you consider the errors inconsequential to your task.

Identifying specific errors

Although you may ignore some errors that you consider inconsequential, you must deal with other, more serious errors. In some cases, it becomes necessary to identify exactly what type of error you are facing. Whenever an error occurs, Excel stores the error number in a variable named Err. You can get a description of the error by using the Error function. For example, the following statement displays the error number and a description:

```
MsgBox Err & ": " & Error(Err)
```

Figure 12-6 shows an example of an error number and description.

Figure 12-6:
Displaying
an error
number
and a
description.

The following subroutine demonstrates how to determine which error occurred. In this case, you can safely ignore errors caused by trying to get the square root of a negative number (that is, error 13). On the other hand, you need to inform the user if the worksheet is protected and the selection contains one or more locked cells (otherwise, the user might think the macro worked when it really didn't). The following event causes error 1005.

```
Sub SelectionSqrt()
    On Error GoTo ErrorHandler
    For Each cell In Selection
        cell.Value = Sqr(cell.Value)
    Next cell
    Exit Sub

ErrorHandler:
    Select Case Err
        Case 13 'Type mismatch
            Resume Next
        Case 1005 'Locked cell, protected sheet
            MsgBox "The selection contains a locked cell. Try _
              again."
            Exit Sub

        Case Else
            ErrMsg= Error(Err)
            MsgBox "ERROR: " & ErrMsg
            Exit Sub
    End Select
End Sub
```

When a run-time error occurs, execution jumps to the ErrorHandler label. The Select Case structure tests for two common error numbers. If the error number is 13, execution resumes at the next statement (in other words, the error is ignored). But if the error number is 1005, the routine advises the user and then ends. The last case, a catch-all, traps all other errors and displays the actual error message.

Error handling in a nutshell

To help you keep all this error-handling business straight, here's a quick-and-dirty summary. An error-handling routine has the following characteristics:

- ✔ It begins immediately after the label specified in the On Error statement.

- ✔ Your macro can only reach it if an error occurs. This means you need to use a statement such as Exit Sub or Exit Function right before the label.

- ✔ If you choose not to abort the procedure when an error occurs, you must execute a Resume statement before returning to the main code.

An Intentional Error

Sometimes, you can use an error to your advantage. For example, suppose you have a macro that only works if a particular workbook (named Prices) is open. How can you determine whether that workbook is open? Perhaps the best solution is to write a general-purpose function that accepts one argument (a workbook name) and returns True if the workbook is open and False if it's not.

Here's the function:

```
Function WorkbookOpen(book) As Boolean
    On Error GoTo NotOpen
    x = Workbooks(book).Name
    WorkbookOpen = True
    Exit Function
NotOpen:
    WorkbookOpen = False
End Function
```

This function takes advantage of the fact that Excel generates an error if you refer to a workbook that is not open. For example, the following statement generates an error if a workbook named MyBook is not open:

```
x = Workbooks("MyBook").Name
```

In the preceding function, the On Error statement tells VBA to resume the macro at the NotOpen statement if an error occurs. Therefore, an error means the workbook is not open, and the function returns False. If the workbook is open, no error occurs and the function returns True.

The following example demonstrates how to use this function in a subroutine. If the workbook is not open, the subroutine informs the user of that fact. If the workbook is open, the macro continues:

```
Sub Macro1()
    If Not WorkbookOpen("Prices") Then
        MsgBox "Please open the Prices workbook first!"
        Exit Sub
    End If
'   Other code goes here
End Sub
```

Learning More

Error handling can be a tricky proposition — after all, many different errors can occur. In general, you should trap errors before Excel intervenes and correct the situation if possible. Writing effective error-trapping code requires a thorough knowledge of Excel and a clear understanding of how VBA's error handling works. Subsequent chapters contain more examples of error handling.

In the next chapter, I cover another type of error: the errors you make when writing code. I demonstrate how to identify and correct bugs in your programs.

Chapter 13

Bug Extermination Techniques

. . . .

In This Chapter

▶ Kinds of bugs and why you should squash them

▶ Types of program bugs you might encounter

▶ Tips for identifying bugs

▶ Techniques for debugging your code

▶ Details on using Excel's built-in debugging tools

. . . .

*I*f the word *bugs* conjures up an image of a cartoon rabbit, this chapter can set you straight. I cover the topic of programming bugs — how to identify them, and how to wipe them off the face of your module.

Species of Bugs

Welcome to Entomology 101. The term *program bug,* as you probably know, refers to a problem with software. In other words, if software doesn't perform as expected, it has a bug. Fact is, all major software has bugs — lots of bugs. It has been said that software that doesn't contain bugs is probably so trivial that it's not worth using. Excel itself has hundreds (if not thousands) of bugs. Fortunately, most of them are relatively obscure and appear only in very unusual circumstances.

Pssst. . . Wanna see an Excel bug in action?

Here's how you can take a peek at one of the bugs in Excel. Activate any worksheet and enter the value **1.40737488355328** into any cell. Press Enter, and the value in the cell changes to 0.64.

It's possible that your version of Excel already has this bug corrected. If not, you can get a *patch* (a collection of software statements designed to be added to existing software) that corrects this well-known bug. You can get the fix from the Microsoft World Wide Web site at the following address:

http://www.microsoft.com/msexcel/

When you write VBA programs, your code may have bugs that fall into any of the following categories:

- ✔ **Logic-flaw bugs.** You can often avoid these bugs by carefully thinking through the problem your program addresses.

- ✔ **Incorrect-context bugs.** This type of bug surfaces when you attempt to do something at the wrong time. For example, when you try to write data to cells in the active sheet when the active sheet is not a worksheet.

- ✔ **Extreme-case bugs.** These bugs rear their ugly heads when you encounter data you didn't anticipate — for example, very large or very small numbers.

- ✔ **Wrong-data bugs.** This type of bug occurs when you try to process data of the wrong type — for example, attempting to take the square root of a text string.

- ✔ **Wrong-version bugs.** This type of bug involves incompatibilities between different versions of Excel. For example, you might develop a worksheet using Excel for Windows 95, and then find out that the worksheet doesn't work with Excel 5. You can usually correct such problems by avoiding Excel for Windows 95-specific features.

- ✔ **Beyond-your-control bugs.** These are the most frustrating. An example occurs when Microsoft upgrades Excel and makes a minor, undocumented change that causes your macro to bomb.

Debugging is the process of identifying and correcting bugs in your program. In the following section, I discuss some debugging techniques you can use. Developing debugging skills takes time, so don't be discouraged if this process seems difficult at first.

It's important to understand the distinction between *bugs* and *syntax errors*. A syntax error is a language error. For example, you might misspell a keyword, omit the Next statement in a For. . . Next loop, or enter a set of mismatched parentheses. Before you can even execute the procedure, you must correct these syntax errors. A program bug is much subtler. You can execute the routine, but it doesn't perform as expected.

Identifying Bugs

Before you can do any debugging, you must determine whether a bug actually exists. You can tell that your macro contains a bug if it doesn't work the way it should. (Gee, this book is just filled with insight, isn't it?) Usually, but not always, you can easily discern if your program contains a bug.

A bug often (but not always) becomes apparent when Excel displays a run-time error message. Figure 13-1 shows an example. Notice that this error message includes a button labeled Debug. More about this in the section "Using the built-in debugger."

Figure 13-1:
An error
message
like this
could mean
your VBA
code
contains
a bug.

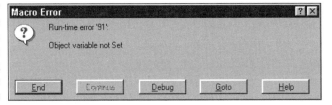

It's important to remember that bugs often appear when you least expect them. For example, just because your macro works fine with one set of data, you can't assume that it works equally as well with all sets of data. The best debugging approach is thorough testing, under a variety of real-life conditions.

Debugging Techniques

In this section, I discuss the three most common methods for debugging Excel VBA code:

- ✔ Examining the code
- ✔ Inserting MsgBox functions at various locations in your code
- ✔ Using Excel's built-in debugging tools

Examining your code

Perhaps the most straightforward debugging technique is simply taking a close look at your code to see if you can find the problem. If you're lucky, the error jumps right out and you can quickly correct it.

Using the MsgBox function

A common problem in many programs involves one or more variables that don't take on the values you expect. In such cases, a helpful debugging technique involves monitoring the variable (or variables) while your code runs. You can do this by inserting temporary MsgBox functions in your routine. For example, if you have a variable named CellCount, you can insert the following statement:

```
MsgBox CellCount
```

When you execute the routine, the MsgBox function displays the value of CellCount.

It's often helpful to display the values of two or more variables in the message box. The following statement displays the current value of LoopIndex and CellCount, as shown in Figure 13-2:

```
MsgBox LoopIndex & " " & CellCount
```

Figure 13-2:
A message box displays the values of two variables.

Notice that I combine the two variables with the concatenation operator (&) and insert a space character between them. Otherwise, the message box strings the two values together, making them look like a single value.

This technique isn't limited to monitoring variables. You can use a message box to display all sorts of useful information while your code is running. For example, if your code loops through a series of sheets, you can use the following statement to display the name and type of the active sheet:

```
MsgBox ActiveSheet.Name & " " & TypeName(ActiveSheet)
```

I use MsgBox functions frequently when I debug my code. Just make sure you remove them after you identify and fix the problem.

Using the built-in debugger

Excel's designers are intimately familiar with the concept of bugs. Consequently, Excel includes a set of debugging tools that can help you correct problems in your VBA code. Figure 13-3 shows the Excel Debug window.

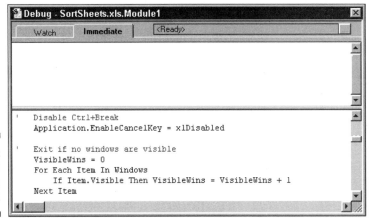

Figure 13-3:
The Excel
Debug
window.

You can open this window in several ways:

- ✔ Choose the View➪Debug Window command (a VBA module must be active).
- ✔ Press Ctrl+G when a VBA module is active.
- ✔ Click the Debug button when Excel displays a run-time error message.
- ✔ Press Ctrl+Break while your code is executing. This generates an error message. Click the Debug button in the Macro Error dialog box.

The Debug window appears automatically when Excel encounters a breakpoint in your code. I discuss breakpoints later in this chapter (see the section "Setting breakpoints in your code").

The Debug window is divided into two panes. The bottom pane (the Code pane) contains the code in the active VBA module. The top pane contains two tabs labeled Watch and Immediate. Clicking these tabs displays either the Watch pane or the Immediate pane (which appears by default). I describe these panes in the next section.

You can change the relative sizes of the two panes by dragging the separator bar up or down.

More about the Debugger

In this section, I discuss the gory details of using the Excel debugger.

Setting breakpoints in your code

Earlier in this chapter, I discuss using MsgBox functions in your code to monitor the values of certain variables. Displaying a message box essentially halts your code in midexecution, and clicking the OK button resumes execution.

Wouldn't it be nice if you could halt the execution of a routine, take a look at some variables, and then continue? Well, that's exactly what you can do by setting a breakpoint.

To set a breakpoint in your code, move the cursor to the line where you want execution to stop, and press F9. As shown in Figure 13-4, Excel highlights the line to remind you that you set a breakpoint there. When you execute the procedure, Excel enters *Break mode* when the line with the breakpoint is executed.

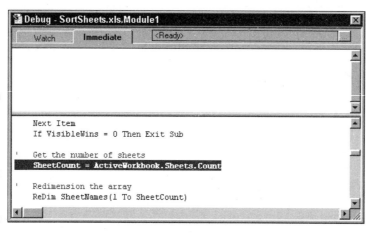

Figure 13-4:
The highlighted line marks a breakpoint in this procedure.

To remove a breakpoint, move the cursor to the highlighted line, and press F9. To remove all breakpoints in the module, choose Run⇨Clear All Breakpoints.

So, what is Break mode? You can think of it as a state of suspended animation. Your VBA code stops running, the Debug window appears automatically, and the Code window displays your code with the current statement highlighted. In Break mode, you can

- ✔ Type VBA statements in the Immediate pane of the Debug window
- ✔ Step through your code one line at a time in the Debug window

Using the Immediate pane

In Break mode, the Immediate pane is particularly useful for finding the current value of any variable in your program. For example, if you want to know the current value of a variable named CellCount, enter the following in the Immediate pane and press Enter:

```
Print CellCount
```

You can save a few milliseconds of time by using a question mark in place of the word *print*, like this:

```
? CellCount
```

Figure 13-5 shows an example of using the Immediate pane.

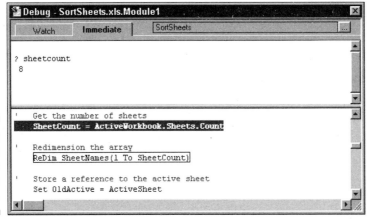

Figure 13-5:
The Immediate pane in action.

The Immediate pane lets you do other things besides checking the values of variables. For example, you can change the value of a variable, activate a different sheet, or even open a new workbook. Just make sure the command you enter is a valid VBA statement.

Stepping through your code

While in Break mode, you can also step through your code line by line. You do this by using the following keystrokes:

Keystroke	*What It Does*
F8	Executes the next statement.
F5	Resumes execution of the code.
F9	Makes the current line a breakpoint. If you already set a breakpoint at the current line, pressing F9 removes the breakpoint.

Throughout this line-by-line execution of your code, you can jump up to the Immediate pane at any time to check the status of your variables.

Using watch variables

In some cases, you might want to know whether a certain variable or expression takes on a particular value. For example, suppose a procedure loops through 1,000 cells. You notice that a problem occurs during the 900th iteration of the loop. Well, you *could* insert a breakpoint within the loop, but that would mean responding to 899 prompts before the code finally gets to the iteration you want to see (and that gets boring real fast). A more efficient solution involves setting a *watch expression*.

For example, you could create a watch expression that puts the procedure into Break mode whenever a certain variable takes on a specific value — for example, Counter=900. To create a watch expression, click the Watch tab at the top of the Debug window. As shown in Figure 13-6, the display changes from the Immediate pane to the Watch pane.

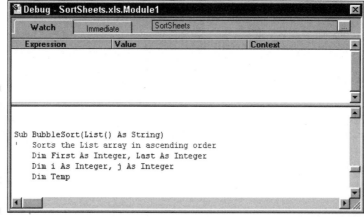

Figure 13-6:
The Debug window with the Watch pane displayed at the top.

Choose the Tools⇨Add Watch command to bring up the Add Watch dialog box, which is shown in Figure 13-7.

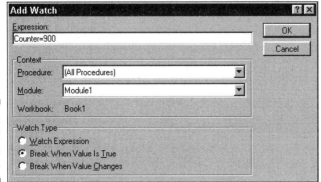

Figure 13-7:
The Add
Watch
dialog box.

The Add Watch dialog has three parts:

- ✔ **Expression:** Enter a valid VBA expression or a variable here. For example, **Counter=900,** or just **Counter.**

- ✔ **Context:** Select the procedure and the module you want to watch. Note that you can select All procedures and All modules.

- ✔ **Watch Type:** Select the type of watch by clicking an option button.

After setting up your watch expression(s), execute your procedure. Things run normally until your watch expression is satisfied (based on the Watch Type you specified). When that happens, Excel puts you in Break mode, and you can step through the code, or use the Immediate pane to debug your code.

Bug Reduction Tips

I can't tell you how to completely eliminate bugs in your programs, but I can provide a few tips to help you keep those bugs to a minimum:

- ✔ **Use an Option Explicit statement at the beginning of your module:** This statement requires you to define the data type for every variable you use. This creates a bit more work, but you avoid the common error of misspelling a variable name. And it has a nice side benefit: Your routines run faster.

- ✔ **Format your code with indentation:** Using indentations helps delineate different code segments. If your program has several nested For. . . Next loops, for example, consistent indentation helps you keep track of them all.

✔ **Regulate use of the On Error Resume Next statement:** As I discuss in Chapter 12, this statement causes Excel to ignore any errors and continue executing the routine. In some cases, using this statement causes Excel to ignore errors that it shouldn't ignore. Your code might have bugs and not even realize it.

✔ **Use lots of comments:** Nothing is more frustrating than revisiting code you wrote six months ago and not having a clue as to how it works. By adding a few comments to describe your logic, you can save lots of time down the road.

✔ **Keep your subroutines and functions simple:** By writing your code in small modules, each of which has a single, well-defined purpose, you simplify the debugging process.

✔ **Use the macro recorder to help you identify properties and methods:** When I can't remember the name or the syntax of a property or a method, I often simply record a macro and look at the recorded code.

✔ **Understand Excel's debugger:** Although it can be a bit daunting at first, Excel's debugger is a useful tool. Invest some time and get to know it.

Learning More

Debugging code is not one of my favorite activities (it ranks right up there with getting audited by the IRS), but it's a necessary evil that goes along with programming. As you gain more experience with VBA, you'll spend less time debugging, and you'll find that it gets easier to do.

Armed with your newfound knowledge of debugging, you're ready to proceed to Chapter 14, which contains lots of useful programming examples.

Chapter 14

VBA Programming Examples

● ●

In This Chapter

▶ Working with ranges

▶ Changing Excel settings using macros

▶ Working with charts

▶ Speeding up your VBA code

● ●

*M*y philosophy for learning how to write Excel macros places heavy emphasis on examples. I find that a well-thought-out example often communicates a concept much better than a lengthy description of the underlying theory — and because you bought this book, you probably agree with me. This chapter presents several examples that demonstrate helpful VBA techniques and some tips on how to make your VBA code run as fast as Carl Lewis on two double lattes. Although you may be able to use some of the examples directly, in most cases, you need to adapt them to your own needs.

Working with Ranges

Most VBA programming involves worksheet ranges. (For a refresher course on working with Range objects, refer to Chapter 8.) When you work with Range objects, keep the following points in mind:

- ✔ You don't need to select a range to work with it.

- ✔ If you do select a range, its worksheet must be active.

- ✔ The macro recorder doesn't always generate the most efficient code. Often, you can create your macro by using the recorder and then editing the code to make it more efficient.

✔ You should use named ranges in your VBA code. For example, Range("Total") is better than Range("D45"). In the latter case, if you add a row above row 45, you need to modify the macro.

✔ The macro recorder doesn't record keystrokes used to select a range. For example, if you press Ctrl+Shift+right-arrow to select to the end of a row, Excel records the actual range selected.

✔ When running a macro that works on the current range selection, you may select entire columns or rows. In most cases, you don't want to loop through every cell in the selection. Your macro should create a subset of the selection consisting of only the nonblank cells.

✔ Excel allows multiple selections. For example, you can select a range, press Ctrl, and select another range. You can test for this in your macro and take appropriate actions.

The examples in the following sections demonstrate these points.

Copying a range

Copying a range is right up there in the Top Ten list of favorite Excel activities. When you turn on the macro recorder and copy a range from A1:A5 to B1:B5, you get this VBA macro:

```
Sub CopyRange()
    Range("A1:A5").Select
    Selection.Copy
    Range("B1").Select
    ActiveSheet.Paste
    Application.CutCopyMode = False
End Sub
```

This macro works, but you can copy a range more efficiently than this. You can produce exactly the same result with the following one-line macro:

```
Sub CopyRange2()
    Range("A1:A5").Copy (Range("B1"))
End Sub
```

This macro takes advantage of the fact that the Copy method can use an argument that specifies the destination. This example also demonstrates that the macro recorder doesn't always generate the most efficient code.

Copying a variable-sized range

In many cases, you need to copy a range of cells but you don't know the exact row and column dimensions. For example, you might have a workbook that tracks weekly sales. The number of rows changes weekly.

Figure 14-1 shows a range on a worksheet. This range consists of several rows, and the number of rows can change from day to day. Because you don't know the exact range address at any given time, writing a macro to copy the range can be challenging. Are you up for the challenge?

The following macro demonstrates how to copy this range from Sheet1 to Sheet2 (beginning at cell A1). It uses the CurrentRegion property, which returns a Range object that corresponds to the block of cells around a particular cell (in this case, A1):

```
Sub CopyCurrentRegion()
    Range("A1").CurrentRegion.Copy
    Sheets("Sheet2").Select
    Range("A1").Select
    ActiveSheet.Paste
    Sheets("Sheet1").Select
    Application.CutCopyMode = False
End Sub
```

	A	B	C	D	E	F	
1	Date	Units Sold	Total Amount				
2	02-Dec-96	143	5,577				
3	03-Dec-96	122	4,758				
4	04-Dec-96	165	6,435				
5	05-Dec-96	101	3,939				
6	06-Dec-96	169	6,591				
7	09-Dec-96	131	5,109				
8	10-Dec-96	94	3,666				
9	11-Dec-96	215	8,385				
10	13-Dec-96	155	6,045				
11							
12							
13							
14							

Book1 — Sheet1 / Sheet2

Figure 14-1: This range can consist of any number of rows.

Using the CurrentRegion property is equivalent to choosing the Edit↷Go To command, clicking the Special button, and selecting the Current Region option.

Selecting to the end of a row or a column

You've probably gotten into the habit of using key combinations such as Ctrl+Shift+right-arrow and Ctrl+Shift+down-arrow to select from the active cell to the end of a row or a column. You might be surprised to discover that the macro recorder doesn't record these types of keystroke combinations. Instead, it records the address of the range that you select.

As I describe in the previous section, you can use the CurrentRegion property to select an entire block. But what if you just want to select, say, one column from a block of cells?

Fortunately, VBA can accommodate this type of action. The following VBA subroutine selects the range beginning at the active cell and extending down to the last cell in the column. After selecting the range, you can do whatever you want with it — copy it, move it, format it, and so on.

```
Sub SelectDown()
    Range(ActiveCell, ActiveCell.End(xlDown)).Select
End Sub
```

This example uses the End method of the Range object, which returns a Range object. The End method takes one argument, which can be any of the following constants:

- ✔ xlUp
- ✔ xlDown
- ✔ xlToLeft
- ✔ xlToRight

Selecting a row or a column

The following subroutine demonstrates how to select the column containing the active cell. It uses the EntireColumn property, which returns a range that consists of a column:

```
Sub SelectColumn()
    ActiveCell.EntireColumn.Select
End Sub
```

As you might expect, VBA also offers an EntireRow property, which returns a range that consists of a row.

Moving a range

You move a range by cutting it to the Clipboard and then pasting it to another area. If you record your actions while performing a move operation, the macro recorder generates code like the following:

```
Sub MoveRange()
    Range("A1:C6").Select
    Selection.Cut
    Range("A10").Select
    ActiveSheet.Paste
End Sub
```

Like the copying example earlier in this chapter, this is not the most efficient way to move a range of cells. In fact, you can do it with a single VBA statement, as follows:

```
Sub MoveRange2()
    Range("A1:C6").Cut (Range("A10"))
End Sub
```

This macro takes advantage of the fact that the Cut method can use an argument that specifies the destination. Notice also that the range is not selected. In fact, the cell pointer remains in its original position.

Looping through a range efficiently

Many macros perform an operation on each cell in a range, or they may perform selected actions based on the content of each cell. These macros usually include a For. . . Next loop that processes each cell in the range.

The following example demonstrates how to loop through a range. In this case, the range is the current selection. A variable named _Cell_ refers to the cell being processed. Within the For. . . Next loop, the single statement evaluates the cell and changes its interior color if the cell contains a positive value.

```
Sub ProcessCells()
    For Each Cell In Selection
        If Cell.Value > 0 Then Cell.Interior.ColorIndex = 6
    Next Cell
End Sub
```

This example works, but what if the selection consists of an entire column or an entire range? (This is not uncommon because Excel lets you perform operations on entire columns or rows.) The macro seems to take forever because it loops through each cell — even the blank cells. To make the macro more efficient, you need a means for processing only the nonblank cells.

The following routine does just that by using the SelectSpecial method (refer to the online help for specific details about its arguments). This routine uses the *Set* keyword to create two new objects: the subset of the selection that consists of cells with constants, and the subset of the selection that consists of cells with formulas. The routine processes each of these subsets, with the net effect of skipping all blank cells. Pretty slick, eh?

```
Sub SkipBlanks()
'    Ignore errors
     On Error Resume Next

'    Process the constants
     Set ConstantCells = Selection.SpecialCells(xlConstants, _
          23)
     For Each cell In ConstantCells
          If cell.Value > 0 Then cell.Interior.ColorIndex = 6
     Next cell

'    Process the formulas
     Set FormulaCells = Selection.SpecialCells(xlFormulas, 23)
     For Each cell In FormulaCells
          If cell.Value > 0 Then cell.Interior.ColorIndex = 6
     Next cell
End Sub
```

The SkipBlanks subroutine works equally fast, regardless of what you select. For example, you can select the range, all columns in the range, all rows in the range, or even the entire worksheet. It's a vast improvement over the ProcessCells subroutine presented earlier in this section.

Notice that I use the following statement in this subroutine:

```
On Error Resume Next
```

This statement tells Excel to ignore any errors and simply process the next statement (see Chapter 12 for a discussion of error handling). This statement is necessary because the SpecialCells method produces an error if no cells qualify.

Prompting for a cell value

As shown in Figure 14-2, you can use VBA's InputBox function to solicit a value
from the user. Then, you can insert that value into a cell. The following subroutine demonstrates how to ask the user for a value and place the value in cell A1
of the active worksheet, using only one statement:

```
Sub GetValue()
    Range("A1").Value = InputBox("Enter the value for cell
        A1")
End Sub
```

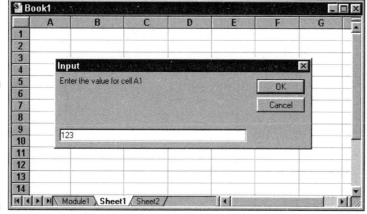

Figure 14-2:
Using VBA's
InputBox
function to
get a value
from the
user.

Determining the type of a selection

If you design your macro to work with a range selection, it must be able to
determine whether a range is actually selected. Otherwise, the macro probably
bombs. The following subroutine identifies what type object is currently
selected:

```
Sub SelectionType()
    MsgBox TypeName(Selection)
End Sub
```

If a Range object is selected, the MsgBox displays *Range*. If your macro works
only with ranges, you can use an If statement to ensure that a range is actually
selected.

Here's an example that beeps, displays a message, and exits the subroutine if the current selection is not a Range object:

```
Sub CheckSelection()
    If TypeName(Selection) <> "Range" Then
        Beep
        MsgBox "Select a range."
        Exit Sub
    End If
'   ... [Other statements go here]
End Sub
```

Identifying a multiple selection

As you know, Excel allows you to make a multiple selection by pressing Ctrl while you select objects or ranges. This can cause problems with some macros. For example, you can't copy a multiple selection that consists of nonadjacent ranges (try it if you don't believe me).

The following macro demonstrates how to determine whether the user made a multiple selection:

```
Sub MultipleSelection()
    If Selection.Areas.Count > 1 Then
        MsgBox "Multiple selections not allowed."
        Exit Sub
    End If
'   ... [Other statements go here]
End Sub
```

This example uses the Areas method, which returns a collection of all objects in the selection. The Count property returns the number of objects in the collection.

Changing Excel Settings Using Macros

Some of the most useful macros are simple subroutines that change one or more of Excel's settings. For example, simply changing the recalculation mode from automatic to manual requires numerous steps. You can save yourself some keystrokes and menu picks (not to mention time) by creating a macro that automates this task.

This section presents two examples that show you how to change settings in Excel. You can apply the general principles demonstrated by these examples to other operations.

Changing Boolean settings

Like a light switch, a *Boolean* setting is either on or off. For example, you might want to create a macro that turns the row and column headings on and off. With the headings turned on, if you record your actions while you access the Options dialog box, Excel generates the following code:

```
ActiveWindow.DisplayHeadings = False
```

On the other hand, if the headings are turned off, Excel generates the following code:

```
ActiveWindow.DisplayHeadings = True
```

This might lead you to suspect that you need two macros: one to turn the headings on, and one to turn them off. Not true. The following subroutine uses the Not operator to effectively toggle the heading display from True to False and from False to True:

```
Sub ToggleHeadings()
    If TypeName(ActiveSheet) <> "Worksheet" Then Exit Sub
    ActiveWindow.DisplayHeadings = Not _
            ActiveWindow.DisplayHeadings
End Sub
```

The first statement ensures that the active sheet is a worksheet; otherwise, an error occurs. You can use this technique with any settings that have Boolean (True or False) values.

Changing non-Boolean settings

For non-Boolean settings, you can use a Select Case structure. This example toggles the calculation mode and displays a message indicating the current mode:

```
Sub ToggleCalcMode()
    Select Case Application.Calculation
        Case xlManual
            Application.Calculation = xlAutomatic
            MsgBox "Automatic Calculation Mode"
```
(continued)

```
(continued)
        Case xlAutomatic
            Application.Calculation = xlManual
            MsgBox "Manual Calculation Mode"
    End Select
End Sub
```

Working with Charts

Because charts are packed with different objects, manipulating charts with VBA can be quite confusing. To get a feel for this, turn on the macro recorder, create a chart, and perform some routine chart-editing tasks. You might be surprised by the amount of code Excel generates. After you understand the objects in a chart, however, you can create some useful macros.

To write macros that manipulate charts, you must understand some terminology. An embedded chart on a worksheet is a ChartObject object. You can activate a chart object much like you activate a sheet. The following statement activates the ChartObject named Chart 1:

```
ActiveSheet.ChartObjects("Chart 1").Activate
```

After you activate the chart, you can refer to it in your VBA code as the ActiveChart. If the chart is on a separate chart sheet, it becomes the active chart as soon you activate that chart sheet.

Modifying the chart type

A ChartObject object acts as a container for a Chart object. To modify a chart with VBA, you don't have to activate it. Rather, you can use the Chart method to return the Chart contained in the ChartObject. This is confusing, I admit. The following subroutines have exactly the same effect: They each change the chart named Chart 1 to an area chart. (The built-in constant xlArea represents an area chart.) This subroutine activates the chart first:

```
Sub ModifyChart1()
    ActiveSheet.ChartObjects("Chart 1").Activate
    ActiveChart.Type = xlArea
    ActiveWindow.Visible = False
End Sub
```

This subroutine does not activate the chart first:

```
Sub ModifyChart2()
    ActiveSheet.ChartObjects("Chart 1").Chart.Type = xlArea
End Sub
```

Looping through the ChartObjects collection

This example changes the chart type of every embedded chart on the active sheet. The subroutine uses a For. . . Next loop to cycle through each Chart object in the ChartObjects collection, accessing each object and changing its Type property:

```
Sub ChartType()
    For Each cht In ActiveSheet.ChartObjects
        cht.Chart.Type = xlArea
    Next cht
End Sub
```

The following macro performs the same function, but works on all the chart sheets in the active workbook:

```
Sub ChartType2()
    For Each cht In ThisWorkbook.Charts
        cht.Type = xlArea
    Next cht
End Sub
```

Modifying properties

The following example changes the legend font for all charts on the active sheet. It uses a For. . . Next loop to process all ChartObject objects:

```
Sub LegendMod()
    For Each cht In ActiveSheet.ChartObjects
        With cht.Chart.Legend.Font
            .Name = "Arial"
            .FontStyle = "Bold"
            .Size = 12
        End With
    Next cht
End Sub
```

Note that the Font object is contained in the Legend object, which is contained in the Chart object, which is contained in the ChartObjects collection. Now do you understand why it's called an object hierarchy?

Applying chart formatting

This example applies several different types of formatting to the active chart:

```
Sub ChartMods()
    ActiveChart.Type = xlArea
    ActiveChart.ChartArea.Font.Name = "Arial"
    ActiveChart.ChartArea.Font.FontStyle = "Regular"
    ActiveChart.ChartArea.Font.Size = 9
    ActiveChart.PlotArea.Interior.ColorIndex = xlNone
    ActiveChart.Axes(xlValue).TickLabels.Font.Bold = True
    ActiveChart.Axes(xlCategory).TickLabels.Font.Bold = True
    ActiveChart.Legend.Position = xlBottom
End Sub
```

Before executing this macro, you must activate a chart. You activate an embedded chart by selecting it. To activate a chart on a chart sheet, you activate the chart sheet.

I created this macro by recording my actions as I formatted a chart. Then I cleaned up the recorded code by removing irrelevant lines.

VBA Speed Tips

VBA is fast, but it's not always fast enough (computer programs are *never* fast enough). This section presents some programming examples that you can use to help speed up your macros.

Turning off screen updating

When executing a macro, you can watch everything that occurs in the macro. Although this can be instructive, after you get the macro working properly, it's often annoying and can slow things down considerably.

Fortunately, you can disable the screen updating when running your macro. To turn off screen updating, insert the following statement:

```
Application.ScreenUpdating = False
```

If you want the user to see what's happening at any point during the macro, use the following statement to turn screen updating back on:

```
Application.ScreenUpdating = True
```

Eliminating those pesky alert messages

As you know, by using a macro, you cause Excel to perform a series of actions automatically. In many cases, you can start a macro and then go hang out at the water cooler while Excel does its thing. However, some operations performed in Excel display messages that require a response. For example, if your macro deletes a sheet, Excel displays the message shown in Figure 14-3. These types of messages mean you can't leave Excel unattended while it executes your macro.

Figure 14-3:
You can instruct Excel not to display these types of alerts.

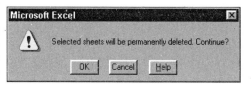

To avoid these alert messages, insert the following VBA statement in your macro:

```
Application.DisplayAlerts = False
```

When the subroutine ends, Excel automatically resets the DisplayAlerts property to True (its normal state).

Simplifying object references

As you already know, references to objects can become very lengthy. For example, a fully qualified reference to a Range object might look like this:

```
Workbooks("MyBook").Worksheets("Sheet1").Range("InterestRate")
```

If your macro frequently uses this range, you might want to create an object variable by using the Set command. For example, the following statement assigns this Range object to an object variable named *Rate:*

```
Set Rate=Workbooks("MyBook").Worksheets("Sheet1"). _
Range("InterestRate")
```

After defining this variable, you can use the variable *Rate* instead of the lengthy reference. For example, you can change the value of the cell named InterestRate by using a simple statement like this:

```
Rate = .085
```

This is much easier to type (and understand) than the following statement:

```
Workbooks("MyBook").Worksheets("Sheet1").Range("InterestRate") _
         = .085
```

In addition to simplifying your coding, using object variables also speeds up your macros considerably. After creating object variables, I've seen some macros run twice as fast as before.

Declaring variable types

If you want your procedures to execute as fast as possible, you should tell Excel what type of data is assigned to each of your variables. This is known as *declaring* a variable's type. (Refer to Chapter 7 for details.)

In general, you should use the data type that requires the smallest number of bytes yet can still handle all the data assigned to it. When VBA works with data, execution speed depends on the number of bytes VBA has at its disposal. In other words, the fewer bytes used by data, the faster VBA can access and manipulate the data.

If you use an object variable (as described in the preceding section), you can declare the variable as an object data type. Here's an example:

```
Dim Rate as Object
     SetRate _
=Workbooks("MyBook").Worksheets("Sheet1").Range("InterestRate")
```

To force yourself to declare all the variables you use, insert the following statement at the beginning of your module:

```
Option Explicit
```

If you use this statement, Excel displays an error message if it encounters a variable that hasn't been declared.

Learning More

By reading this chapter, you have learned several useful tricks — and probably gained some new insights about VBA in the process. I could fill the entire book with short routines like this, but my publisher wouldn't like that. Instead, I settled on several that I consider to be particularly useful and informative.

This chapter concludes Part III. You're now ready to move on to a new topic: custom dialog boxes.

Part IV
Developing Custom Dialog Boxes

The 5th Wave   By Rich Tennant

WANDA HAD THE DISTINCT FEELING HER HUSBAND'S NEW SOFTWARE PROGRAM WAS ABOUT TO BECOME INTERACTIVE.

In this part. . .

The four chapters in this part show you how to develop custom dialog boxes. This VBA feature is fairly easy to use, once you get a few basic concepts under your belt. And, if you're like me, you may actually *enjoy* creating dialog boxes.

Chapter 15

Custom Dialog Box Alternatives

• •

In This Chapter

▶ Saving time by using alternatives to custom dialog boxes

▶ Using the InputBox and MsgBox functions to get information from the user

▶ Getting a filename and path from the user (two ways)

▶ Writing VBA code to display any of Excel's built-in dialog boxes

• •

*Y*ou can't use Excel very long without being exposed to dialog boxes. They seem to pop up every time you select a command. Excel — like most Windows programs — uses dialog boxes to obtain information, clarify commands, and display messages. If you develop VBA macros, you can create your own dialog boxes that work just like Excel's built-in dialogs.

Why Create Dialog Boxes?

Some VBA macros you create behave exactly the same every time you execute them. For example, you might develop a macro that enters a list of your employees. Running this macro always produces the same result and requires no additional user input.

However, you might develop other macros that behave differently under various circumstances, or that offer some options for the user. In such cases, the macro may benefit from a custom dialog box.

A custom dialog box provides a simple means for getting information from the user. Your macro then uses that information to determine what it should do.

Do You Really Need a Custom Dialog?

Custom dialog boxes can be quite useful, but (as you'll soon see), creating them takes time. Before I cover the topic of creating custom dialog boxes, you need to know about some time-saving alternatives.

VBA lets you display four different types of dialog boxes that you can sometimes use in place of a custom dialog box. You can customize these built-in dialog boxes in some ways, but they certainly don't offer the options available in a custom dialog box. In some cases, however, they are just what the doctor ordered.

In this chapter, you learn about

- ✔ The MsgBox function
- ✔ The InputBox function
- ✔ The GetOpenFileName method
- ✔ The GetSaveAsFileName method

I also describe how to display Excel's built-in dialog boxes.

The MsgBox Function

You may already be familiar with VBA's MsgBox function — I use it quite often in the examples throughout this book. The MsgBox function provides a very handy means for displaying information and getting simple input from users.

Here's a simplified version of the syntax for the MsgBox function:

```
MsgBox(prompt[,buttons][,title])
```

The MsgBox function accepts the following arguments:

Argument	*What It Does*
prompt	Supplies the text Excel displays in the message box
buttons	Specifies which buttons appear in the message box (optional)
title	Defines the text that appears in the message box's title bar (optional)

Displaying a simple message box

You can use the MsgBox function by itself or assign its result to a variable. If you use this function by itself, don't include parentheses around the arguments. The following example displays a message and does not return a result:

```
Sub MsgBoxDemo()
    MsgBox "Click OK to continue"
End Sub
```

Figure 15-1 shows this message box.

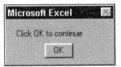

Getting a response from a message box

To get a response from a message box, you can assign the result of the MsgBox function to a variable. In the following code, I use some built-in constants (which I describe later in Table 15-1) that make it easy to work with the values returned by MsgBox:

```
Sub GetAnswer()
    Ans = MsgBox("Continue?", vbYesNo)
    Select Case Ans
        Case vbYes
'           ...[code if Ans is Yes]...
        Case vbNo
'           ...[code if Ans is No]...
    End Select
End Sub
```

When you execute this procedure, the *Ans* variable is assigned a value of either vbYes or vbNo. The Select Case statement uses the value of *Ans* to determine which action the routine should perform.

Customizing message boxes

You can easily customize your message boxes because of the flexibility of the *buttons* argument. You can specify which buttons to display, whether an icon appears, and which button is the default. Table 15-1 lists the built-in constants you can use for the buttons argument.

Table 15-1		Constants Used in the MsgBox Function
Constant	*Value*	*What It Does*
vbOKOnly	0	Displays OK button only
vbOKCancel	1	Displays OK and Cancel buttons
vbAbortRetryIgnore	2	Displays Abort, Retry, and Ignore buttons
vbYesNoCancel	3	Displays Yes, No, and Cancel buttons
vbYesNo	4	Displays Yes and No buttons
vbRetryCancel	5	Displays Retry and Cancel buttons
vbCritical	16	Displays Critical Message icon
vbQuestion	32	Displays Warning Query icon
vbExclamation	48	Displays Warning Message icon
vbInformation	64	Displays Information Message icon
vbDefaultButton1	0	First button is default
vbDefaultButton2	256	Second button is default
vbDefaultButton3	512	Third button is default
vbSystemModal	4096	System modal; all applications are suspended until the user responds to the message box

To use more than one of these constants as an argument, just connect them with a + operator. For example, to display a message box with Yes and No buttons and an exclamation icon, use the following expression as the second MsgBox argument:

```
vbYesNo + vbExclamation
```

The following example uses a combination of constants to display a message box with a Yes button and a No button (vbYesNo) as well as a question mark icon (vbQuestion). The constant vbDefaultButton2 designates the second button (the No button) as the default button — that is, the button Excel executes if the user presses Enter. For simplicity, I assign these constants to the *Config* variable. I then use *Config* as the second argument in the MsgBox function:

```
Sub GetAnswer()
    Config = vbYesNo + vbQuestion + vbDefaultButton2
    Ans = MsgBox("Process the monthly report?", Config)
    If Ans = vbNo Then End
    If Ans = vbYes Then RunReport
End Sub
```

Figure 15-2 shows the message box Excel displays when you execute the
GetAnswer subroutine. If the user clicks the No button (or presses Enter), the
routine ends with no action. If the user clicks the Yes button, the routine
executes the procedure named RunReport (which is not shown). Because I
omitted the title argument in the MsgBox function, Excel uses the default title,
Microsoft Excel.

Figure 15-2:
The
GetAnswer
subroutine
displays this
message
box.

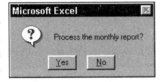

The following routine provides another example of using the MsgBox function:

```
Sub GetAnswer2()
    Msg = "Do you want to process the monthly report?"
    Msg = Msg & Chr(13) & Chr(13)
    Msg = Msg & "Processing the monthly report will take "
    Msg = Msg & "approximately 15 minutes. It will generate a _
            30-"
    Msg = Msg & "page report for all sales offices for the _
            current "
    Msg = Msg & "month."
    Title = "XYZ Marketing Company"
    Config = vbYesNo + vbQuestion
    Ans = MsgBox(Msg, Config, Title)
    If Ans = vbYes Then RunReport
    If Ans = vbNo Then End
End Sub
```

This example demonstrates an efficient way to specify a longer message in a message box. I use a variable (Msg) and the concatenation operator (&) to build the message in a series of statements. The Chr(13) function inserts a character that starts a new line. I also use the title argument to display a different title in the message box. Figure 15-3 shows the message box Excel displays when you execute this procedure.

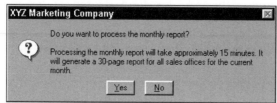

Figure 15-3:
The
dialog box
displayed by
the MsgBox
function.

The InputBox Function

The InputBox function is useful for obtaining a single value from the user. When you only need to get one value from a user (rather than several), this is a good alternative to developing a custom dialog box.

InputBox syntax

Here's a simplified version of the syntax for the InputBox function:

```
InputBox(prompt[,title][,default])
```

The InputBox function accepts the following arguments:

Argument   *What It Does*

prompt   Supplies the text Excel displays in the input box

title   Specifies the text Excel displays in the input box's title bar
              (optional)

default   Defines the default value (optional)

An InputBox example

Here's an example showing how you can use the InputBox function:

```
TheName = InputBox("What is your name?","Greetings, user")
```

When you execute this VBA statement, Excel displays the dialog box shown in Figure 15-4. Notice that this example uses only the first two arguments and does not supply a default value. When the user enters a value and clicks OK, the routine assigns the value to the variable *TheName*.

Figure 15-4:
The
InputBox
function
displays this
dialog box.

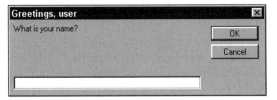

The following example uses the third argument and provides a default value. The default value is the user name stored by Excel.

```
Sub GetName()
    DefName = Application.UserName
    TheName = InputBox("What is your name?", "Greetings, _
            user", DefName)
End Sub
```

VBA's InputBox function always returns a string, and so you may need to convert the result to a value. You can convert a string to a value by using the Val function.

The following example uses the Val function to convert the user's entry to a value:

```
Sub GetName()
    Prompt = "How many sheets do you want to add?"
    Caption = "Tell me..."
    Default = 1
    NumSheets = Val(InputBox(Prompt, Caption, Default))
End Sub
```

Figure 15-5 shows the dialog box this routine produces.

Figure 15-5:
Another
example of
using the
InputBox
function.

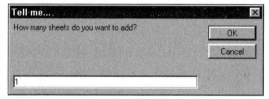

The GetOpenFilename Method

If your VBA procedure needs to get a filename from the user, you *could* use the InputBox function to ask the user to enter the filename. However, an InputBox isn't usually the best tool for this job because most users find it difficult to remember paths and directory names, and typographic errors often result.

For a better solution to this problem, use the GetOpenFilename method of the Application object, which ensures that your application gets a valid filename (and its complete path).

This method displays the familiar Open dialog box (the same dialog box Excel displays when you choose File⇨Open). However, the GetOpenFileName method doesn't actually open the specified file. This method simply returns the filename selected by the user. Then, you can do whatever you want with the filename.

GetOpenFilename syntax

The official syntax for this method is

```
object.GetOpenFilename(fileFilter,filterIndex,title)
```

The GetOpenFileName method takes the following arguments:

Argument	What It Does
fileFilter	Determines the types of files that appear in the dialog box (for example, *.TXT). You can specify several different filters from which the user can choose
filterIndex	Determines which of the file filters the dialog box displays by default
title	Specifies the caption for the dialog box's title bar

GetOpenFilename example

The fileFilter argument determines what appears in the dialog box's List Files of Type drop-down list. This argument consists of pairs of file filter strings followed by the wild-card file filter specification, with each part and each pair separated by commas. If omitted, this argument defaults to

```
"User (*.*),*.*"
```

Notice that this string consists of two parts:

```
User (*.*)
```

and

```
*.*
```

The first part of this string is the text displayed in the List Files of Type drop-down list. The second part actually determines which files the dialog box displays.

The following example pops up a dialog box that asks the user for a filename. The subroutine defines five file filters. Notice that I use VBA's line continuation sequence to set up the Filter variable; doing so helps simplify this rather complicated argument.

```
Sub GetImportFileName()
'    Set up list of file filters

    Filter = "Text Files (*.txt),*.txt," & _
             "Lotus Files (*.prn),*.prn," & _
             "Comma Separated Files (*.csv),*.csv," & _
             "ASCII Files (*.asc),*.asc," & _
             "All Files (*.*),*.*"

'    Display *.* by default
    FilterIndex = 5

'    Set the dialog box caption
    Title = "Select a File to Import"

'    Get the filename
    FileName = Application.GetOpenFilename(Filter, _
        FilterIndex, Title)

'    Exit if dialog box canceled
    If FileName = False Then
        MsgBox "No file was selected."
        Exit Sub
    End If
```

(continued)

```
(continued)
'   Display full path and name of the file
    MsgBox "You selected " & FileName
End Sub
```

Figure 15-6 shows the dialog box Excel displays when you execute this procedure.

Figure 15-6:
The
GetOpen
Filename
method
displays a
customizable
dialog box
and returns
the path and
name of the
selected file,
but it does
not open
the file.

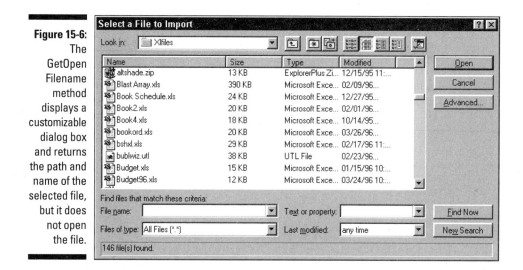

The GetSaveAsFilename Method

Excel's GetSaveAsFilename method works just like the GetOpenFilename method, but it displays Excel's SaveAs dialog box. It gets a path and filename from the user, but doesn't do anything with it.

The syntax for this method is

```
object.GetSaveAsFilename(initialFilename, fileFilter, _
    filterIndex, title)
```

The GetSaveAsFilename method takes the following arguments:

Argument	*What It Does*
initialFilename	Specifies a default filename that appears in the File name box
fileFilter	Determines the types of files Excel displays in the dialog box (for example, *.TXT). You can specify several different filters from which the user can choose

filterIndex   Determines which of the file filters Excel displays by default

title   Defines a caption for the dialog box's title bar

Displaying Excel's Built-In Dialogs

You can write VBA code that executes Excel's menu commands. And, if a command leads to a dialog box, your code can make choices in the dialog — although Excel doesn't actually display the dialog.

For example, the following statement has the same effect as selecting the Edit⇨Go To command, specifying a range named InputRange, and clicking OK:

```
Application.Goto Reference:="InputRange"
```

However, when you execute this statement, the Go To dialog box does not appear. This is almost always what you want to happen; you don't want dialog boxes flashing across the screen while your macro executes.

In some cases, however, you might want to simply display one of Excel's 226 built-in dialog boxes and let the user make the choices. You can easily do this by using the Dialogs method of the Application object. Here's an example:

```
Result = Application.Dialogs(xlDialogFormulaGoto).Show
```

When executed, this statement displays the Go To dialog box, as shown in Figure 15-7. The user can specify a named range or enter a cell address. This dialog box works exactly as it does when you choose Edit⇨Go To (or press F5). The value assigned to Result is True if the user clicks OK, and False if the user clicks Cancel or presses Escape.

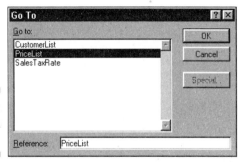

Figure 15-7:
The Go To
dialog box.

The preceding example uses the predefined constant xlDialogFormulaGoto. This constant determines which dialog box Excel displays.

You can get a list of all the dialog box constants by using the Object Browser:

1. **In a VBA module, press F2 to bring up the Object Browser.**

2. **In the Object Browser dialog box, select Excel from the Libraries/Workbooks list.**

3. **Select Constants from the Objects/Modules list.**

4. **Scroll down the Methods/Properties list until you find the constants that begin with** *xlDialog***.**

5. **If you like, you can click the Paste button to paste the selected constant into your code.**

If you try to display a built-in dialog box in an incorrect context, Excel displays an error message. For example, if you display the xlDialogFormatFont dialog box when a VBA module is active, Excel displays an error message because that dialog box is not appropriate when a module is the active sheet.

Learning More

This chapter doesn't tell you anything about creating custom dialog boxes. Rather, it describes some techniques you can use in place of custom dialog boxes.

The next three chapters tell you everything you need to know to jazz up your applications with some award-winning dialogs.

Chapter 16
Dialog Box Basics

● ●

In This Chapter

▶ Learning when to use custom dialog boxes

▶ Understanding how Excel uses dialog sheets

▶ Displaying a custom dialog box

▶ Creating a custom dialog box that works with a useful macro

● ●

*I*f your VBA macro needs to get only a few pieces of information from the user (for example, a Yes/No answer, or a text string), the techniques described in the previous chapter may just do the job. But if you need to obtain more information, you need to create a custom dialog box. In this chapter, you learn the essential skills you need to create and work with custom dialog boxes.

When a Custom Dialog Is Useful

The following simple but useful macro changes the text in each cell in the selection to uppercase. It does this by using VBA's built-in UCase function.

```
Sub ChangeCase()
    For Each cell In Selection
        cell.Value = UCase(cell.Value)
    Next cell
End Sub
```

You can make this macro even more useful. For example, it would be nice if the macro could also change the cells to either lowercase or *proper* case (the first letter in each word is capitalized). You can easily modify the macro to do this. But if you give the macro this capability, you need some method of asking the user which type of change to make to the cells.

The solution is to display a dialog box like the one shown in Figure 16-1. You create this dialog box on a dialog sheet in the workbook, and you display it by using a VBA macro. Later in this chapter, I provide step-by-step instructions for creating this dialog box. But before I get into that, I need to set the stage with some introductory material.

Figure 16-1:
You can get information from the user by displaying a custom dialog box.

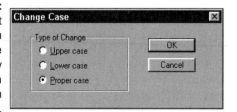

Creating Custom Dialog Boxes: An Overview

To create a custom dialog box, you usually follow these steps:

1. **Determine exactly how the dialog box will be used and where it fits in your VBA macro.**

2. **Insert a new dialog sheet and add the appropriate controls to it.**

3. **Link the controls to worksheet cells (if appropriate).**

   In some cases, you may want to attach a macro to a control.

4. **Modify your macro so that it displays the dialog box.**

5. **Modify your macro code so that it obtains and uses the information from the dialog box.**

I provide more details about each of these steps in the following sections.

Working with Dialog Sheets

Excel stores custom dialog boxes on dialog sheets (one dialog box per sheet). When you insert a dialog sheet (using the Insert⊅Macro⊅Dialog command), Excel displays a sheet with a nearly empty dialog box, as shown in Figure 16-2. The dialog box includes only an OK button and a Cancel button, which most dialog boxes use.

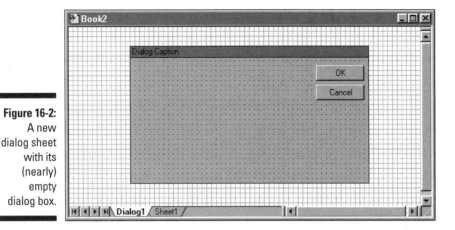

Figure 16-2:
A new
dialog sheet
with its
(nearly)
empty
dialog box.

When you activate a dialog sheet, Excel displays the Forms toolbar, which
makes it easy to add controls to the dialog box. Figure 16-3 shows the Forms
toolbar.

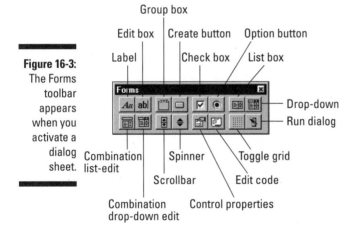

Figure 16-3:
The Forms
toolbar
appears
when you
activate a
dialog
sheet.

You add controls to the dialog box by using the tools on the Forms toolbar.
After you add a control, you can move and resize it by using standard techniques. The next chapter covers this process in detail.

You can also insert some of the dialog box controls directly on an Excel worksheet. The following controls work on both dialog sheets and worksheets:

- ✔ Check box
- ✔ Create button
- ✔ Drop-down
- ✔ Group box
- ✔ Label
- ✔ List box
- ✔ Option button
- ✔ Scrollbar
- ✔ Spinner

Linking Controls

You can link some types of dialog box controls to a worksheet cell or range. For example, you might link a check box control to a cell. When the check box is checked, the cell contains True; when it's not checked, the cell contains False. You can link a drop-down list box control to a single-column vertical range of cells. In this case, each cell in the range contains one of the choices in the drop-down list box. You can also link another cell to hold the user's choice from the drop-down list.

Linking a control to a cell is not the only way to obtain the information from the dialog box. In fact, if speed is essential, you should usually avoid linking a control to a cell. Instead, you can write VBA code to read the control's value directly — thus avoiding a worksheet link. I discuss this method later in this chapter (see "Using Information from Custom Dialog Boxes").

To link a dialog box control to a cell, right-click the control, and then you choose Format Object from the shortcut menu. Excel displays the Format Object dialog box. Click the Control tab in the Format Object dialog box and specify the cells to which the control should be linked. The easiest way to do this is by clicking in the edit box and then pointing to the appropriate cell or range in the worksheet.

Figure 16-4 shows the Format Object dialog box for a drop-down list box control (the dialog box varies with each type of control). In this case, the range A1:A12 on Sheet1 contains the entries for the list that's displayed, and the user's selection appears in cell B16 of Sheet1. You can also control the number of lines that drop down when the user selects the drop-down list box control (in this example, eight).

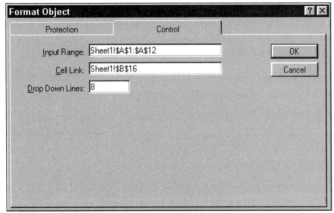

Figure 16-4:
This Format
Object
dialog box
enables you
to link a
drop-down
list box to
cells in a
worksheet.

Displaying Custom Dialog Boxes

The only way you can display a custom dialog box is by using the Show method in a VBA macro. The following procedure displays the dialog box located on the Dialog1 sheet:

```
Sub ShowDialog()
    DialogSheets("Dialog1").Show
'    ... [other statements]
End Sub
```

When Excel displays the dialog box, the macro halts until the user closes the dialog box by clicking either OK or Cancel. Then, VBA executes the remaining statements in the procedure.

The Show method also generates a value. If the dialog box closes normally (that is, the user clicks the OK button), the Show method generates the value True. If the user cancels the dialog box (by clicking the Cancel button), the Show method generates the value False.

In most cases, you don't want to continue if the user clicks the Cancel button. Therefore, you need to test for this in your macro. The following example demonstrates how to do this:

```
Sub ShowDialog()
    DBoxOK = DialogSheets("Dialog1").Show
    If Not DBoxOK Then Exit Sub
'    ... [other statements]
End Sub
```

This subroutine assigns the dialog box result to the variable *DBoxOK*. When the user closes the dialog box, VBA executes the next statement, which checks the value of DBoxOK. If DBoxOK is False, VBA exits the subroutine with no further action. If DBoxOK is True, the subroutine continues.

The following routine shows how you can accomplish this without using a variable. If the user clicks OK, VBA executes all the statements between the If. . . Then and End If statements. If the user clicks Cancel, VBA does not execute these statements.

```
Sub ShowDialog2()
    If DialogSheets("Dialog1").Show Then
'        ... [other statements]
    End If
End Sub
```

Using Information from Custom Dialog Boxes

You use a dialog box to get information from the user. After the user responds to a dialog box, your macro needs to obtain the user's response and do something with it. Your macro can get the response in one of two ways:

- ✔ You can read the result from the cell if you linked the dialog box control to a cell.
- ✔ You can read the result directly from the dialog box control.

Dialog box controls are objects, and you can access their properties by using VBA. For example, to determine whether an option button (named *Option1*) on dialog sheet Dialog1 is selected, you can check its Value property by using the following statement:

```
Selected = DialogSheets("Dialog1").OptionButtons("Option1").Value
```

If the variable *Selected* is equal to the built-in constant xlOn, the option button is selected. If the value of Selected is the built-in constant xlOff, the option button is not selected. I present an example of this in the next section.

Excel provides a name for each control you add to a dialog box. You can use those names or change the names to something more meaningful. To change the name of a control, use the Name box on the edit line (this is the same tool you use for naming cells and ranges).

A Custom Dialog Box Example

In this section, I demonstrate how to develop a custom dialog box. The example is an enhanced version of the ChangeCase routine from the beginning of the chapter. Recall that the original version of this macro changes the text in the selected cells to uppercase. This modified version asks the user which type of case change to make: uppercase, lowercase, or proper case.

Creating the dialog box

This dialog box needs to obtain one piece of information from the user: the type of change to make to the text. Because the user has three choices, you can't get the input by using a MsgBox function. You *could* use an input box, but that's not a very efficient solution.

To allow the user to select only one option at a time, your best bet is a custom dialog box with option button controls. Here are the steps required for creating the custom dialog box. Start with an empty workbook:

1. **Insert a new dialog sheet by choosing Insert⇨Macro⇨Dialog.**

   The new sheet contains a dialog box with two controls: an OK button and a Cancel button.

2. **Make sure the Forms toolbar is displayed.**

   If it isn't, choose View⇨Toolbars and select Forms from the list of toolbars.

3. **Click the Option Button tool and drag the option button into the dialog box.**

   The option button has a default name (*Option Button 4*) and the name appears as text. If you can't see all the text, drag the right handle to make the option button wider.

4. **In the Name box (located on the left side of the edit line), change the name of this option button to *Upper*.**

   To do this, click the option button to select it, type **Upper** in the Name box, and press Enter.

5. **Change the text displayed in this option button by double-clicking it and entering the new text, *Upper Case*.**

6. **Add two more option buttons to the dialog box.**

7. **Name the second option button *Lower* and change its text to *Lower Case*.**

8. **Name the third option button *Proper* and change its text to *Proper Case*.**

9. **Click the Group Box tool and drag the new group box so that it encloses the three option buttons.**

Make sure the group box completely encloses the option buttons. You may need to make the option buttons narrower so that they fit. Or, you can increase the width of the group box. If the group box doesn't completely enclose the option buttons, the dialog box might not work properly.

10. Change the dialog box's title bar text to *Change Case*.

11. Adjust the dialog box's size so that it looks something like Figure 16-5.

To do this, simply select the dialog box and drag its borders.

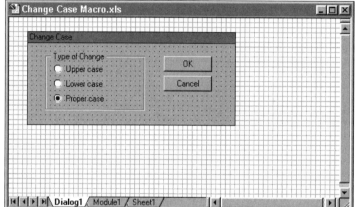

Figure 16-5:
The completed dialog box.

Modifying the macro

Insert a VBA module and enter the following macro:

```
Sub ChangeCase()
'    Exit if a range is not selected
     If TypeName(Selection) <> "Range" Then Exit Sub

'    Show the dialog box
     DBoxOK = DialogSheets("Dialog1").Show

'    Exit if dialog is canceled
     If Not DBoxOK Then Exit Sub

'    Uppercase
```

```
If DialogSheets("Dialog1").OptionButtons("Upper") _
        .Value = xlOn Then
    For Each cell In Selection
        cell.Value = UCase(cell.Value)
    Next cell
End If

'   Lowercase
    If DialogSheets("Dialog1").OptionButtons("Lower") _
            .Value = xlOn Then
        For Each cell In Selection
            cell.Value = LCase(cell.Value)
        Next cell
    End If

'   Proper case
    If DialogSheets("Dialog1").OptionButtons("Proper") _
            .Value = xlOn Then
        For Each cell In Selection
            cell.Value = Application.Proper(cell.Value)
        Next cell
    End If
End Sub
```

This is a much-enhanced version of the original ChangeCase macro that I presented at the beginning of the chapter.

Here's how the new version works:

- ✔ The macro starts by checking the type of the selection. If it's not a range, the procedure ends.
- ✔ Next, the macro displays the dialog box and assigns the result to the DBoxOK variable.
- ✔ If the dialog is canceled, VBA exits the subroutine. Otherwise, the macro continues.
- ✔ The rest of the macro consists of three separate blocks. Only one block is executed, determined by which option button the user selects. In this example, I read the value directly from the dialog box (instead of using a cell link).

Notice that VBA has a UCase function and an LCase function, but not a function to convert text to proper case. Therefore, I use Excel's PROPER worksheet function (preceded by Application) to do the conversion.

When you execute the macro, the controls in the dialog box retain their settings from one execution to the next. In other words, each time VBA displays the dialog box, the option button selected the previous time remains selected (until the user chooses another option, of course). If you want the dialog box to default to the uppercase option, insert the following statement before the statement that shows the dialog:

```
DialogSheets("Dialog1").OptionButtons("Upper").Value = xlOn
```

Making the macro available

At this point, everything should work properly. However, you still need an easy way to execute the macro. You can meet this need by adding a new command to the Tools menu.

Activate the VBA module and choose Tools⇨Macro. Select ChangeCase from the list in the Macro Name/Reference box and click the Options button. Excel displays its Macro Options dialog box, as shown in Figure 16-6.

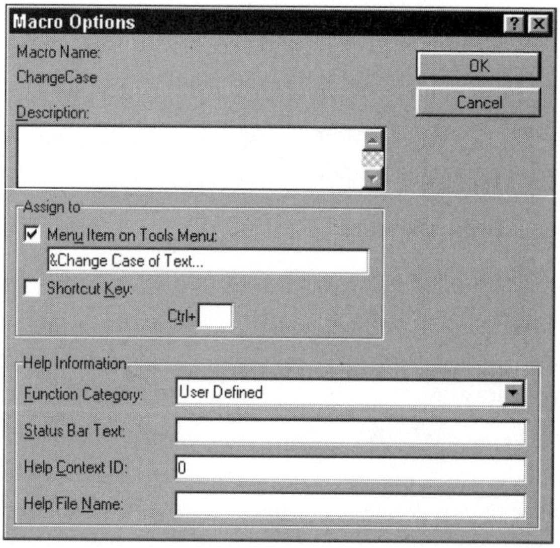

Figure 16-6:
The Macro
Options
dialog box.

Enter the following in the box labeled Menu Item on Tools Menu and click OK:

```
&Change Case of Text...
```

Then click Close to close the Macro dialog box.

NOTE

Using an ampersand (&) before a letter in this entry causes that letter to be underlined in the menu. After you perform this operation, the Tools menu has a new command: Change Case of Text.

Testing the macro

Finally, you need to test the macro and the dialog box to make sure that they work properly. Activate a worksheet and select some cells that contain text. Choose Tools⇨Change Case of Text and the custom dialog box appears. Make your choice and click OK. If you did everything correctly, the macro should make the specified change to the text in the selected cells.

The user wants to be able to execute this general-purpose macro from any workbook. However, the macro has a problem. If you attempt to execute the macro and the active workbook does not contain the macro, you get the error message shown in Figure 16-7.

Figure 16-7:
This error occurs if you attempt to execute the macro from a different workbook.

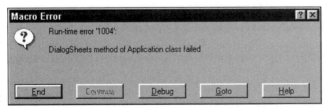

What's the problem? Excel looks for the Dialog1 sheet in the active workbook. If Excel can't find the macro in the active workbook, an error occurs. You need to correct this macro so that it can be executed from any workbook.

Correcting the macro

You can correct the problem in a few different ways. You could precede the reference to the dialog sheet with a workbook qualifier. Here's an example:

```
DBoxOK = Workbooks("Dialog _
          Example").DialogSheets("Dialog1").Show
```

This is not a good solution, because the macro fails if you rename the workbook.

A better solution uses the ThisWorkbook property of the Application object. ThisWorkbook returns the workbook in which the macro is stored — and it works regardless of the workbook's name. Here's an example that shows how you use this property:

```
DBoxOK = ThisWorkbook.DialogSheets("Dialog1").Show
```

You must make this change in every statement that refers to the dialog sheet.

Yet another approach is to create an object variable that refers to the dialog sheet. An object variable lets you refer to an object by a simpler name and also speeds up execution of the macro.

Use the keyword *Set* to create an object variable. For example, to create an object variable named *Dialog* that refers to the dialog sheet named Dialog1, insert the following statement at the beginning of the subroutine:

```
Set Dialog = ThisWorkbook.DialogSheets("Dialog1")
```

After defining the object variable, you can replace every instance of ThisWorkbook.DialogSheets("Dialog1") with Dialog.

The following is the code for the finalized macro, which uses an object variable:

```
Sub ChangeCase()
'    Create object variable
     Set Dialog = ThisWorkbook.DialogSheets("Dialog1")

'    Exit if a range is not selected
     If TypeName(Selection) <> "Range" Then Exit Sub

'    Show the dialog box
     DBoxOK = Dialog.Show

'    Exit if dialog is canceled
     If Not DBoxOK Then Exit Sub

'    Uppercase
     If Dialog.OptionButtons("Upper").Value = xlOn Then
         For Each cell In Selection
             cell.Value = UCase(cell.Value)
         Next cell
     End If
```

```
'    Lowercase
    If Dialog.OptionButtons("Lower").Value = xlOn Then
        For Each cell In Selection
            cell.Value = LCase(cell.Value)
        Next cell
    End If

'    Proper case
    If Dialog.OptionButtons("Proper").Value = xlOn Then
        For Each cell In Selection
            cell.Value = Application.Proper(cell.Value)
        Next cell
    End If
End Sub
```

Learning More

This chapter provides an introductory overview of custom dialog boxes, as well as a hands-on example. By working through this exercise, you gain a pretty good feel for custom dialog boxes — and you create a useful Excel utility as a bonus.

You still have more to learn — the next two chapters show you even more about custom dialog boxes.

Chapter 17

Using Dialog Box Controls

A user responds to a dialog box by using the various controls (buttons, edit boxes, option buttons, and so on) that the dialog box contains. Your VBA code then makes use of these responses to determine which actions to take. You have lots of controls at your disposal, and this chapter tells you about them.

Getting Started with Dialog Box Controls

In this section, I tell you how to add controls to a dialog box, give them meaningful names, and adjust some of their properties.

Before you can get started with dialog box controls, you must have a dialog sheet — which you get by choosing Insert⇨Macro⇨Dialog.

Adding controls

Oddly enough, no menu commands let you add controls to a dialog box. To add controls, you must use the Forms toolbar, which I describe in Chapter 16. Normally, the Forms toolbar pops up automatically when you activate a dialog sheet. If it doesn't, you can display the Forms toolbar by choosing View⇨Toolbars, and then placing a check mark next to the Forms option.

To add a control to the dialog box, click the toolbar button that corresponds to the control you want to add. Then click in the dialog box and drag the control into position (this is easier to do than describe). Figure 17-1 shows a dialog box in which I've added a few controls.

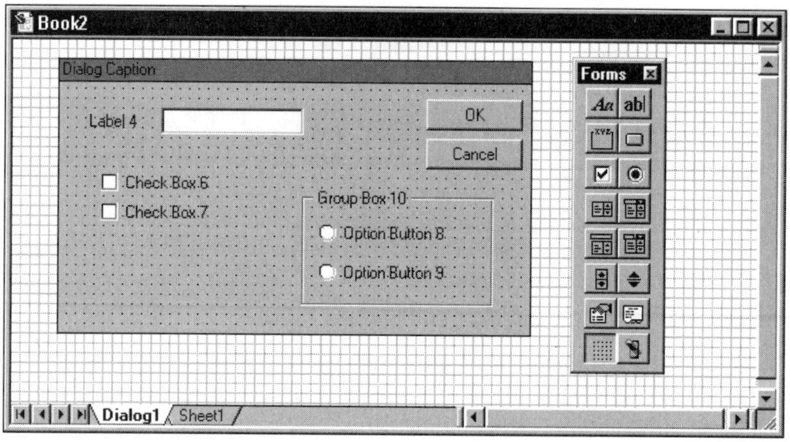

Figure 17-1:
A dialog box
with a few
controls
added.

Each object on a dialog sheet has a name, which appears in the Name box on the edit line. When you insert a new dialog sheet, the sheet already has three objects:

✔ The dialog box's frame, named Dialog Frame 1

✔ The OK button, named Button 2

✔ The Cancel button, named Button 3

When you add a new control, Excel assigns a name by combining the control type with the numeric sequence. For example, if you add a button to an empty dialog box, Excel names it Button 4. If you then add an edit box, Excel names it Edit Box 5.

Normally, dialog boxes contain vertical and horizontal grid lines. These lines exist to help you align the controls you add. When you add or move a control, it *snaps* (or automatically aligns) to the grid. If you don't like this, you can turn off the grids by clicking the Toggle Grid button on the Forms toolbar.

Naming controls

You should rename all the controls you add; the new names make the controls easier to work with, and you avoid any possible confusion caused by the numbering of the default names. For example, a button named *Button 12* is the 12th object added to the dialog box. It is *not* the 12th object in the Buttons collection.

To change the name, just select the object, type a new name in the Name box (the same Name box you use for naming ranges), and press Enter. If you type the name and then just click in the workbook, then the name does not stick.

Adjusting control properties

Each dialog box control has a set of properties that determines how the control works. You can adjust some properties of these controls from the Control tab of the Format dialog box. The easiest way to display the Format dialog box is by right-clicking the control and then choosing Format Object from the shortcut menu.

Figure 17-2 shows the Control tab for a button control (the options in this tab vary depending on the type of control).

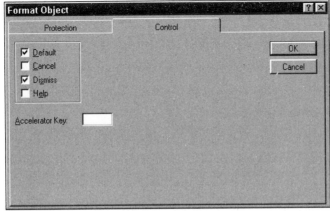

Figure 17-2:
The Control
tab of the
Format
Object
dialog box.

Dialog Box Controls: The Details

In the following sections, I introduce you to each type of control you can use in your custom dialogs.

Buttons

Every dialog box begins its life with two button controls (OK and Cancel). You can add as many other buttons as you need. Clicking a dialog box button can execute a procedure, close the dialog box (OK or Cancel), or display a custom help topic.

Figure 17-3 shows some buttons in a dialog box.

Buttons in a dialog box can display only one line of text. Although the text may appear to wrap around when you type it, Excel displays the text in a single line when displaying the dialog box. As a result, when you use the dialog box, some text may be cut off.

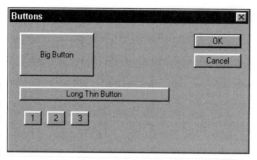

Figure 17-3:
Button
controls.

The Control tab of the Format Object dialog box for a button control lets you set the following properties:

- ✔ **Default:** Makes this button the default button for the dialog box. In other words, the user can activate the button by pressing Enter and by double-clicking certain other controls. Only one button at a time can be the default button. If the user clicks the default button, the Show method used to display the dialog returns True.

- ✔ **Cancel:** Specifies that activating the button aborts the dialog box (this has the same effect as pressing Esc). If the user clicks the Cancel button, the Show method used to display the dialog returns False.

- ✔ **Dismiss:** Specifies that activating the button dismisses the dialog box. Usually, OK and Cancel buttons both have this setting.

- ✔ **Help:** Specifies that activating the button displays a help topic of your choice.

- ✔ **Accelerator Key:** Lets you specify a *hot key*. The corresponding letter in the button's text is underlined.

Labels

A label control, which is as simple as a control gets, holds up to 255 characters of text. You can resize labels, and the words rewrap when you do so. You have no control over the type format in a label — the type font and type size are always the same.

You can enter more than 255 characters into a label, but only the first 255 appear when Excel displays the dialog box.

Figure 17-4 shows some labels in a dialog box.

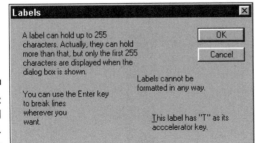

Figure 17-4:
Label
controls.

You can also specify an accelerator key (an underlined letter) for a label. Doing so enables users to use the keyboard to access objects that don't have accelerator keys, such as edit boxes. If the label appears directly before an edit box in the dialog box's tab order, for example, pressing the label's hot key activates the edit box. If this doesn't make sense, stay tuned. I discuss tab order later in this chapter (see "Accommodating keyboard users").

Edit boxes

An edit box accepts user input. The Format Object dialog box for an edit box control lets you adjust the following properties:

- ✔ **Edit Validation:** Determines which data type the edit box can hold
- ✔ **Multiline Edit:** Specifies whether the text wraps if it exceeds the width of the edit box
- ✔ **Vertical Scrollbar:** Specifies whether the edit box has a vertical scroll bar
- ✔ **Password Edit:** If checked, specifies that the edit box displays an asterisk for each character the user enters

Password Edit is a new feature in Excel for Windows 95. If you use this feature, be warned that it doesn't work if the workbook is used with Excel 5. In other words, the actual characters (not asterisks) appear when an Excel 5 user enters text into the password edit box.

Edit box controls are actually quite flexible because users can also enter formulas and cell references in an edit box. Just make sure the Edit Validation setting corresponds to the type of entry the edit box can hold.

Figure 17-5 shows edit boxes in a dialog box.

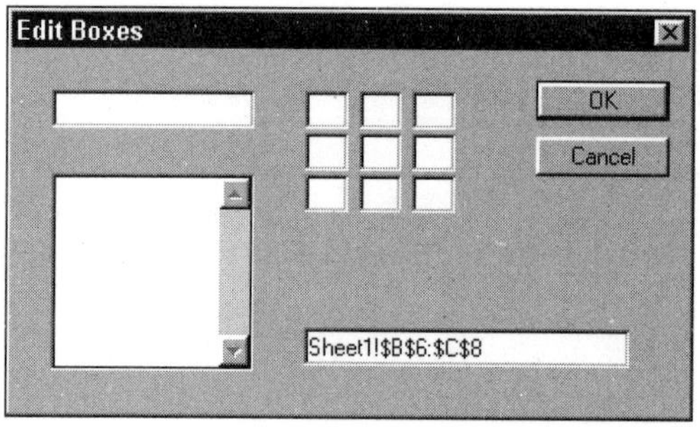

Figure 17-5:
Edit box
controls.

Group boxes

A group box doesn't really do anything, except visually (and functionally) combine a group of related controls, such as option buttons. You might add a descriptive label for the group box, but this isn't necessary.

Figure 17-6 shows three group boxes in a dialog box. Two of them have labels and one doesn't. None of them contain any objects.

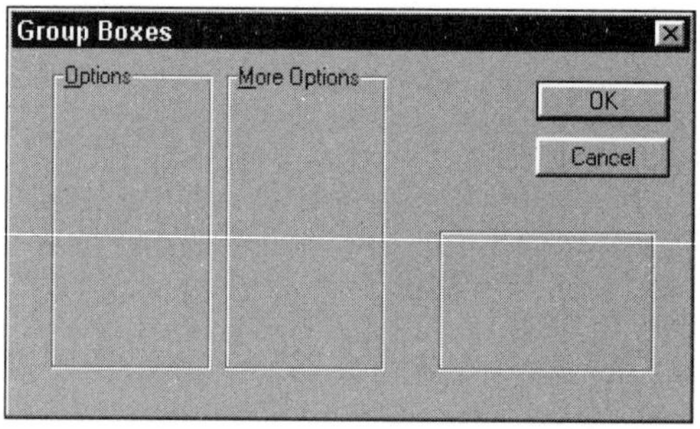

Figure 17-6:
Group box
controls.

Check boxes

Check boxes enable users to specify a binary choice — that is, a check box is either checked or not checked. When a check box is checked, its value is the constant xlOn. When it's not checked, the check box's value is xlOff. A check box can have a value of xlMixed, which is useful when the value is not consistent.

You can link a check box to a cell in a worksheet. With such a link, the cell displays True when the check box is checked, False when it's not checked, and #N/A when it's mixed.

Figure 17-7 shows three check boxes enclosed in a group box. The group box is not required, but it looks nice.

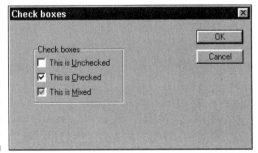

Figure 17-7:
Check box
controls.

Activating a check box's accelerator key toggles its value between xlOn and xlOff. If the check box has a value of xlMixed when displayed, however, pressing the hot key cycles through all three options.

Option buttons

Option buttons enable users to select one option from several possibilities. When the user selects one option button, the other buttons in the group are dese-lected. As a result, option buttons are useful only when you put two or more in a group; an option button by itself is useless (use a check box instead). When an option button is selected, it has a value of xlOn; otherwise, its value is xlOff.

You can link an option button to a cell. The cell displays an integer that corre-sponds to the selected option button in its group. If you have more than one set of option buttons in a dialog box, you need to enclose at least one group in a group box.

Figure 17-8 shows two sets of option buttons in a dialog box. One set is en-closed in a group box; the other set is not.

If an option button is selected, you can press the arrow keys to select another option button in the same group. Or, you can press an accelerator key to select one option button and deselect the others in its group.

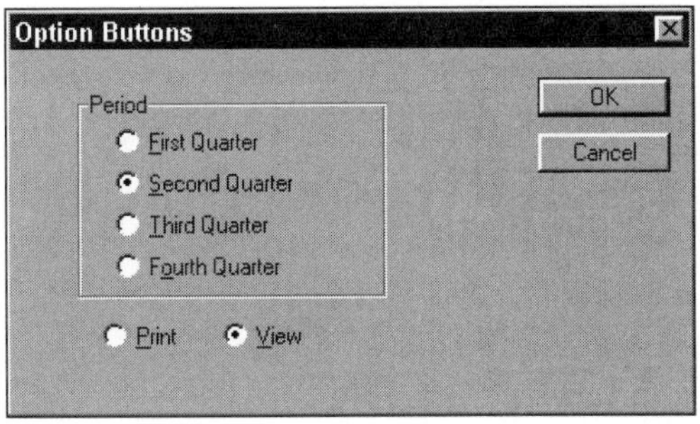

Figure 17-8:
Option
button
controls.

If you have more than one set of option buttons in a dialog, you must use a group box to enclose at least one set — otherwise, all the option buttons in the dialog box work as though they belong to the same set, and the user can select only one of them.

List boxes

List boxes let the user choose one or more items from a list. The Format Object dialog box lets you control the following properties of a list box:

- ✔ **Input Range:** Specifies a vertical range of cells that contains the options to be displayed in the list box.

- ✔ **Cell Link:** Identifies a cell for storing the selected item (an integer that corresponds to the selected item's position in the list).

- ✔ **Selection Type:** Determines whether the user can select one or several items. *Single* means only one item can be selected. *Multi* lets the user select more than one item by holding down Ctrl while selecting items from the list box. *Extend,* similar to Multi, lets the user select a range of options by holding down Shift.

If the selection type is Multi or Extend, Excel ignores the Cell Link option. To determine which items the user selects, you need to write some VBA code.

Figure 17-9 shows a list box in a dialog box.

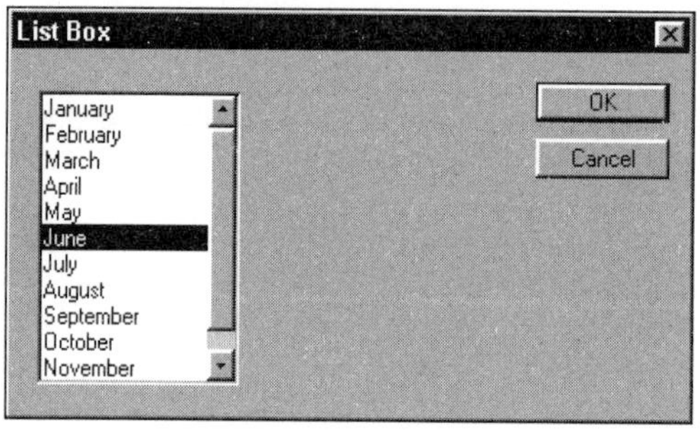

Figure 17-9:
A list box
control.

You can use a worksheet range to store the list box's options, or you can set the options with VBA code. You can also change the selection type with VBA. You can set up a single dialog box to accept a single selection in some circumstances and a multiple selection in others.

Drop-down list boxes

Drop-down list boxes can substitute for list boxes if you don't need to allow for a multiple selection. The advantage is that this control saves space — only one item appears initially. When the drop-down list is activated, it opens to display other items.

The Format Object dialog box lets you control the following properties of a drop-down list:

- ✔ **Input Range:** Specifies a vertical range of cells that contains the options to be displayed in the drop-down list.
- ✔ **Cell Link:** Identifies a cell for storing the selected item (an integer that corresponds to the selected item's position in the list).
- ✔ **Drop-down Lines:** Indicates the number of lines that drop down when the user activates the control. If the number of items exceeds the number of drop-down lines, scroll bars appear.

Figure 17-10 shows two drop-down list boxes in a dialog box. One is activated; the other isn't.

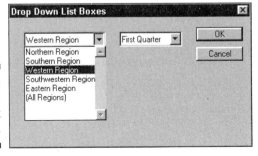

Figure 17-10:
Drop-down
list box
controls.

In general, the methods and properties for a list box can also be used in a drop-down list box. However, those that deal with multiple selections do not apply.

Combination list-edit boxes

A combination list-edit control actually comprises two controls: a drop-down list box and an edit box. These controls are independent of each other; you need to write VBA code to use them together.

Figure 17-11 shows a combination list-edit box in a dialog box.

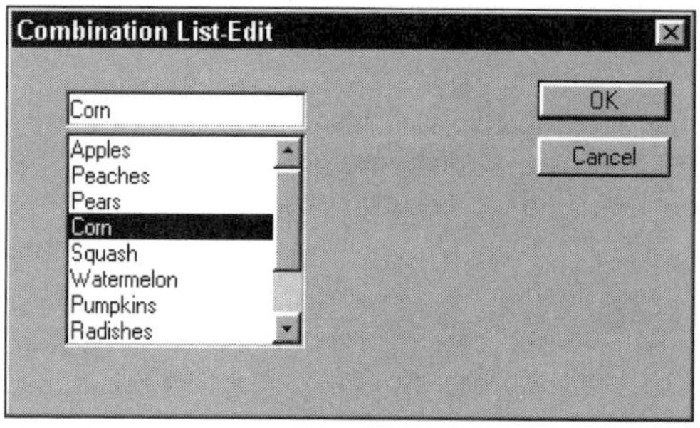

Figure 17-11:
A
combination
list-edit box.

Combination drop-down edit boxes

A combination drop-down edit box is similar to a drop-down list box, but it also lets the user type an option into the list. In other words, this control is useful when you can't display all possible options in the list.

The Format Object dialog box for this control has the same options as a drop-down list box. If the user enters an option that's not on the list, the linked cell has a value of 0. To determine what the user entered, you need to use VBA code.

Scroll bars

A scroll bar provides a convenient means for changing a value. These controls work just like the scroll bars used in Excel's windows. When you add a scroll bar to a dialog box, you can orient it either vertically or horizontally. A scroll bar doesn't display its value, and so you usually team these controls with a label or an edit box control.

The Format Object dialog box lets you control the following properties of a scroll bar:

- ✔ **Current Value:** The value of the scroll bar
- ✔ **Minimum Value:** The minimum allowable value
- ✔ **Maximum Value:** The maximum allowable value (up to 30,000)
- ✔ **Incremental Change:** The change in value when the user clicks either of the arrows
- ✔ **Page Change:** The change in value when the user clicks the scroll bar button
- ✔ **Cell Link:** A cell to store the scroll bar's value (an integer that corresponds to the selected item's position in the list)

Figure 17-12 shows scroll bars — lots of scroll bars — in a dialog box.

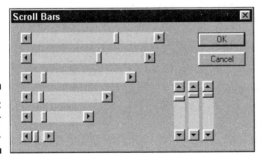

Figure 17-12:
Scroll bar
controls.

Spinners

A spinner is similar to a scroll bar, but it's smaller, it displays only the arrows, and it can only be placed vertically. A spinner's Format Object dialog box has the same options as a scroll bar's, except for the Page Change option. Like a scroll bar, a spinner doesn't display its value, so you might want to use an edit box or a label control to provide feedback to the user.

Figure 17-13 shows some spinner controls in a dialog box.

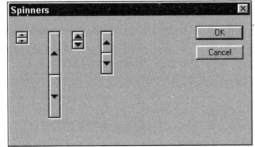

Figure 17-13:
Spinner
controls.

Working with Dialog Box Controls

In this section, I discuss how to work with dialog box controls in a dialog sheet.

Moving and resizing controls

After you place a control in a dialog box, you can move it and resize it by using standard mouse techniques. You can't completely resize some controls — for example, you can make a check box wider, but not taller.

You can select multiple controls by Ctrl-clicking or clicking and dragging to lasso a group.

A control can hide another control; in other words, you can stack one control on top of another. Usually, this is not a good idea. For best results, make sure you do not overlap controls.

Aligning controls

As I mention earlier in this chapter, dialog boxes normally display a grid. As you move or resize a control, it automatically snaps to the grid lines. If you want more precise control over a control's size or location, turn off the grid (the fastest way to do this is by clicking the Toggle Grid button on the Forms toolbar).

Excel doesn't have any commands to help you align or resize your controls, but you may find the Object Size and Align utility — which is included with the Power Utility Pak — particularly useful (you can order a free copy of this package by using the coupon in the back of the book).

Accommodating keyboard users

Many users prefer to navigate through a dialog box by using the keyboard: pressing Tab and Shift+Tab cycles through the controls, while pressing a hot key instantly activates a particular control.

To make sure your dialog box works properly for keyboard users, you must be mindful of two issues:

- ✔ Tab order
- ✔ Accelerator keys (or *hot keys*)

Changing the tab order

The tab order determines the order in which the controls are activated when the user presses Tab or Shift+Tab. It also determines which control has the initial *focus* — that is, which control is the active control when the dialog box first appears. For example, if a user is entering text into an edit box, the edit box has the focus. If the user clicks an option button, the option button has the focus. The first control in the tab order has the focus when Excel opens a dialog box.

To set the tab order of your controls, choose the Tools⇨Tab Order command while the dialog sheet is active. Or, right-click the dialog box and choose Tab Order from the shortcut menu. In either case, Excel displays the Tab Order dialog box shown in Figure 17-14.

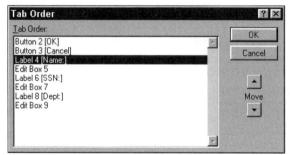

Figure 17-14:
The Tab
Order dialog
box.

The Tab Order dialog box lists all the controls. The tab order in the dialog box corresponds to the order of the items in the list. To move a control, select it and click the arrow buttons up or down. You can choose more than one control (click while pressing Shift or Ctrl), and move them all at once.

Setting hot keys

As I mention in the previous section, you can assign an accelerator key, or *hot key*, to the following dialog box controls:

- Buttons
- Labels
- Group boxes
- Check boxes
- Option buttons

If a control doesn't have an accelerator key (an edit box, for example), you can still allow direct keyboard access to it by using a label control. That is, assign an accelerator key to the label, and put the label directly before the control in the tab order.

Figure 17-15 shows several edit boxes. The labels that describe the edit boxes have accelerator keys, and each label precedes its corresponding edit box in the tab order. Therefore, pressing Alt+N activates the edit box next to the Name label.

Figure 17-15:
Accelerator
keys are
underlined
in this edit
box.

Employee Data	
Name:	OK
SSN:	Cancel
Dept:	

Testing a dialog box

Accelerator key assignments don't appear in the dialog box until Excel displays the dialog box. However, Excel offers three ways for you to test a dialog box without actually calling it from a VBA procedure:

- ✔ Choose the Tools⇨Run Dialog command.
- ✔ Right-click the dialog box and choose Run Dialog from the shortcut menu.
- ✔ Choose the Run Dialog tool on the Forms toolbar.

When Excel displays a dialog box in this test mode, you can try out the tab order and the accelerator keys.

Dialog Box Aesthetics

A good-looking dialog box is easy on the eye, has nicely sized and aligned controls, and makes its function perfectly clear to the user. Bad-looking dialogs confuse the user, have misaligned controls, and give the impression that the developer didn't have a plan (or a clue).

A good rule of thumb is to make your dialog boxes look like Excel's built-in dialogs. As you gain more experience with dialog box construction, you'll be able to duplicate almost all the features of Excel's dialog boxes — with a few exceptions. You cannot create

- ✔ Tabbed dialog boxes, such as the Options dialog box
- ✔ Check box list boxes, such as the Toolbars dialog box

Also, custom dialog boxes do not display the little help icon in their title bars. If you want to provide help for the dialog, you must add a button.

Learning More

This chapter gives you more information about custom dialog boxes — specifically, the controls that make up a dialog box. The next chapter concludes this topic by explaining how to take action in your VBA code using the information you get from a custom dialog box.

Chapter 18

Dialog Box Techniques and Tricks

• •

In This Chapter

▶ Steps for using a custom dialog box in your application

▶ A hands-on example of creating a dialog box

▶ More dialog box examples

• •

*T*he previous chapters show you how to insert a dialog sheet, add controls to the dialog, and adjust some of the control's properties. These skills won't do you much good unless you understand how to make use of custom dialogs in your VBA code. This chapter provides these missing details, and it presents some useful techniques and tricks in the process.

Using Dialog Boxes

When you use a custom dialog box in your application, you normally write VBA code to do the following:

1. **Initialize the dialog box controls.**

   This optional step involves clearing out edit boxes, setting default options, and so on.

2. **Display the dialog box by using the Show method.**

3. **Determine whether the user canceled the dialog box.**

   If so, you probably want to abort the procedure that follows.

4. **Validate the information provided by the user (if the user did not cancel the dialog box, of course).**

   This step is optional.

5. **Take some action with the information provided by the user (if the information is valid).**

An Example

In Chapter 16, I present a hands-on dialog box example. Here's yet another example that can help you understand how dialog boxes work.

In this section, I present an example that demonstrates the five steps I describe in the previous section. This example uses a dialog box to get two pieces of information: a person's name and sex. The dialog box uses an edit box control to get the name, and two option buttons to get the sex.

Creating the dialog box

Figure 18-1 shows the custom dialog box for this example. It is on a dialog sheet named Dialog1.

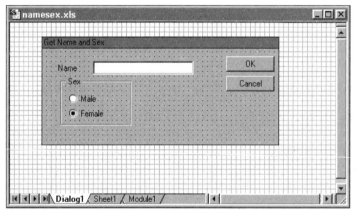

Figure 18-1:
This dialog box asks the user to enter a name and a sex.

This dialog box has seven controls:

- ✔ **An OK button named OKButton.** This button has its Default and Dismiss properties set.

- ✔ **A Cancel button named CancelButton.** This button has its Dismiss property set.

- ✔ **A label (*Name*).** This has its Accelerator Key property set to *N*.

- ✔ **An edit box named EditName.** This control has its Edit Validation property set to Text.

- ✔ **An option button named OptionMale (with the text *Male*).** This button has its Accelerator Key property set to *M*.

> ✔ **An option button named OptionFemale (with the text *Female*).** This control has its Accelerator Key property set to *F*.

> ✔ **A group box.** This box completely encloses the two option buttons, and displays the text, *Sex*.

I changed the dialog box's caption to *Get Name and Sex.* I also resized the dialog box so it doesn't show so much empty space.

If you're following along on your computer (and you should be), take a few minutes to create this dialog box using the preceding information.

Displaying the dialog box

Your next step is developing some VBA code to display this dialog box. Insert a VBA module and enter the following subroutine:

```
Sub GetData()
    DialogSheets("Dialog1").Show
End Sub
```

This subroutine uses the Show method of an object (Dialog1) in the DialogSheets collection of the active workbook. In other words, the code displays the dialog box. This is just the basic code — in the following sections, I show you how to extend its capabilities.

The next step makes it easy to execute this subroutine. Click on Sheet1 and display the Drawing toolbar. Add a button to the worksheet and attach it to the GetData macro. Click the button, and Excel executes the subroutine — and displays the dialog box. Figure 18-2 shows the result.

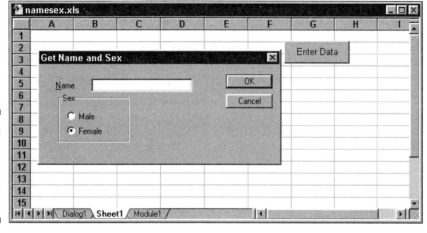

Figure 18-2:
Executing the GetData routine displays the dialog box.

Trying it out

Enter some text into the edit box. Click OK or Cancel to dismiss the dialog box. Now, execute the subroutine again, and notice that the dialog box still contains the text you entered. This is because the GetData routine doesn't *initialize* the dialog box.

Initializing the dialog box

Modify the subroutine so that it clears out any text in the edit box before displaying the dialog box:

```
Sub GetData()
    DialogSheets("Dialog1").EditBoxes("EditName").Text = ""
    DialogSheets("Dialog1").Show
End Sub
```

The new statement changes the Text property of the edit box object. Notice that this new statement refers to an object (EditName) in the EditBoxes collection, which is contained in the Dialog1 DialogSheets object. You need to fully qualify the reference because the Dialog1 sheet is not the active sheet when the subroutine is executed. In fact, references to objects in dialog boxes can be very lengthy. I describe a solution for fixing these long references later in this chapter (see "Using object variables").

Modifying this subroutine causes the dialog box to open with an empty edit box whenever you execute the GetData routine.

If this routine doesn't work properly, make sure you named the edit box EditName. Use the Name box to change the control's name.

To make Male the default sex, insert the following statement:

```
DialogSheets("Dialog1").OptionButtons("OptionMale").Value = _
        xlOn
```

Using the dialog box information

So far, this dialog box just pops up, but it doesn't do anything useful. It's time to change that. Modify the GetData subroutine so that it looks like the following code (I also added some comments):

```
Sub GetData()
'    Initialize the dialog
     DialogSheets("Dialog1").EditBoxes("EditName").Text = ""

'    Display the dialog
     DialogSheets("Dialog1").Show

'    Determine the next empty row
     NextRow = Application.CountA(ActiveSheet.Range("A:A")) + _
              1

'    Make sure Sheet1 is active
     Sheets("Sheet1").Activate

'    Transfer the name
     Cells(NextRow, 1) = _
             DialogSheets("Dialog1").EditBoxes("EditName").Text

'    Transfer the sex
     Select Case _
             DialogSheets("Dialog1").OptionButtons("OptionMale").Value
         Case xlOn
             Cells(NextRow, 2) = "Male"
         Case xlOff
             Cells(NextRow, 2) = "Female"
     End Select
End Sub
```

When you run the subroutine again, notice that it transfers the information to the worksheet. Figure 18-3 shows how this looks in action.

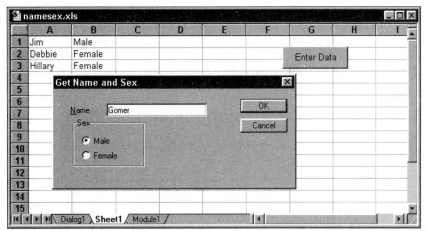

Figure 18-3:
Using the custom dialog box.

Here's how it works. The routine uses Excel's COUNTA function to determine the next blank row in the worksheet. It then activates Sheet1, just in case that's not the active sheet. Next, it transfers the text from the edit box to column 1 of the next empty row. It then uses Select Case to determine which option button the user selected, and it writes the appropriate text (Male or Female) to column 2 of the next empty row.

What if the macro is canceled?

You may notice that clicking the Cancel button doesn't cancel the macro. The subroutine still enters the information into the worksheet. The macro needs another modification. Here it is:

```
'    Display the dialog
     DBoxOK = DialogSheets("Dialog1").Show

'    Exit if canceled
     If Not DBoxOK Then Exit Sub
```

I changed the statement that shows the dialog box. With this change, the subroutine assigns the result of the dialog to a variable, DBoxOK. A value of False for the variable DBoxOK means the user clicked Cancel or pressed Escape. In that case, the Exit Sub statement kicks in and nothing happens.

The following statement shows another way to perform this same action (without using a variable):

```
If Not DialogSheets("Dialog1").Show Then Exit Sub
```

What if no name is entered?

Play around with this routine some more, and you find that the macro has another problem: It doesn't ensure that the user enters a name into the edit box. The following modification ensures that the user enters a name (well, at least some text) in the edit box. If the edit box is empty, a message appears and the routine stops.

```
'    Make sure a name was entered
     If DialogSheets("Dialog1").EditBoxes("EditName").Text = _
         "" Then
         MsgBox "You must enter a name!"
         Exit Sub
     End If
```

Now, it works

After making all these modifications, the dialog box works flawlessly. In real life, you'd probably need to collect more information than just name and sex. However, the same basic principles apply. You just have to deal with more dialog box controls.

More about Dialog Boxes

This section describes some additional details you should know about custom dialog boxes.

Referencing dialog sheet objects

When working with dialog box controls (also known as *objects*), you must fully qualify your object references because the dialog sheet that contains the object is not the active sheet. For example, a statement such as the following causes an error unless the active sheet has an EditBoxes collection and an edit box named EditName:

```
EditBoxes("EditName").Text = ""
```

In almost all cases, when you display a dialog box, its dialog sheet is not the active sheet. Therefore, you must fully qualify the reference by referring to the dialog sheet object, as in the following example:

```
DialogSheets("Dialog1").EditBoxes("EditName").Text = ""
```

If you execute a dialog box that's in a different workbook, you also need to qualify your references with the workbook object's name. Rather than use the actual name, use ThisWorkbook, which returns a reference to the workbook that contains the dialog box. In fact, you should always precede a dialog sheet reference with ThisWorkbook, as in

```
ThisWorkbook.DialogSheets("MyDialog").Show
```

The reason for this becomes clear when you create add-ins. Stay tuned. . . I reveal this information in Chapter 22.

Using object variables

An object variable is a variable that holds an object. You use a Dim statement to declare an object variable, and you use a Set statement to assign an object to that variable. For example, the following code assigns a Range object to an object variable named InputArea:

```
Dim InputArea as Range
Set InputArea = Worksheets("Sheet1").Range("A1:D4")
```

Thereafter, you can use InputArea whenever you need to refer to cells A1:D4 on Sheet1.

The Dim statement isn't really necessary. If you omit it, VBA uses a variant data type. However, it's a good practice to declare your variables.

As you may expect, you can use object variables for objects in a dialog sheet. Here is the example from the preceding section, rewritten to use object variables. I also declare all the variables used in this subroutine:

```
Sub GetData2()
'    Declare normal variables
     Dim DBoxOK As Boolean
     Dim NextRow As Integer

'    Declare object variables
     Dim Dialog As DialogSheet
     Dim EditName As EditBox
     Dim OptionMale As OptionButton
     Dim DataSheet As Worksheet
     Dim FirstCol As Range

'    Create object variables
     Set Dialog = DialogSheets("Dialog1")
     Set EditName = Dialog.EditBoxes("EditName")
     Set OptionMale = Dialog.OptionButtons("OptionMale")
     Set DataSheet = Sheets("Sheet1")
     Set FirstCol = DataSheet.Range("A:A")

'    Initialize the dialog
     EditName.Text = ""

'    Display the dialog
     DBoxOK = Dialog.Show
```

```
'   Exit if canceled
    If Not DBoxOK Then Exit Sub

'   Make sure a name was entered
    If EditName.Text = "" Then
        MsgBox "You must enter a name!"
        Exit Sub
    End If

'   Determine the next empty row
    NextRow = Application.CountA(FirstCol) + 1

'   Make sure Sheet1 is active
    DataSheet.Activate

'   Transfer the name
    Cells(NextRow, 1) = EditName.Text

'   Transfer the sex
    Select Case OptionMale.Value
        Case xlOn
            Cells(NextRow, 2) = "Male"
        Case xlOff
            Cells(NextRow, 2) = "Female"
    End Select
End Sub
```

The routine is quite a bit longer than its predecessor. However, the code is much easier to read. In addition, using object variables can make your code run significantly faster — especially in more complicated applications.

By the way, the variable name you choose for an object variable does not have to correspond to the object's name. However, I find that doing so helps me keep things straight.

More Dialog Box Examples

I could probably fill an entire book with interesting and useful tips for working with dialog boxes. Unfortunately, this book has a limited number of pages. I wrap up the topic of custom dialog boxes with a few more examples.

A list box example

List boxes are useful controls, but working with them can be a bit tricky. Before displaying a dialog box that uses a list box, you need to fill the list box with items. Then you need to determine which item(s) the user selected.

When dealing with list boxes, you need to know about the following properties and methods:

- **AddItem:** You use this method to add an item to a list box.
- **RemoveAllItems:** You use this method to remove all items from a list box.
- **ListCount:** This property returns the number of items in the list.
- **ListIndex:** This property returns the index number of the selected item or sets the item that's selected (single selections only).
- **List:** This property returns or sets the text in an item in a list.
- **Selected:** This property returns an array indicating selected items (multiple selections only).

Filling a list box

The example in this section assumes the following:

- You have a dialog box on a sheet named *ListBoxDlg*.
- This dialog box contains a list box control named *TheList*.

The procedure fills the list box with the names of the months. It starts by assigning the list box to an object variable. It then clears the list by using the RemoveAllItems method. Finally, the procedure uses the AddItem method to add 12 items to the list box. For complete details on these methods, consult the program's online help.

```
Sub ShowMonthNames()
    Dim ListBoxDlg As DialogSheet
    Dim TheList As ListBox

    Set ListBoxDlg = ThisWorkbook.DialogSheets("ListBoxDlg")
    Set TheList = ListBoxDlg.ListBoxes("TheList")

'   Clear list box
    TheList.RemoveAllItems

'   Fill the list box
```

```
    With TheList
        .AddItem Index:=1,  Text:="January"
        .AddItem Index:=2,  Text:="February"
        .AddItem Index:=3,  Text:="March"
        .AddItem Index:=4,  Text:="April"
        .AddItem Index:=5,  Text:="May"
        .AddItem Index:=6,  Text:="June"
        .AddItem Index:=7,  Text:="July"
        .AddItem Index:=8,  Text:="August"
        .AddItem Index:=9,  Text:="September"
        .AddItem Index:=10, Text:="October"
        .AddItem Index:=11, Text:="November"
        .AddItem Index:=12, Text:="December"
    End With

'   Show the dialog
    If Not ListBoxDlg.Show Then Exit Sub
End Sub
```

Figure 18-4 shows the dialog box with the list box filled with month names.

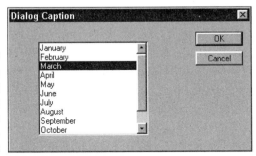

Figure 18-4:
A list box
filled with
month
names.

Determining the selected item

The preceding code merely displays a dialog box with a list box filled with month names. The procedure doesn't determine which item the user selected.

The following statement accesses the ListIndex property, and it also displays a message box with the index number of the selected item:

```
MsgBox TheList.ListIndex
```

You also can use the Value property, which returns the selected item's index number:

```
MsgBox TheList.Value
```

If you need to know the text of the selected item, use the List property along with the ListIndex property:

```
MsgBox TheList.List(TheList.ListIndex)
```

Selecting a range

In some cases, you might want the user to select a range while a dialog box is displayed. An example of this occurs in the first step of the Excel Chart Wizard. The Chart Wizard guesses the range, but the user is free to change it from the dialog box.

To allow a range selection in your dialog box, add an edit box, and set its Edit Validation property to Reference. Then, when the dialog box is displayed, the user can click in the edit box and then select a range in the worksheet.

The following example displays a dialog box with the current region's range address displayed in an edit box, as shown in Figure 18-5. The user can accept this range or change it. When the user closes the dialog box, the subroutine makes the range bold.

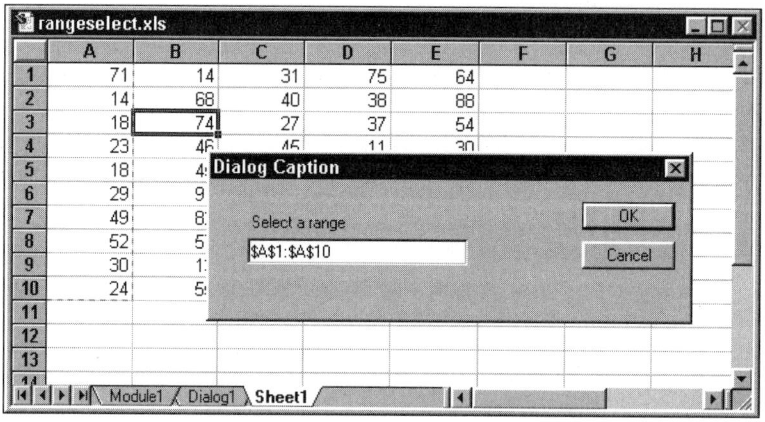

Figure 18-5: This dialog box lets the user select a range.

This example assumes the following:

- ✔ You have a dialog sheet named *Dialog1*.
- ✔ Dialog1 contains an edit box named *RangeBox*.
- ✔ RangeBox has its Edit Validation property set to *Reference*.

Here's the VBA code:

```
Sub BoldCells()
    Set Dialog = DialogSheets("Dialog1")
    Set Boldbox = Dialog.EditBoxes("RangeBox")

'   Exit if worksheet is not active
    If TypeName(ActiveSheet) <> "Worksheet" Then Exit Sub

'   Initialize with active area
    Boldbox.Text = ActiveCell.CurrentRegion.Address

'   Show dialog, exit if canceled
    If Not Dialog.Show Then Exit Sub

'   Make the range bold
    Range(Boldbox.Text).Font.Bold = True
End Sub
```

A spinner and an edit box

A spinner control and an edit box form a natural pair. Excel uses them frequently (check out the Print dialog box for a few examples). A spinner is useful for letting the user specify a number, which then appears in the companion edit box. Ideally, the spinner and its edit box should be in synch — that is, if the user clicks the spinner, the spinner's value should appear in the edit box. And if the user enters a value directly into the edit box, the spinner should take on that value.

Figure 18-6 shows a custom dialog box with a spinner and an edit box.

Figure 18-6:
A custom dialog box with a spinner and its companion edit box.

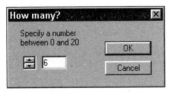

This dialog box contains the following controls:

- A spinner named *Spin,* with its Minimum Value property set to 0, its Maximum Value property set to 20, and its Incremental Change property set to 1. The spinner has a macro (SpinClick) attached to it.

- An edit box named *EdBox,* with its Edit Validation property set to Integer. The edit box has a macro (EdBoxClick) attached to it.

To attach a macro to a dialog control, right-click the control, and choose Assign Macro from the shortcut menu. If the macro already exists, you can choose it from the list Excel displays. If you haven't written it yet, you can enter the macro's name. When you assign a macro to a dialog control, the macro is executed whenever the control is accessed.

Here are the macros for this example:

```
'    Delcare global variables
     Public DBox As DialogSheet
     Public Spin As Spinner
     Public EdBox As EditBox

Sub GetInteger()
     Set DBox = DialogSheets("Dialog1")
     Set Spin = DBox.Spinners("Spin")
     Set EdBox = DBox.EditBoxes("EdBox")

'    Initialize to zero
     Spin.Value = 0
     EdBox.Text = Spin.Value

     If Not DBox.Show Then Exit Sub
     MsgBox "The integer is: " & Spin.Value
End Sub

Sub SpinClick()
     EdBox.Text = Spin.Value
End Sub

Sub EdBoxClick()
     Spin.Value = EdBox.Text
End Sub
```

Notice that I declare public variables — variables that I use in all three subroutines. The GetInteger subroutine initializes the controls to zero. When the user clicks the spinner, the SpinClick routine changes the edit box to correspond to the spinner's value. Similarly, when the user enters a value in the edit box, the spinner's value changes to match the entry.

Using a linked picture

One of my favorite dialog box tricks is to use a linked picture object. A linked picture in a dialog box lets you display a formatted cell or range in your dialog box. The nice part is that this involves a link. If the cell or range changes while the dialog box is displayed, the picture is updated.

Here's a simple example that demonstrates the technique. Figure 18-7 shows a worksheet set up to display the day of the week, the date, and the time:

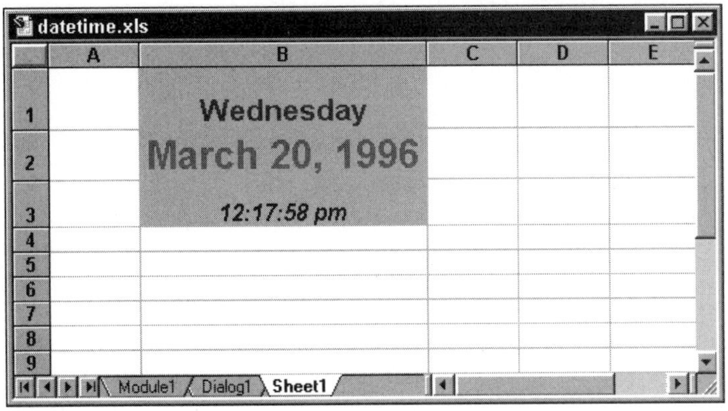

Figure 18-7: This range becomes a linked picture in a dialog box.

- ✔ **Cell B1:** Contains the formula =NOW( ), with *dddd* as the number format.
- ✔ **Cell B2:** Contains the formula =NOW( ), with *mmmm d, yyyy* as the number format.
- ✔ **Cell B3:** Contains the formula =NOW( ), with *hh:mm:ss am/pm* as the number format.

Apply a gray shading to the cells and make each cell a different color.

To create the linked picture:

1. **Insert a dialog sheet.**

2. **Activate the worksheet and select the range B1:B3.**

3. **Choose Edit⇨Copy.**

4. **Activate the dialog sheet.**

5. **Press Shift, and then choose Edit⇨Paste Picture Link (this command appears only when you press Shift).**

6. **Move the pasted picture into the dialog box.**

   You might want to remove the border from the picture.

Insert a VBA module and enter the following code:

```
Sub ShowDateTime()
    Update
    DialogSheets("Dialog1").Show
End Sub

Sub Update()
    With Sheets("Sheet1").Range("B3")
        .Formula = "=NOW()"
        .NumberFormat = "hh:mm:ss am/pm"
    End With
End Sub
```

Reactivate the dialog sheet and then add a new button with *Update the time* as its text. Attach the Update macro to the button. Now, when you run the ShowDateTime dialog, it displays the current date and time. To update the time, click the button. Figure 18-8 shows the finished product.

Figure 18-8:
This dialog box displays the current date and time by using a linked picture object.

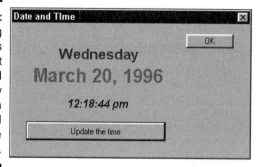

Using a linked picture is helpful for adding nicely formatted text to your dialog box. Just apply the formatting in a worksheet, and create the linked picture in your dialog box.

You can also use this technique to display a chart in a dialog box. Just position the chart on a worksheet, and then *take a picture* of the underlying range. Figure 18-9 shows an example of this.

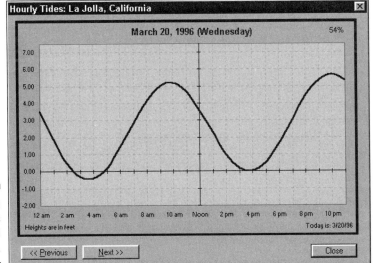

Figure 18-9:
This chart is
a linked
picture.

A Dialog Box Checklist

To wrap up this chapter, here's a checklist you can use when creating dialog boxes:

- Are the controls aligned with each other?
- Are similar controls the same size?
- Are controls evenly spaced?
- Does the dialog box have an appropriate caption?
- Is the dialog box too overwhelming? If so, you might want to use a series of dialogs.
- Can the user access every control with an accelerator key?
- Are any of the accelerator keys duplicated?
- Are the controls grouped logically (by function)?

✔ Is the tab order set correctly? The user should be able to tab through the dialog box and access the controls sequentially.

✔ If you plan to store the dialog in an add-in (which I discuss in Chapter 22), did you test it thoroughly after creating the add-in? Remember that an add-in is never the active workbook.

✔ Does your VBA code take appropriate action if the user cancels the dialog box or presses Esc?

✔ Are there any misspellings in the text? The Excel spelling checker works with dialog sheets.

✔ Does the dialog box have an appropriate caption?

✔ Does your dialog box fit on the screen in 640 × 480 mode? In other words, if you develop your dialog box using a high resolution video mode, your dialog box may be too big to fit on a screen in lower resolution.

✔ If your dialog box is used by Excel 5 and Excel For Windows 95 users, have you tested the application on both platforms? Text that looks good in Excel For Windows 95 doesn't always display properly in Excel 5.

✔ Do all edit boxes have the appropriate validation setting?

✔ Do all scroll bars and spinner controls allow valid values only?

✔ Are list boxes set properly (Single, Multi, or Extend)?

Learning More

This concludes the discussion of custom dialog boxes. The best way to master this feature is by creating dialog boxes — lots of them. Start simply, and then add more bells and whistles as you gain more experience.

Part V
Creating Custom Menus and Toolbars

The 5th Wave   By Rich Tennant

"HOW'S THAT FOR FAST SCROLLING?"

In this part...

This part consists of only two chapters, both of which deal with customizing Excel. Chapter 19 focuses on how to modify Excel's menu system. In Chapter 20, I discuss customizing toolbars.

Chapter 19

When Excel's Normal Menus Aren't Good Enough

*Y*ou may not realize it, but you can change almost every aspect of Excel's menus. Typical Excel users get by just fine with the standard menus. Because you're reading this book, however, you're probably not the typical Excel user. You might modify menus to make life easier for you and for your applications' users. In this chapter, I describe how to make changes to the Excel menu system.

Why Bother?

Most of the Excel applications you develop will get along just fine with the standard menu system. In some cases, however, you might want to add a new menu to make it easier to run your VBA macros. In other cases, you may want to remove certain menu items to prevent users from accessing certain features. If these sorts of changes seem useful, you should read this chapter. Otherwise, you can safely skip this chapter until the need arises.

Menu Terminology

Before I get too far into this, I need to discuss terminology. At first, menu terminology confuses people because many of the terms are similar. The following list describes official Excel menu terminology, which I use throughout this book:

✔ **Menu Bar:** The row of words that appears directly below the application's title bar. Excel has nine different menu bars that appear automatically, depending on the context. For example, the menu bar displayed when a worksheet is active differs from the menu bar displayed when a chart sheet is active.

✔ **Menu:** A single, top-level element of a menu bar. For example, each of Excel's menu bars has a menu called File.

✔ **Menu Item:** An element that appears in the drop-down list when you select a menu. For example, the first menu item under the File menu is New. Menu items also appear in submenus and shortcut menus.

✔ **Separator Bar:** A horizontal line that appears between two menu items. This is used to *group* similar menu items.

✔ **Submenu:** A second-level menu that is under some menus. For example, the Edit menu has a submenu called Clear.

✔ **Submenu Item:** A menu item that appears in the list when you select a submenu. For example, the Edit⇨Clear submenu contains the following submenu items: All, Formats, Contents, and Notes.

✔ **Shortcut Menu:** The floating list of menu items that appears when you right-click a selection or an object. Excel has 25 different shortcut menus.

✔ **Enabled:** A menu item that can be used. If a menu item isn't enabled, its text is grayed and the menu item can't be used.

✔ **Status Bar Text:** Text that appears in Excel's status bar when you select a menu or a menu item. For custom menu items, the status bar text is associated with the macro that the menu item executes.

✔ **OnAction:** The macro that is executed when a custom menu item command is executed.

Ways to Modify Menus

You can modify the Excel menus by removing elements, adding elements, and changing elements. I discuss these topics in the following sections.

Excel offers two ways to modify its menus:

✔ Using the built-in menu editor

✔ Using VBA code

Technically, Excel offers a third way to modify a menu, but it affects only the Tools menu. As you know, choosing the Tools⇨Macro command brings up the Macro dialog box. Clicking the Options button opens the Macro Options dialog box, which lets you assign a macro to a new menu item in the Tools menu.

This chapter focuses primarily on the menu editor, which can handle most of your menu modification chores. However, for those who just can't get enough of this menu editing stuff, I also introduce some of the VBA commands you can use to modify menus.

Using the Menu Editor

The menu editor is a tool that lets you add, remove, or modify elements in Excel's menus. The menu editor is available only when a VBA module is active. The Tools⇨Menu Editor command brings up the dialog box shown in Figure 19-1.

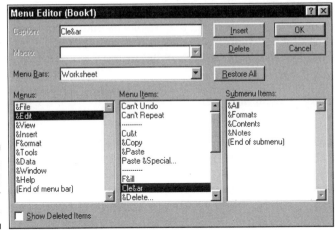

Figure 19-1:
The Excel
Menu Editor
dialog box.

The Menu Editor dialog box has several parts. To modify a menu, choose the appropriate menu bar from the Menu Bars drop-down list. Table 19-1 describes the items in this list.

Table 19-1	The Excel Menu Bars
Menu Bar	*What It Does*
Worksheet	The menu bar that appears when a worksheet is active
Chart	The menu bar that appears when a chart sheet is active or when an embedded chart is activated

(continued)

Table 19-1 (continued)	
Menu Bar	**What It Does**
No Documents Open	The menu bar that appears when no documents are open
Visual Basic Module	The menu bar that appears when a VBA module is active
Shortcut Menus 1	Lets you edit shortcut menus
Shortcut Menus 2	Lets you edit shortcut menus
Shortcut Menus 3	Lets you edit shortcut menus

When you select a menu bar, its menus appear in the Menus list box. Select a menu from the Menus list box, and its menu items appear in the Menu Items list box. Select a menu item from the Menu Items list box, and its submenu items (if any) appear in the Submenu Items list box.

Inserting a new menu

To insert a new menu, first select the existing menu that you want to appear *after* the new menu. Then click the Insert button. For example, if you want to insert a new menu called *Utilities* right before the Window menu, select the Window menu in the Menus list box, and then click Insert.

Next, enter the menu caption. Use an ampersand (&) to specify the hot key for the menu.

After you insert a new menu, you should insert at least one menu item for the menu. Click in the Menu Items list box, and click Insert. Enter the caption for the menu item, and specify the macro that Excel should run when the menu item is selected. Repeat this procedure until you've entered all the menu items for the new menu. To insert a separator bar, just enter a single hyphen as the caption and leave the Macro field empty.

Figure 19-2 shows a menu I created with four new menu items.

Deleting a menu or a menu item

To delete a menu or a menu item, select it from the Menus list box or the Menu Items list box, and then click the Delete button.

Deleting a menu item doesn't necessarily prevent the user from issuing a particular command. For example, if you delete the Open menu item from the File menu, you can still open a file by pressing Ctrl+O.

Figure 19-3 shows the Data menu after I deleted most of its menu items.

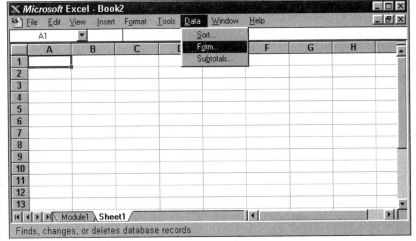

Restoring the original menus

The Restore All button resets the selected item to its built-in state. This is useful if you accidentally delete a menu or a menu item.

Modifying shortcut menus

As you know, a shortcut menu appears when you right-click an object or a selection. To modify a shortcut menu, choose one of the three Shortcut Menu listings in the menu bar's drop-down list. The Menu Items list box displays the shortcut menus you can choose. Table 19-2 lists all of the Excel shortcut menus and the context in which they appear.

Table 19-2	The Excel Shortcut Menus
Shortcut Menu	*Appears When You Click This*
Toolbar	A toolbar
Toolbar Button	A toolbar button
Worksheet Cell	A cell or a range
Column	An entire worksheet column
Row	An entire worksheet row
Workbook Tab	A workbook tab
Macrosheet Cell	A cell or range on an XLM macro sheet
Title Bar	The title bar of a workbook
Desktop	Excel's background area
Module	A VBA module
Watch Pane	The Watch pane in the VBA Debug window
Immediate Pane	The Immediate pane in the VBA Debug window
Debug Code Pane	The Debug Code pane in the VBA Debug window
Drawing Object	A drawing object
Button	A button
Text Box	A text box
Dialog Sheet	A dialog sheet
Chart Series	A data series in a chart
Chart Text	Text in a chart
Chart Plot Area	The plot area of a chart
Entire Chart	The entire chart
Chart Axis	An axis in a chart
Chart Gridline	A gridline in a chart
Chart Floor	The floor of a 3-D chart
Chart Legend	The legend of a chart

Menu-making conventions

You may have noticed that menus in Windows programs typically adhere to some established conventions. No one knows where these conventions came from, but if you want to give the impression that you know what you're doing, you should follow them. When you modify menus — with the menu editor or with VBA — keep the following points in mind:

- The File menu is always first, and the Help menu is always last.

- Menu item text is always proper case — the first letter of words are uppercase, except for minor words such as *the, a,* and *and.*

- Menu items are usually limited to three or fewer words.

- Every menu item should have a hot key (underlined letter) that's unique to the menu.

- Menu items that display a dialog box are followed by ellipses (. . .).

- Avoid having a long list of menu items. Sometimes, submenus provide a good alternative. If you must have a lengthy list of menu items, use a separator bar (a menu item with its Caption property set to "-") to group items into logical groups.

- Menu items that are not appropriate in the current context are *grayed.* In VBA terminology, the menu item's Enabled property is set to False.

- Some menu items serve as a toggle. When the option is on, the menu item is preceded by a check mark. In VBA terminology, the menu item's Checked property is True.

Menu editor limitations

Although the menu editor is quite straightforward and easy to use, it has some limitations:

- You can't use the menu editor to create a new menu bar.

- You can't change the captions for built-in menus or menu items.

- The menu editor doesn't recognize any menu changes you've made using VBA statements. Therefore, the menu structure displayed in the menu editor may not correspond to the actual menu structure.

What to look out for

Modifying menus can be useful, but you need to be careful. Excel stores the menu modifications you make with the menu editor in the workbook that is active when you invoke the editor. If you open that workbook, the customized menus remain in effect until you close the workbook. This can cause some strange things to happen if you have several workbooks open, each with its own customized menu. For reliable results, it's best to have only one workbook open that has a customized menu.

Manipulating Menus with VBA

Use the menu editor for simple modifications only. If you want to do anything fancy — for example, change menus on the fly, add check marks to menu items, or disable menu items under certain conditions — you need to write VBA macro code.

If you're thinking about using the macro recorder to record your actions while using the menu editor, forget it. Recording grinds to a halt when Excel displays the Menu Editor dialog box. So, this is one area in which turning on the macro recorder won't do you any good.

It's important to understand that menus manipulated with VBA remain in effect until you exit Excel, or until you change them with more VBA code. These menus differ from menus manipulated with the menu editor; when you close the workbook that contains menus edited with the menu editor, the menus return to their normal state. Therefore, when you modify menus with VBA, you must ensure that your menu changes remain in effect only as long as required. In other words, you probably need to write code to reset the menus when your application closes.

More object stuff

Before you jump into writing VBA code to work with menus, you must understand the object hierarchy, which is as follows:

```
Application
    MenuBar
        Menu
            MenuItem
                MenuItem
```

The Application object contains the MenuBars collection. A MenuBar object contains Menu objects, and Menu objects contain MenuItem objects. MenuItem objects may contain other MenuItem objects, as in the case of submenus. To reference the New menu item in the worksheet's File menu, use the following syntax:

```
MenuBars(xlWorksheet).Menus("File").MenuItems("New...")
```

xlWorksheet is a constant that represents the displayed menu bar when a worksheet is active. *File* is the caption for the first Menu object in the menu bar, and *New. . .* is the caption for the first menu item in the menu. This may be a bit confusing at first, but it becomes clear with practice.

Some menu examples

In the following sections, I present a few examples of using VBA code to modify the Excel menus.

Deleting menus

The Delete method of the Menus collection deletes a menu (either custom or built-in) from a menu bar. The following example deletes the Help menu from all the built-in menu bars. Notice that it uses an On Error statement to ignore errors that occur if the menu bar does not have a Help menu.

```
Sub RemoveHelpMenus()
    On Error Resume Next
    For Each Bar In MenuBars
        Bar.Menus("Help").Delete
    Next Bar
End Sub
```

The following subroutine uses the Add method to restore all the Help menus to the built-in menu bars:

```
Sub RestoreHelpMenus()
    On Error Resume Next
    For Each Bar In MenuBars
        If Bar.BuiltIn Then _
            Bar.Menus.Add "Help", Restore:=True
    Next Bar
End Sub
```

Changing menu text

You can change the text displayed for menu items (both custom and built-in). You do so by changing the Caption property. This example changes the Help menu in the worksheet menu bar to display *Assistance:*

```
Sub ChangeHelp()
        MenuBars(xlWorksheet).Menus("Help").Caption = _
        "&Assistance"
End Sub
```

The following example changes the text of all the menus in all the menu bars to uppercase — probably not something you'd want to do, but it *does* give Excel a new look:

```
Sub UpperCaseMenus()
    For Each Bar In MenuBars
        For Each Menu In Bar.Menus
            Menu.Caption = UCase(Menu.Caption)
        Next Menu
    Next Bar
End Sub
```

Figure 19-4 shows how the menus look after you execute this routine.

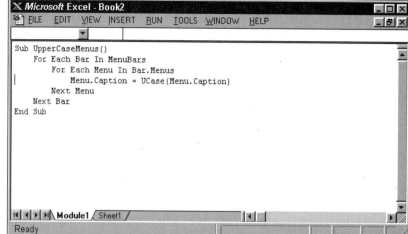

To return the menus to normal, use the following routine. The On Error statement avoids the error message that appears when attempting to reset a custom menu.

```
Sub ResetMenus()
    On Error Resume Next
    For Each Bar In MenuBars
        Bar.Reset
    Next Bar
End Sub
```

Deleting menu items

Use the Delete method to delete custom or built-in menu items. The following statement deletes the Exit menu item from the File menu on the worksheet menu bar:

```
MenuBars(xlWorksheet).Menus("File").MenuItems("Exit").Delete
```

To get this menu item back, use the Add method, with the Restore option. For example:

```
MenuBars(xlWorksheet).Menus("File").MenuItems.Add "Exit", _
    Restore:=True
```

Disabling shortcut menus

You may want to disable one or more shortcut menus while your application is running. For example, you may not want the user to access the commands by right-clicking a cell. You can't use the menu editor to remove shortcut menus. This tool allows you to add or remove shortcut menu items, but not entire menus.

If you want to disable all shortcut menus, you can't use a For Each structure, because the shortcut menus aren't part of a collection. Therefore, you must loop through them, as shown in the following code:

```
Sub DisableShortcuts()
    For i = 1 To 25
        ShortcutMenus(i).Enabled = False
    Next i
End Sub
```

Adding menu items to a shortcut menu

Adding a menu item to a shortcut menu works just like adding one to a regular menu. The following example demonstrates how to add a menu item to the shortcut menu that appears when you right-click a cell. This menu item is added before the first menu item, so it will appear at the top of the list. Selecting the new menu item executes the ToggleWordWrap subroutine.

```
Sub AddItemToTop()
    ShortcutMenus(xlWorksheetCell).MenuItems.Add _
        Caption:="Toggle Word Wrap", _
        Before:=1, _
        OnAction:="ToggleWordWrap"
End Sub
```

The following routine adds two menu items to a shortcut menu. The first is a separator bar. Because I omit the Before argument, Excel adds the menu item to the end of the menu items.

```
Sub AddItemToBottom()
    With ShortcutMenus(xlWorksheetCell).MenuItems
        .Add Caption:="-"
        .Add Caption:="Toggle Word Wrap", _
            OnAction:="ToggleWordWrap"
    End With
End Sub
```

Learning More

This chapter shows you how to use Excel's menu editor — which is usually all you need. For more advanced menu modification, you need to write VBA code. This chapter presents a few examples, but complete coverage of this topic is beyond the scope of this book. Check out the online help for additional details and examples.

In the next chapter, I discuss how to modify another user interface element: toolbars.

Chapter 20

Customizing the Excel Toolbars

. . . .

In This Chapter

▶ An overview of using toolbars in Excel

▶ Different ways you can customize toolbars

▶ How to create different images on toolbar buttons

▶ Examples of using VBA to manipulate toolbars

. . . .

*E*xcel is definitely *not* a toolbar-challenged product. It comes with more than 200 toolbar buttons and 13 built-in toolbars. You won't find all the available toolbar buttons on the prebuilt toolbars. In fact, some of the more useful toolbar buttons don't appear on any of the prebuilt toolbars (almost as if Microsoft was trying to keep them a secret). And, you might decide that many of the buttons on the prebuilt toolbars are not all that useful. Consequently, you might decide to create one or more custom toolbars containing the toolbar buttons you use most often. This chapter shows you how.

What You Can Do with Toolbars

The following list summarizes the ways in which you can customize toolbars (I discuss these topics in detail later in this chapter):

- **Remove toolbar buttons from built-in toolbars.** You can get rid of toolbar buttons that you never use — and free up a few pixels of screen space.

- **Add toolbar buttons to built-in toolbars.** You can add as many toolbar buttons as you want to any toolbar. The buttons can be custom buttons or buttons from other toolbars, or they can come from the stock of toolbar buttons that Excel provides for you.

- **Create new toolbars.** You can create as many new toolbars as you like, with toolbar buttons from any source.

✔ **Change the function of built-in toolbar buttons.** You do this by attaching your own macro to a built-in toolbar button.

✔ **Change the image that appears on any toolbar button.** Excel includes a rudimentary but functional toolbar button editor. You can also do this by using several other techniques.

Don't be afraid to experiment with toolbars. If you mess up a built-in toolbar, you can easily reset it to its default state. Just choose View➪Toolbars, select the toolbar, and click the Reset button.

Hiding and Displaying Toolbars

You can display as many toolbars as you like. A toolbar can be either *floating* or *docked*. A docked toolbar is fixed in place at the top, bottom, left, or right edge of Excel's workspace. Toolbars that contain nonstandard buttons (for example, the Zoom Control) can't be docked on the left or right edges of the workspace because the larger control makes the toolbar too wide. Floating toolbars appear in an *always-on-top* window, which means that they are never obscured by other windows. You can change the dimensions of a floating toolbar by dragging a border.

As shown in Figure 20-1, right-clicking any toolbar or toolbar button displays a shortcut menu that lets you hide or display a toolbar. However, not all toolbars appear in this shortcut menu. To get a complete list of the toolbars, use the Toolbars dialog box. This dialog box lets you hide or display toolbars (among other things).

How Excel handles toolbars

When you start up Excel, it displays the same toolbar configuration that was in effect the last time you used the program. Did you ever wonder how Excel keeps track of this information? When you exit Excel, it updates a file called EXCEL5.XLB — this file is located in your Windows folder. This file stores all your custom toolbars, as well as information about which toolbars are visible, and the onscreen location of each toolbar.

If you ever need to restore the toolbars to their previous configuration, you can use the File➪Open command to open EXCEL5.XLB. This restores your toolbar configuration to the way it was when you started the current session of Excel. You also can make a copy of the EXCEL5.XLB file and give it a different name. Doing so lets you store multiple toolbar configurations that you can load at any time.

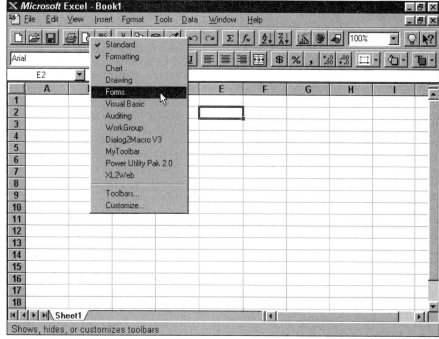

Figure 20-1:
Right-
clicking
a toolbar or
a toolbar
button
displays this
shortcut
menu.

You can access the Toolbars dialog box in two ways:

▹ Choose View▹Toolbars.

▹ Right-click a toolbar, and choose Toolbars from the shortcut menu.

Either of these methods displays the dialog box shown in Figure 20-2. This
dialog box lists all the available toolbars, including custom toolbars you have
created.

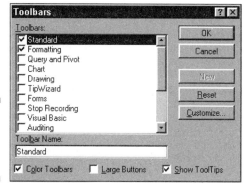

Figure 20-2:
The
Toolbars
dialog box.

The Toolbars dialog box lets you perform the following actions:

- ✔ **Hide or display any toolbar in the list.** Add a check mark to display a toolbar; remove the check mark to hide a toolbar. The changes take effect when you close the dialog box.

- ✔ **Create a new toolbar.** Enter a name in the Toolbar Name edit box, and click the New button. Excel creates and displays an empty toolbar. You can then add buttons to the new toolbar.

- ✔ **Reset a built-in toolbar.** Select a built-in toolbar from the list, and click the Reset button (when you select a custom toolbar, this button says Delete). Excel restores the toolbar to its default state.

- ✔ **Delete a custom toolbar.** Select a custom toolbar from the list, and click the Delete button (when you select a built-in toolbar, this button says Reset).

- ✔ **Toggle the toolbar button color.** Check or uncheck the Color Toolbars check box.

- ✔ **Toggle the toolbar button size.** Check or uncheck the Large Buttons check box. If you use a high-resolution video mode, you might prefer working with large toolbar buttons.

- ✔ **Toggle the tooltips display.** Tooltips are the pop-up messages that display the button names when you pause the mouse pointer over a button. If you find the tooltips distracting, remove the check mark from the Show ToolTips check box. When you move the mouse pointer over a button, the status bar still displays a description of the button.

In addition, you can make the following changes while the Toolbars dialog box is displayed:

- ✔ **Move a toolbar button from any displayed toolbar to any other displayed toolbar.** Click a button and drag it to its new location.

- ✔ **Copy a toolbar button from any displayed toolbar to any other displayed toolbar.** Ctrl-click a button and drag it to another location.

- ✔ **Copy the image on a toolbar button to another button.** Right-click a button, and choose Copy Button Image from the shortcut menu. Then right-click another button, and choose Paste Button Image from the shortcut menu.

I describe additional customization options in the next section.

Toolbar autosensing

Normally, Excel displays a particular toolbar automatically when you change contexts. For example, when you activate a chart, Excel displays the Chart toolbar. You can easily override this feature, called *autosensing,* by hiding the toolbar (to do so, click its Close button, or use the View➪Toolbars command). After doing so, Excel no longer displays that toolbar when you switch to its former context. However, you can restore autosensing by displaying the appropriate toolbar when you're in the appropriate context. Thereafter, Excel automatically displays the toolbar when you switch to that context.

The table below lists the contexts in which Excel automatically displays each toolbar.

User Action	Toolbar Displayed
Activates a chart sheet	Chart
Activates an embedded chart	Chart
Activates a VBA module	Visual Basic
Activates a dialog sheet	Forms
Starts recording a macro	Stop Recording
Enters full-screen mode	Full Screen
Activates a sheet with a pivot table	Query and Pivot

Using the Customize Dialog Box

You customize toolbars by using the Customize dialog box, shown in Figure 20-3. You can bring up this dialog box in either of two ways:

- ✔ Choose View➪Toolbars, and click the Customize button in the Toolbars dialog box.
- ✔ Right-click a toolbar or a toolbar button, and choose Customize from the shortcut menu.

The Customize dialog box contains the built-in toolbar buttons, arranged in 13 categories. A 14th category, Custom, contains 28 additional buttons that don't do anything (you can use these to execute macros). When you select a category, the dialog box displays the buttons in that category. To find out what a button does, click it and then read its description at the bottom of the dialog box.

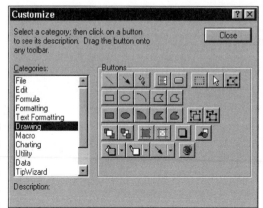

Figure 20-3:
The
Customize
dialog box.

Table 20-1 lists the toolbar button categories.

Table 20-1	Toolbar Button Categories
Category	*What It Handles*
File	Files, sheets, and printing
Edit	Worksheet editing
Formula	Characters listed in the formula bar
Formatting	Borders, shading, and styles
Text Formatting	Fonts and alignment
Drawing	Drawing tools, colors, and patterns
Macro	VBA macro tools
Charting	Chart types and customization
Utility	Miscellaneous tools, including workgroup tools
Data	Pivot tables and outlining
TipWizard	TipWizard tools
Auditing	Auditing tools
Forms	Dialog box and worksheet controls
Custom	Button faces that don't do anything (you supply the macro)

With the Customize dialog box displayed, you can copy and move buttons freely among any visible toolbars. To copy a button, Ctrl-click the button and drag the copy into position. To move a button, just click it and drag it to its new location. Note that you also can create *gaps* by moving a toolbar button slightly to the left or the right.

Changing a Toolbar Button's Image

If you don't like the image displayed on a toolbar button, change it. You can use several methods to change a button's image:

- ✔ Modify or create the image by using the Excel Button Editor dialog box.
- ✔ Copy an image from another toolbar button.
- ✔ Using the Clipboard, copy an image from another application.

I discuss these methods in the following sections.

Creating images from scratch

The Excel Button Editor is simple and easy to use. To create a new image from scratch, you have to start with some button. You might want to use the blank toolbar button in the Custom category of the Customize dialog box. Or maybe you just want to make some minor changes to an existing button image.

To edit a button image, you must be in *toolbar customization mode* (either the Toolbars or the Customize dialog box must be visible). To begin editing, right-click the button you want to edit, and choose Edit Button Image from the shortcut menu. As shown in Figure 20-4, the image appears in the Button Editor dialog box, where you can change individual pixels and shift the entire image up, down, to the left, or to the right. (If you've never worked with icons before, you may be surprised at how difficult it is to create attractive images in such a small area.)

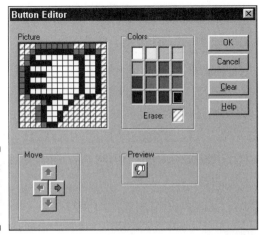

Figure 20-4:
The Button Editor dialog box.

The Button Editor dialog box is straightforward. Just click a color and then click a pixel (or drag across pixels). When you're satisfied with the image, click OK. Or if you don't like what you've done, click Cancel and the button retains its original image.

Toolbar buttons can be displayed in regular size or in a larger size. Users with high-resolution video drivers often choose the large button options because the buttons are more legible. If your custom toolbar button images will be displayed in both sizes, you *must* create them while the toolbar buttons are displayed at regular size. If you create the button images in large button mode, you'll be in for a rude awakening when you switch to normal-sized buttons. Excel scales the images to fit the smaller space, but the results are almost always disappointing.

Copying and modifying other buttons

Another way to get a button image on a custom toolbar is to copy it from another toolbar button. In toolbar customization mode, right-clicking a toolbar button displays a shortcut menu that lets you copy a button image to the Clipboard or paste the Clipboard contents to the selected button.

Copying from the Clipboard

You also can copy any image from the Clipboard to a toolbar button. This works best when the copied image is exactly the right size. You can copy an image of any size to a toolbar button, but it will be scaled to fit — and usually won't look very good.

Distributing Toolbars

If you want to distribute a custom toolbar to other users, you can store it in a workbook. To store a toolbar in a workbook file, you must insert a VBA module sheet (unless one already exists). Store a toolbar in a workbook file by choosing the Insert⇨Macro⇨Module command.

Activate a VBA module, and choose Tools⇨Attach Toolbars. Excel displays the Attach Toolbars dialog box, shown in Figure 20-5. In the list box on the left, this dialog box lists all the custom toolbars on your system. The list box on the right lists toolbars already stored in the workbook. To attach a toolbar, select it and then click the Copy button. When a toolbar in the right list box is selected, the Copy button says Delete; you can click the Delete button to remove the selected toolbar from the workbook.

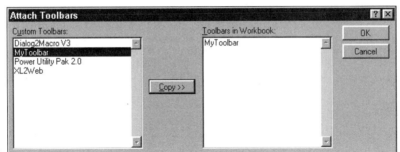

When you open a workbook, any toolbar attached to the workbook appears automatically, unless the workspace already has a toolbar with the same name.

The toolbar that's stored in the workbook is an exact copy of the toolbar at the time you attach it. If you modify the toolbar after attaching it, the changed version is not automatically stored in the workbook. You must manually remove the old toolbar and then add the edited toolbar.

Using VBA to Manipulate Toolbars

As you might expect, you can write VBA code to do fun things with toolbars. In this section, I present a few examples to get you started.

More object stuff

When you work with toolbars, you can turn on the macro recorder to see what's happening in terms of VBA code. Unless you're editing buttons, the steps you take while customizing toolbars generate code. By examining this code, you can discover how Excel arranges the object model for toolbars. The model actually is pretty simple:

```
Application
    Toolbars
        ToolbarButtons
```

The Toolbars collection — which is contained in the Application object — is a collection of all Toolbar objects, and each Toolbar object has a collection of ToolbarButtons. These objects have properties and methods that allow you to control toolbars by using VBA procedures.

Resetting all built-in toolbars

The following procedure resets all built-in toolbars to their virgin state:

```
Sub ResetAll()
    For Each Bar In Toolbars
        Bar.Reset
    Next Bar
End Sub
```

Using the Reset method on a custom toolbar has no effect (and does not generate an error).

Be careful with the preceding routine. Calling this routine erases all customizations to all built-in toolbars. The toolbars will be just as they were when you first installed Excel.

Toggling the display of all toolbars

The following example isn't all that useful, but it causes lots of onscreen action (try it!). It simply reverses the Visible property of each toolbar. Hidden toolbars are displayed, and visible toolbars are hidden. To return to normal, just rerun the subroutine:

```
Sub ToggleDisplay()
    For Each Bar In Toolbars
        Bar.Visible = Not Bar.Visible
    Next Bar
End Sub
```

Displaying a toolbar when a worksheet is activated

Assume you have a workbook that holds your budget information in a worksheet named Budget. In addition, assume that you've developed a custom toolbar named Budget Tools, which you use with this workbook. The toolbar should be visible when you work on the Budget sheet; otherwise, it should remain hidden and out of the way.

The following Auto_Open subroutine sets up Excel so that activating the Budget worksheet executes the ShowToolbar routine, which shows the Budget Tools toolbar. Deactivating the Budget worksheet executes the HideToolbar routine, which hides the Budget Tools toolbar.

```
Sub Auto_Open()
'    Set up toolbar display
    With ThisWorkbook.Worksheets("Budget")
        .OnSheetActivate = "ShowToolbar"
        .OnSheetDeactivate = "HideToolbar"
    End With
End Sub
```

The following routines are executed when the Budget worksheet is activated or deactivated, respectively:

```
Sub ShowToolbar()
    Toolbars("Budget Tools").Visible = True
End Sub

Sub HideToolbar()
    Toolbars("Budget Tools").Visible = False
End Sub
```

OnSheetActivate and OnSheetDeactivate remain in effect until canceled or until the current Excel session ends. To cancel, assign an empty string to the properties. The following Auto_Close routine cancels the OnSheetActivate and OnSheetDeactivate settings:

```
Sub Auto_Close()
'    Cancel the toolbar display
    With ThisWorkbook.Worksheets("Budget")
        .OnSheetActivate = ""
        .OnSheetDeactivate = ""
    End With
End Sub
```

For more information about using automatic procedures, take a look at Chapter 11.

Hiding and restoring toolbars

In some cases, you may want to remove all the toolbars when a workbook is opened. It's only polite, however, to restore the toolbars when your application closes.

The following subroutine, SaveToolbars, saves the names of all visible toolbars in column A of Sheet1 and then hides all the toolbars. Notice that the routine saves the toolbar names in a worksheet range rather than an array, ensuring that the toolbar names are still available when the RestoreToolbars routine is executed. Values stored in an array may be lost between the time SaveToolbars is executed and RestoreToolbars is executed.

```
Sub SaveToolbars()
    ThisWorkbook.Sheets("Sheet1").Range("A:A").Clear
    Set SaveRange = _
        ThisWorkbook.Sheets("Sheet1").Range("A1")
    BarCount = 0
    For Each Bar In Toolbars
        If Bar.Visible Then
            BarCount = BarCount + 1
            SaveRange.Offset(BarCount - 1, 0).Value = _
                Bar.Name
            Bar.Visible = False
        End If
    Next Bar
End Sub
```

RestoreToolbars displays the toolbars that were saved by SaveToolbars:

```
Sub RestoreToolbars()
    Set SaveRange = _
        ThisWorkbook.Sheets("Sheet1").Range("A1")
    Set ColumnA = ThisWorkbook.Sheets("Sheet1").Range("A:A")
    For i = 1 To Application.CountA(ColumnA)
        Toolbars(SaveRange.Offset(i - 1, 0).Value).Visible = _
            True
    Next i
End Sub
```

Learning More

In this chapter, you learn all about toolbars, and I even provide some useful VBA examples. This concludes Part V.

In the next part, I tie lots of the preceding information together as well as discuss some new topics.

Part VI
Putting It All Together

Re·al Pro'gram·mers

Real Programmers don't look stylish. To do so would indicate a belief in society.

In this part...

The preceding 20 chapters cover quite a bit of material. At this point, you may still feel a bit disjointed about all of this VBA stuff. The three chapters in this part fill in the gaps and otherwise tie everything together. I discuss custom worksheet functions (a very useful feature), describe add-ins, provide more programming examples, and wrap up with a discussion of user-oriented applications.

Chapter 21

Creating Worksheet Functions — and Living to Tell about It

*F*or many people, the main attraction of VBA is the capability to create custom worksheet functions — functions that look, work, and feel just like those that Microsoft built into Excel. A custom function offers the added advantage of working exactly how you want it to. I introduce custom functions in Chapter 5. In this chapter, I get down to the nitty-gritty and describe some tricks of the trade.

Why Create Custom Functions?

You are undoubtedly familiar with the Excel worksheet functions — even Excel novices know how to use common worksheet functions such as SUM, AVERAGE, and IF. By my count, Excel contains 319 predefined worksheet functions. And if that's not enough, you can create custom functions by using VBA.

With all the functions available in Excel and VBA, you may wonder why you would ever need to create new functions. The answer: to simplify your work. With a bit of planning, you can create custom functions that are very useful in worksheet formulas and VBA procedures. Often, for example, you can significantly shorten a formula by creating a custom function. After all, shorter formulas are more readable and easier to work with.

What custom worksheet functions can't do

As you develop custom functions for use in your worksheet formulas, it's important that you understand a key point: VBA worksheet function procedures are essentially *passive*. For example, code within a function procedure cannot manipulate ranges, change formatting, or perform many of the other actions that a subroutine can perform. An example may help your understanding of this important point.

You might try to write a custom function that changes the formatting of a cell. For example, it might be useful to create a function that changes the color of text in a cell, based on the cell's value. Try as you might, however, you can't write such a function. Just remember this: A function returns a value — it does not perform actions with objects.

Function Arguments

To work with functions, you need to understand how to work with arguments. The following points apply to the arguments for both Excel's worksheet functions and custom VBA functions:

- Arguments can be variables (including arrays), constants, literals, or expressions.
- Some functions have no arguments.
- Some functions have a fixed number of required arguments (from 1 to 60).
- Some functions have a combination of required and optional arguments.

Function Examples

The examples in the following sections demonstrate how to work with various types of arguments.

A function with no argument

Like subroutines, functions need not have arguments. For example, Excel has a few built-in worksheet functions that don't use arguments, including RAND, TODAY, and NOW.

Here's a simple example of a function with no arguments. The following function returns the UserName property of the Application object. This name appears in the Options dialog box (General tab). This simple but useful example shows the only way you can get the user's name to appear in a worksheet formula:

```
Function User()
'    Returns the name of the current user
     User = Application.UserName
End Function
```

When you enter the following formula into a worksheet cell, the cell displays the name of the current user:

```
=User()
```

As with the built-in functions in Excel, when you use a function with no arguments, you must include a set of empty parentheses.

A function with one argument

This section describes a function designed for sales managers who need to calculate the commissions earned by their sales forces. The commission rate depends on the monthly sales volume — those who sell more earn a higher commission rate. The function returns the commission amount, based on the monthly sales (which is the function's only argument — a required argument). The calculations in this example are based on the following table:

Monthly Sales	Commission Rate
0 – $9,999	8.0%
$10,000 – $19,999	10.5%
$20,000 – $39,999	12.0%
$40,000+	14.0%

You can use several approaches to calculate commissions for various sales amounts entered into a worksheet. You *could* write a formula such as this:

```
=IF(AND(A1>=0,A1<=9999.99),A1*0.08,IF(AND(A1>=10000,A1<=19999.99),A1*0.105,
IF(AND(A1>=20000,A1<=39999.99),A1*0.12,IF(A1>=40000,A1*0.14,0))))
```

This is a bad approach for a couple of reasons. First, the formula is overly complex. Second, the values are hard-coded into the formula, making the formula difficult to modify if the commission structure changes.

A better approach is to use a lookup table function to compute the commissions, as shown in the following example:

```
=VLOOKUP(A1,Table,2)*A1
```

An even better approach is to create a custom function such as the following:

```
Function Commission(Sales)
'    Calculates sales commissions
    Tier1 = 0.08
    Tier2 = 0.105
    Tier3 = 0.12
    Tier4 = 0.14
    Select Case Sales
        Case 0 To 9999.99: Commission = Sales * Tier1
        Case 1000 To 19999.99: Commission = Sales * Tier2
        Case 20000 To 39999.99: Commission = Sales * Tier3
        Case Is >= 40000: Commission = Sales * Tier4
    End Select
End Function
```

After you define this function in a VBA module, you can use it in a worksheet formula. Entering the following formula into a cell produces a result of 3,000 (the amount, 25,000, qualifies for a commission rate of 12 percent):

```
=Commission(25000)
```

Figure 21-1 shows a worksheet that uses this new function.

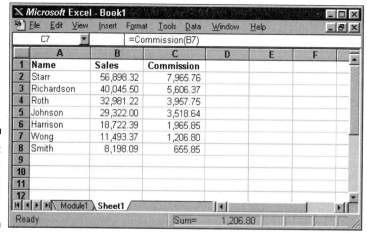

Figure 21-1:
Using the
Commission
function in a
worksheet.

A function with two arguments

This example builds on the previous one. Imagine that the sales manager implements a new policy: The total commission paid increases by 1 percent for every year the salesperson has been with the company.

I modify the custom Commission function (defined in the preceding section) so that it takes two arguments — both of which are required arguments. Call this new function *Commission2:*

```
Function Commission2(Sales, Years)
'    Calculates sales commissions based on years in service
     Tier1 = 0.08
     Tier2 = 0.105
     Tier3 = 0.12
     Tier4 = 0.14
     Select Case Sales
          Case 0 To 9999.99: Commission2 = Sales * Tier1
          Case 1000 To 19999.99: Commission2 = Sales * Tier2
          Case 20000 To 39999.99: Commission2 = Sales * Tier3
          Case Is >= 40000: Commission2 = Sales * Tier4
     End Select
     Commission2 = Commission2 + (Commission2 * Years / 100)
End Function
```

I simply add the second argument (Years) to the Function statement and include an additional computation that adjusts the commission before exiting the function.

Here's an example of how you can write a formula by using this function (it assumes that the sales amount is in cell A1; cell B1 specifies the number of years the salesperson has worked):

```
=Commission2(A1,B1)
```

A function with a range argument

The following example demonstrates how to use a worksheet range as an argument. Actually, it's not at all tricky; Excel takes care of the behind-the-scenes details.

Assume that you want to calculate the average of the five largest values in a range named Data. Because Excel doesn't have a function that can calculate this value, you would probably write a formula such as the following:

```
=(LARGE(Data,1)+LARGE(Data,2)+LARGE(Data,3)+LARGE(Data,4)+ _
LARGE(Data,5))/5
```

This formula uses the Excel LARGE function, which returns the *n*th largest value in a range. The formula adds the five largest values in the range named Data and then divides the result by 5. The formula works fine, but it's rather unwieldy. And what if you decide that you need to compute the average of the top *six* values? You would need to rewrite the formula — and make sure that you update all copies of the formula.

Wouldn't it be easier if Excel had a function named TopAvg? Then you could compute the average by using the following (nonexistent) function:

```
=TopAvg(Data,5)
```

This example shows a case in which a custom function can make things much easier for you. The following custom VBA function, named *TopAvg*, returns the average of the *N* largest values in a range:

```
Function TopAvg(InRange, N)
'    Returns the average of the highest N values in InRange
    Sum = 0
    For i = 1 To N
        Sum = Sum + Application.LARGE(InRange, i)
    Next i
    TopAvg = Sum / N
End Function
```

This function takes two arguments: InRange (which is a worksheet range) and N (the number of values to average). It starts by initializing the Sum variable to 0. It then uses a For. . .Next loop to calculate the sum of the *N* largest values in the range. Note that I use Excel's LARGE function within the loop. Because the function is part of the Application object, I have to precede it with *Application*. Finally, TopAvg is assigned the value of Sum divided by N.

You can use all of Excel's worksheet functions in your VBA procedures *except* those that have equivalents in VBA. For example, VBA has a RAND function that returns a random number. Therefore, you can't use Excel's RND function in a VBA procedure.

A function with an optional argument

Many of Excel's built-in worksheet functions use optional arguments. An example is the LEFT function, which returns characters from the left side of a string; its official syntax is

```
LEFT(text,num_chars)
```

The first argument is required, but the second is optional. If you omit the optional argument, Excel assumes a value of 1. Therefore, the following formulas return the same result:

```
=LEFT(A1,1)
=LEFT(A1)
```

The custom functions you develop in VBA also can have optional arguments. You specify an optional argument by preceding the argument's name with the keyword *Optional*.

The following example shows a custom function that uses an optional argument. This function randomly chooses one cell from an input range. If the second argument is 1, the selected value changes whenever the worksheet is recalculated (the function is made *volatile*). If the second argument is 0 (or omitted), the function is not recalculated unless one of the cells in the input range is modified. I used VBA's IsMissing function to determine whether the second argument is supplied.

```
Function DrawOne(InputRange As Variant, Optional Recalc)
'    Chooses one cell at random from a range

'    Assign default value (0) if 2nd argument is missing
     If IsMissing(Recalc) Then Recalc = 0

'    Make function volatile if Recalc is 1
     If Recalc = 1 Then Application.Volatile True

'    Determine a random cell
     DrawOne = InputRange(Int((InputRange.Count) * Rnd + 1))
End Function
```

You might use this function for choosing lottery numbers, picking a winner from a list of names, and so on.

Debugging custom functions

Debugging a function can be a bit more challenging than debugging a subroutine. If you develop a function for use in worksheet formulas, you find that an error in the function procedure simply results in an error display in the formula cell (usually #VALUE!). In other words, you don't receive the normal run-time error message that helps you locate the offending statement.

Here are three methods you can use for debugging custom functions:

✔ **Place MsgBox functions at strategic locations to monitor the value of specific variables.** Fortunately, message boxes in function procedures do pop up when you execute the procedure. However, make sure

only one formula in the worksheet uses your function, or message boxes appear for each formula that's evaluated — which could get very annoying.

✔ **Test the procedure by calling it from a subroutine procedure.** Run-time errors display as normal, and you can either fix the problem (if you know it) or jump right into the debugger.

✔ **Set a breakpoint in the function and then use Excel's debugger to step through the function.** You can then access all the usual debugging tools. Refer to Chapter 13 to learn about the debugger.

A function with an indefinite number of arguments

Some of Excel's worksheet functions take an indefinite number of arguments. A familiar example is the SUM function, which has the following syntax:

```
SUM(number1,number2. . .)
```

The first argument is required, but you can have as many as 30 additional arguments. Here's an example of a SUM function with four range arguments:

```
=SUM(A1:A5,C1:C5,E1:E5,G1:G5)
```

Here's a function that can have any number of single-value arguments (it doesn't work with multicell range arguments):

```
Function Concat(string1, ParamArray string2())
'    Demonstrates indefinite number of function arguments

'    Process the first argument
    Concat = string1
```

```
'   Process additional arguments (if any)
    If UBound(string2) <> 0 Then
        For args = 1 To UBound(string2)
            Concat = Concat & " " & string2(args)
        Next args
    End If
End Function
```

This function is similar to Excel's CONCATENATE function, which combines text arguments into a single string. The difference is that this custom function inserts a space between each pair of concatenated strings.

The second argument, string2( ), is an array preceded by the ParamArray keyword. The UBound function determines how many elements the array contains. If the number of elements is not zero (that is, additional arguments exist), the For. . .Next loop processes each additional argument.

ParamArray can apply only to the *last* argument in the procedure. It is always a variant data type, and it is always an optional argument (although you don't use the Optional keyword).

Figure 21-2 shows this function in use. It also shows how the results differ from those produced by Excel's CONCATENATE function.

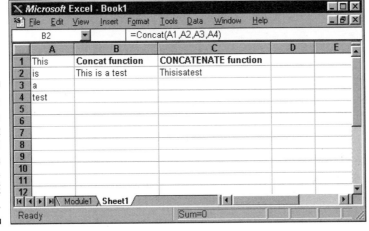

Figure 21-2: Using the Concat function and Excel's CONCATENATE function.

Function Wizardry

The Function Wizard in Excel is a handy tool that lets you choose a worksheet function; you can even choose one of your custom worksheet functions. The Function Wizard also prompts you for the function's arguments.

Function procedures defined with the Private keyword do not appear in the Function Wizard.

Displaying the function's description

The Function Wizard displays a description of each function. You can also display a description of your custom function in the Function Wizard. You add a description in the Description field in the Macro Options dialog box, shown in Figure 21-3. To display this dialog box, move the cursor anywhere within the custom function procedure, and press F2. This displays the Object Browser dialog box. Click the Options button to display the Macro Options dialog box.

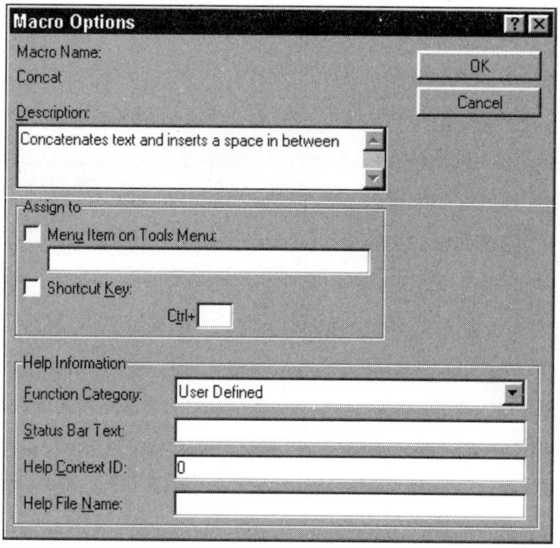

Figure 21-3: Entering a description for a custom function. This description appears in the Function Wizard dialog box.

Macro Options	? X
Macro Name: Concat	OK / Cancel
Description: Concatenates text and inserts a space in between	
Assign to	
☐ Menu Item on Tools Menu:	
☐ Shortcut Key: Ctrl+	
Help Information	
Function Category: User Defined	
Status Bar Text:	
Help Context ID: 0	
Help File Name:	

Function categories

Custom functions are listed under the User Defined category; there is no straightforward, reliable way to create a new function category for your custom functions.

Figure 21-4 shows the first Function Wizard dialog box, listing the custom functions in the User Defined category. The second Function Wizard dialog box prompts you to enter arguments for a custom function — just like using a built-in worksheet function.

Figure 21-4:
The Function Wizard also can insert custom functions.

Argument descriptions

When you access a built-in function from the Function Wizard, the second dialog box displays a description of each argument. Unfortunately, you can't provide such descriptions for custom functions.

Learning More

This chapter provides lots of information about creating custom worksheet functions. Use these examples as models when you create functions for your own work. As usual, the program's online help provides additional details.

In the next chapter, you learn how to make your custom functions more accessible by storing them in an add-in. And, you learn that add-ins are useful in other ways.

Chapter 22
Creating Excel Add-Ins

. . . .

. . . .

*O*ne of Excel's slickest features — at least in *my* opinion — is the capability to create add-ins. In this chapter, I explain why this feature is so slick, and I show you how to create your own add-ins by using only the tools built into Excel.

Okay ... So What Is an Add-In?

What's an add-in? Glad you asked. A spreadsheet add-in is something you add to enhance a spreadsheet's functionality. Some add-ins provide new worksheet functions that you can use in formulas. The new features usually blend in well with the original interface, and so they often appear to be part of the program.

Excel ships with several add-ins you can use. The more popular add-ins include the Analysis ToolPak, View Manager, Report Manager, and Solver. You can also get Excel add-ins from third-party suppliers or as shareware (my Power Utility Pak is an example of Excel add-in shareware).

Any knowledgeable user can create Excel add-ins (no special C++ programming skills are required). An Excel add-in is basically a different form of an XLS workbook file — in fact, you can convert any XLS file into an add-in. Add-ins are always hidden, however, so you can't display worksheets or chart sheets that an add-in contains. But you can access an add-in's VBA subroutines and functions, and you can display dialog boxes contained on dialog sheets.

Why Create Add-Ins?

You might decide to convert your XLS application into an add-in for any of the following reasons:

- **Prevent access to your code:** When you distribute an application as an add-in, users can't view the sheets in the workbook. If you use proprietary techniques in your VBA code, you can prevent anyone from copying the code (or at least make it more difficult to do so).

- **Avoid confusion:** If a user loads your application as an add-in, the file is not visible and is therefore less likely to confuse novice users or get in the way. Unlike a hidden XLS workbook, an add-in can't be unhidden.

- **Simplify access to worksheet functions:** Custom worksheet functions that you store in an add-in don't require the workbook name qualifier. For example, if you store a custom function named MOVAVG in a workbook named NEWFUNC.XLS, you must use syntax like the following to use this function in a different workbook:

```
=NEWFUNC.XLS!MOVAVG(A1:A50)
```

But if this function is stored in an add-in file that's open, you can use much simpler syntax because you don't need to include the file reference:

```
=MOVAVG(A1:A50)
```

- **Provide easier access for users:** Once you identify the location of your add-in, it appears in the Add-Ins dialog box, with a friendly name and a description of what it does.

- **Gain better control over loading:** Add-ins can be opened automatically when Excel starts, regardless of the directory in which they are stored.

- **Avoid displaying prompts when unloading:** When an add-in is closed, the user never sees the prompt *Save change in . . . ?*

Working with Add-Ins

The most efficient way to work with add-ins is by using Excel's add-in manager, which you access by choosing Tools⇨Add-Ins. This command displays the dialog box shown in Figure 22-1. The list box contains the names of all available add-ins. In this list, check marks identify any currently open add-ins. You can open and close add-ins from this dialog box by checking or unchecking the appropriate check boxes.

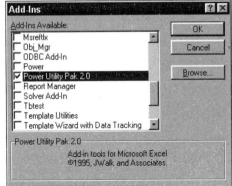

Figure 22-1:
The Add-Ins
dialog box.

You can also open most add-in files by choosing the File⊃Open command. However, you can't close an open add-in by choosing File⊃Close. You can only remove the add-in by exiting and restarting Excel or by writing a macro to close the add-in.

When you open an add-in, you may or may not notice anything different. In almost every case, however, the menu changes in some way — Excel displays either a new menu or one or more new menu items on an existing menu. For example, when you open the Analysis ToolPak add-in, this add-in gives you a new menu item on the Tools menu: Data Analysis. When you open my Power Utility Pak add-in, you get a new Utilities menu, which is located between the Data menu and the Window menu.

Creating an Add-In

Although you can convert any workbook to an add-in, not all workbooks benefit from this change. Workbooks that consist only of worksheets become unusable because the add-ins are hidden.

In fact, the only types of workbooks that benefit from being converted to an add-in are those with macros. For example, a workbook that consists of general-purpose macros (subroutines and functions) makes an ideal add-in.

Creating an add-in is simple. The following steps describe how to create an add-in from a normal workbook file:

1. **Develop your application and make sure everything works properly.**

   Don't forget to include a method for executing the macro or macros. You may want to add a new menu item to the Tools menu.

2. Test the application by executing it when a *different* workbook is active.

This simulates the application's behavior when it's used as an add-in, because an add-in is never the active workbook. You might find that some references no longer work. For example, the following statement works fine when the code resides in the active workbook, but it fails when a different workbook is active:

```
Dialogsheets("MyDialog").Show
```

You could qualify the reference with the name of the workbook object, like this:

```
Workbooks("MYBOOK.XLS").Dialogsheets("MyDialog").Show
```

I don't recommend this method because the name of the workbook changes when you convert it to an add-in. The solution is to use the ThisWorkbook qualifier, as follows:

```
ThisWorkbook.Dialogsheets("MyDialog").Show
```

3. Choose File⇨Summary Info and enter a brief descriptive title in the Title field and a longer description in the Comments field.

This step is not required, but it makes the add-in easier to use.

4. Activate any VBA module or any dialog sheet in the workbook and choose Tools⇨Make Add-In.

Excel responds with its Make Add-In dialog box, which suggests the current workbook name, with an XLA extension. Click OK and Excel creates the add-in.

Remember that once you create an add-in, you can't modify it. You can think of the original XLS version of the file as the source file and the XLA version as the compiled file. If you need to modify your add-in, make your changes in the XLS version and then create a new add-in from that file.

An Add-In Example

In this section, I discuss the basic steps involved in creating a useful add-in. The example uses the ChangeCase text conversion utility that I describe in Chapter 16.

Setting up the workbook

The workbook consists of two sheets: a dialog sheet (named Dialog1) and a VBA module (named Module1).

The dialog sheet

Figure 22-2 shows Dialog1. It consists of three option buttons, named Upper, Lower, and Proper.

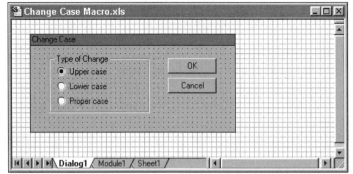

Figure 22-2:
The dialog sheet used in this example.

The VBA module

This version of ChangeCase differs slightly from the version in Chapter 16. For this example, I use the SpecialCells Method to create an object variable that consists of only those cells in the selection that contain constants (that is, not formulas) or text. This makes the routine run much faster. See Chapter 14 for more information on this technique.

Here's the code for the macro:

```
Sub ChangeCase()
'    Create object variable
     Set Dialog = ThisWorkbook.DialogSheets("Dialog1")

'    Exit if a range is not selected
     If TypeName(Selection) <> "Range" Then Exit Sub

'    Show the dialog box
     DBoxOK = Dialog.Show

'    Exit if dialog is canceled
     If Not DBoxOK Then Exit Sub

'    Create an object with just text constants
```

(continued)

```
(continued)
    On Error Resume Next
    Set TextCells = Selection.SpecialCells(xlConstants, _
        xlTextValues)

'   Uppercase
    If Dialog.OptionButtons("Upper").Value = xlOn Then
        For Each cell In TextCells
            cell.Value = UCase(cell.Value)
        Next cell
    End If

'   Lowercase
    If Dialog.OptionButtons("Lower").Value = xlOn Then
        For Each cell In TextCells
            cell.Value = LCase(cell.Value)
        Next cell
    End If

'   Proper case
    If Dialog.OptionButtons("Proper").Value = xlOn Then
        For Each cell In TextCells
            cell.Value = Application.Proper(cell.Value)
        Next cell
    End If
End Sub
```

To refresh your memory, here's a quick rundown on how ChangeCase works. The macro first creates an object variable for the dialog box. Then it checks to make sure a range is selected. It displays the dialog box and exits if the user clicks Cancel or presses Esc. Next, the procedure creates an object variable named TextCells. This object consists of all the nonformula cells in the selection that contain text. I use the On Error statement to avoid the error message that appears if no cells in the selection qualify. Finally, I use three If . . . Then constructs to perform the appropriate conversions. A For . . . Next loop converts each cell in TextCells.

Adding a menu item to the Tools menu

Next, you need to make this macro accessible. You can do this by creating a new menu item on the Tools menu. Activate the module and choose the Tools⇨Macro command. Select the ChangeCase macro from the list that's displayed and click the Options button. Complete the Macro Options dialog box as shown in Figure 22-3.

Figure 22-3:
Use the
Macro
Options
dialog box
to make this
macro
accessible
from the
Tools menu.

Testing the workbook

Before converting this workbook to an add-in, you need to test it. To simulate what happens when the workbook is an add-in, you should test the workbook when a different workbook is active. Remember, an add-in is never the active sheet.

Open a new workbook and enter information into some cells. For testing purposes, enter various types of information, including text, values, and formulas. Or just open an existing workbook and use it for your tests. Select one or more cells and execute the ChangeCase macro by choosing the new command you added to the Tools menu. I think you'll find that it works just fine.

Adding descriptive information

I recommend entering a description of your add-in, but this step is not required. Choose the File➪Properties command, which opens the Properties dialog box. Then click the Summary tab, as shown in Figure 22-4.

Enter a title for the add-in in the Title field. This text appears in the Add-Ins dialog box. In the Comments field, enter a description. This information appears at the bottom of the Add-Ins dialog box when the add-in is selected.

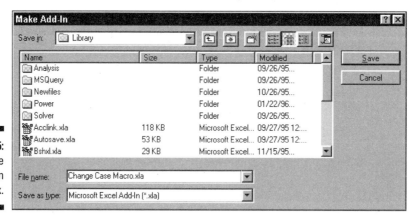

Figure 22-4:
Use the
Properties
dialog box to
enter
descriptive
information
about your
add-in.

Creating the add-in

Before creating the add-in, save the workbook. To create the add-in, activate the VBA module and choose Tools⇨Make Add-In. Excel displays the Make Add-In dialog box shown in Figure 22-5. Use this dialog box to select a location and enter a name for the add-in file. You usually want to keep the add-in's name the same as the XLS version's name.

Figure 22-5:
The Make
Add-In
dialog box.

Click the Save button to create the add-in. Congratulations! You've created your first add-in.

Opening the add-in

To avoid confusion, close the XLS workbook before opening the add-in created from that workbook. If you don't close the XLS workbook, the Tools menu will have two Change Case menu items (one for the XLS version, and one for XLA version).

Choose the Tools⇨Add-Ins command. Excel displays the Add-Ins dialog box. Click the Browse button, and locate the add-in you just created. After you find your new add-in, the Add-Ins dialog box displays the add-in in its list. As shown in Figure 22-6, the Add-Ins dialog box also displays the descriptive information you provided in the Properties dialog box. Click OK to close the dialog box and open the add-in.

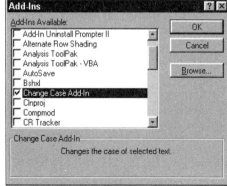

Figure 22-6: The Add-Ins dialog box with the new add-in selected.

After you open the add-in, the Tools menu displays the new menu item that executes the ChangeCase macro in the add-in.

Distributing the add-in

You can distribute this add-in to other Excel users by simply giving them a copy of the XLA file (they don't need the XLS version). When they open the add-in, the new Change Case command appears on the Tools menu. Your macro code is hidden.

Although XLA files appear to be secure, they really aren't. In fact, it's possible to convert an XLA file back to the original XLS file. What's the bottom line? If you use proprietary techniques, don't consider an add-in to be encrypted.

Modifying the add-in

If you want to modify the add-in, you must do so in the XLS version of the file. Then use the Tools⇨Make Add-In command to recreate the add-in. Use the same name to replace the old copy with the updated version.

Manipulating Add-Ins with VBA

It should come as no surprise that you can manipulate add-ins by using VBA code. This section provides an introduction to the topic, and (as usual) you can find additional details in the Excel online help.

The AddIns collection

The AddIns collection consists of all add-ins that Excel knows about, regardless of whether these add-ins are installed. The Tools⇨Add-Ins command displays the Add-Ins dialog box, which lists all add-ins in the AddIns collection. Check marks identify the currently installed add-ins in this list.

An AddIn object is a single add-in in the AddIns collection. For example, to display the filename of the first add-in in the AddIns collection, use the following:

```
Msgbox AddIns(1).Name
```

You can use the Add method to add an add-in to the AddIns collection, but — oddly — there is no direct way to remove an add-in from the AddIns collection (the AddIns collection doesn't have a Delete method). To remove an add-in from the AddIns collection, delete or move the add-in file. As shown in Figure 22-7, Excel displays a warning the next time you try to install or uninstall the add-in — and gives you an opportunity to remove the add-in from the AddIns collection.

Determining whether a file is an add-in

You can access a Workbook object's FileFormat property to determine whether a particular workbook is an add-in. This might seem useless, but there are some good uses for this property. For example, if you're working on an application that you plan to convert to an add-in, you may not want the Auto_Open procedure to run while you test the application. In other words, you only want

Figure 22-7:
Removing
an add-in
from the
AddIns
collection.

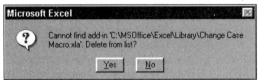

Auto_Open to execute in the XLA version of the file. You *could* press the Shift
key when you open the file (this prevents Auto_Open from executing), but a
better approach is to use the following code, which simply exits the subroutine
if the FileFormat property is not equal to the xlAddIn constant:

```
Sub Auto_Open()
    If ThisWorkbook.FileFormat <> xlAddIn Then Exit Sub
'   [... code goes here ...]
End Sub
```

Uninstalling all add-ins

The following example loops through all add-ins in the AddIns collection and
uninstalls any installed add-ins. This procedure does not affect add-ins that
were opened with the File⇨Open command.

```
Sub UninstallAll()
    Count = 0
    For Each Item In AddIns
        If Item.Installed Then
            Item.Installed = False
            Count = Count + 1
        End If
    Next Item
    MsgBox Count & " Add-Ins Uninstalled."
End Sub
```

Learning More

In this chapter, I discuss the concept of add-ins — files that add new capabilities to Excel. You now know how to work with add-ins and why you may want to create your own add-ins. One example in this chapter shows you the steps for creating an add-in that changes the case of text in selected cells. Other examples show how you can use VBA to work with add-ins. The best way to learn more about add-ins is by creating a few.

Chapter 23

Creating Excel Applications for Other Users

In This Chapter

▶ Features of a good spreadsheet application

▶ Differences between developing spreadsheets for you and developing spreadsheets for others

▶ Guidelines for developing applications that others will use

*E*xcel programmers develop two basic types of spreadsheets: (1) spreadsheets that only they use, and (2) spreadsheets that other people use. This distinction often determines how much effort you need to put into creating a spreadsheet. Developing spreadsheets for your use is much easier than developing spreadsheets that others will use. In this chapter, I provide general guidelines for developing spreadsheets that others use. But even if you're the only person who uses your spreadsheet creations, you might discover some helpful hints.

What Is a Spreadsheet Application?

Excel programming is essentially the process of building applications that use a spreadsheet rather than a traditional programming language such as C, Pascal, or BASIC. In many cases, people other than the application developer use these applications.

The definition

Without further ado, here's my working definition of a *spreadsheet application*:

A spreadsheet file (or a group of related files) designed so that someone other than the developer can perform useful work without extensive training.

Based on this definition, most of the spreadsheet files you develop probably don't qualify as spreadsheet applications. You may have hundreds of spreadsheet files on your hard disk, but you probably didn't design many of them so others can use them.

Throughout this chapter, I use the terms *developer* and *end users.* The developer is the person who creates and maintains the application (that's you!), and the end users are the folks who benefit from your efforts (this group also could include you).

What makes a good application?

Like good witches and bad witches, you find good and bad spreadsheet applications. How can you tell them apart? This list describes the qualities of a good spreadsheet application:

- ✔ Allows end users to perform a task they couldn't otherwise perform
- ✔ Provides an appropriate solution to a problem
- ✔ Produces accurate, bug-free results
- ✔ Traps errors and helps the user correct them
- ✔ Prevents the user from accidentally (or intentionally) deleting or modifying important application components
- ✔ Offers a clear, consistent user interface so the user always knows how to proceed
- ✔ Offers well-documented formulas, macros, and user interface elements
- ✔ Enables developers to make simple modifications without making major structural changes
- ✔ Offers an easily accessible help system that provides useful information on the most common procedures
- ✔ Offers a *portable* design that runs on any system that has the proper software (in this case, Excel for Windows 95 or Excel 5)

You can create spreadsheet applications at many different levels, ranging from simple fill-in-the-blank templates to extremely complex applications that use custom menus and dialog boxes — your application may not even look like a spreadsheet.

Application Development, Step by Step

No simple recipe exists for developing a spreadsheet application — besides, this isn't a cookbook. The fact is, everyone develops his or her own style for creating a spreadsheet application.

Here's a list of activities that a spreadsheet developer typically performs. You won't necessarily perform all of these steps for every application, and the order in which you perform the steps may vary from project to project:

- Determine the needs of the user.
- Plan an application that meets user needs.
- Determine the most appropriate user interface.
- Create the spreadsheet, the formulas, the macros, and the user interface.
- Test and debug the application.
- Make the application *bulletproof*.
- Make the application aesthetically appealing and intuitive.
- Document the development effort.
- Develop user documentation and online help.
- Distribute the application to the user.
- Update the application when necessary.

Determining user needs

The first step in developing an application usually involves identifying exactly what the end user requires. Skipping this step (or guessing what the user *might* need) often results in additional work later in the development process.

Here are a few tips for making this phase easier:

- ✔ Don't assume that you know what the users need. Making assumptions at this early stage almost always causes problems later in the development process.

- ✔ Talk directly to the end users of the application, not just with their supervisor or manager.

- ✔ Learn what, if anything, the users currently do to solve the problem. You might be able to save some work by adapting an existing application.

- ✔ Identify the resources available at the users' site. For example, try to determine whether you must work around any hardware or software limitations.

- ✔ Find out which systems will be used for running your application. You need to consider whether your application must run on slower systems.

- ✔ Understand the skill levels of the end users. This information helps you design the application appropriately.

- ✔ Determine how long the application will be used. This factor often influences the amount of effort you put into the project.

One final note: Don't be surprised if the project specifications change before you complete the application. This often happens, and you're better off *expecting* changes rather than being surprised by them.

Planning an application that meets user needs

After you determine the end users' needs, you may be tempted to jump right in and start fiddling around in Excel. Take it from someone who suffers from this problem: Try to restrain yourself. Builders don't construct a house without a set of blueprints, and you shouldn't develop a spreadsheet application without a plan.

Take some time to consider the various ways you can approach the problem. A thorough knowledge of Excel pays off here by helping you avoid blind alleys before you get to them.

More specifically, you need to consider some general options at this stage, including the following:

- ✔ **File structure:** Should you use one workbook with multiple sheets, several single-sheet workbooks, or a template file?

- ✔ **Data structure:** Should the application use external database files or store everything in worksheets?

- ✔ **Formulas or VBA:** Should you use formulas to perform calculations or write VBA procedures? Both have advantages and disadvantages.

- ✔ **Add-in or XLS file:** In most cases, you probably want your final product to be an XLA add-in, but an XLS file is sometimes preferable.

- ✔ **Version of Excel:** Does your Excel for Windows 95 application need to work with Excel 5? What about Excel 4? Excel for the Macintosh?

- ✔ **Error handling:** You need to determine how your application will detect and deal with error conditions.

- ✔ **Use of special features:** Don't reinvent the wheel. For example, if your application needs to summarize lots of data, consider using Excel's built-in pivot table feature.

- ✔ **Performance issues:** The approach you take ultimately determines the overall performance of your application. Start thinking about the speed and efficiency of your application now — don't wait until the application is complete and users are complaining about it.

- ✔ **Level of security:** Excel provides several protection options for restricting access to particular elements of a workbook. You can make your job easier by determining up front exactly what you need to protect — and what level of protection you want.

You have to deal with many other project-dependent considerations in this phase. The important point is that you should consider all options and avoid settling on the first solution that comes to mind.

I've learned from experience that you can't let the end user completely guide your approach to solving the problem. For example, suppose you meet with a manager who tells you the department needs an application that writes text files, which will be imported into another application. Don't confuse the user's perceived need with the solution. In this example, the real need is to share data — using an intermediate text file is just one possible solution. In other words, don't let the users define their problem by stating it in terms of a solution approach. Finding the right approach is *your* job.

Determining the most appropriate user interface

When you develop spreadsheets that others will use, you need to pay special attention to the user interface. By *user interface,* I mean the method by which the user interacts with the application — clicking buttons, using menus, pressing keys, accessing toolbars, and so on.

Excel provides several features that relate to user interface design:

- Dialog box controls placed directly on a worksheet
- Custom dialog boxes
- Custom menus
- Custom toolbars
- Custom shortcut keys

Consider all your options, as well as the skill level and motivation of the end users. Then decide on the interface elements that make the most sense.

Developing the application

Okay, you've identified user needs, determined the approach you'll take, and decided on the user interface. Now, you can get down to the nitty-gritty and start creating the application — the step that comprises most of the time you spend on a project.

The approach you take for developing the application depends on your personal style and the nature of the application. Except for simple template-type applications, your application will probably use VBA macros.

I can't be more specific here, because each application is different. In general, try to keep your VBA procedures short and modular.

Testing the application

Every computer user encounters software bugs. In most cases, such problems result from insufficient testing that fails to catch all the bugs.

After you create your application, you need to test it. This is a crucial step, and you might spend as much time testing and debugging an application as you do creating the application in the first place. Actually, you should test extensively during the development phase. After all, while you write a VBA routine or create formulas in a worksheet, you want to make sure that the application works as it should.

Although you can't test for all possibilities, your macros should handle common types of errors. For example, what if the user enters a text string instead of a value? What if the user cancels a dialog box without making any selections? What happens if the user presses Ctrl+F6 and jumps to the next window?

As you gain experience, issues like these become second nature, and you account for them with little effort.

Making an application bulletproof

A user can easily destroy a worksheet. Erasing one critical formula or value often causes errors throughout the entire worksheet — and perhaps in other dependent worksheets. Even worse, if the user saves the damaged workbook, the corrupt version replaces the good copy on disk. Unless the user of your application has a backup procedure in place, the user could be in trouble — and *you'll* probably be blamed!

If other users — especially novices — will be using your worksheets, you need to add some protection. Excel provides several techniques for protecting worksheets and parts of worksheets:

- ✔ Locking specific cells (using the Protection tab in the Format Cells dialog box) so they can't be changed. This takes effect only when you protect the document with the Tools⇨Protection⇨Protect Sheet command.

- ✔ Protecting an entire workbook — the structure of the workbook, the window position and size, or both — by using the Tools⇨Protection⇨Protect Workbook command.

- ✔ Hiding the formulas in specific cells (using the Protection tab in the Format Cells dialog box) so other users can't see them. Again, this takes effect only when you protect the document with the Tools⇨Protection⇨Protect Sheet command.

- ✔ Locking objects on the worksheet (using the Protection tab in the Format Object dialog box). This takes effect only when you protect the document with the Tools⇨Protection⇨Protect Sheet command.

- ✔ Hiding rows (Format⇨Row⇨Hide), columns (Format⇨Column⇨Hide), sheets (Format⇨Sheet⇨Hide), and documents (Window⇨Hide). This helps prevent the worksheet from looking cluttered and provides some protection against prying eyes.

✔ Designating Excel workbooks as read-only to ensure that they cannot be overwritten with any changes. You access this option by choosing the Options button in the Save As dialog box.

✔ Assigning a password to prevent unauthorized users from opening your file (using the Options button in the Save As dialog box).

✔ Using an add-in, which doesn't allow the user to change *anything* on the worksheets.

The appropriate level of protection, and how you implement it, depends on the application and who will be using it.

Making it look good

You've undoubtedly seen examples of poorly designed user interfaces, difficult-to-use programs, and just plain ugly screens. If you develop spreadsheets for other people, you should pay particular attention to how the application looks.

The way a computer program looks can make all the difference in the world to users. And so it goes with the applications you develop with Excel. End users appreciate a good-looking user interface, and you can give your applications a much more polished and professional look if you devote some additional time to design and aesthetic considerations.

Evaluating aesthetic qualities is very subjective. When in doubt, keep your worksheets simple and generic looking. Here are a few tips:

✔ **Strive for consistency.** This includes fonts, text sizes, and formatting. When designing dialog boxes, for example, try to emulate the look and feel of the Excel dialog boxes as much as possible.

✔ **Avoid the gaudy.** Just because Excel lets you work with 56 colors, you don't have to use them all. In general, use only a few colors and no more than two fonts.

✔ **Keep it simple.** Developers often make the mistake of trying to cram too much information into a single screen or dialog box. A good rule of thumb is to present only one or two chunks of information at a time.

✔ **Consider the hardware.** If your application will be used on laptops, make sure you use color combinations that also look good (and are legible) in monochrome.

✔ **Think modular.** Make it easy for the user to figure out what's what. For example, you can separate different parts of a worksheet by using background colors or borders.

Documenting your efforts

Assembling a spreadsheet application is one thing — making it understandable to other people is another. It's important that you thoroughly document your work. This helps *you* if you need to modify the application (and you will), and it helps anyone else who needs to work on the application (after you get that big promotion).

How do you document a workbook application? You can either store the information in a worksheet or use another file. You can even use a paper document if you prefer. Perhaps the easiest way is to create a separate worksheet in which you store comments and key information about the project.

Use comments liberally throughout your VBA code. An elegant piece of VBA code may seem perfectly understandable to you today — but come back to it in a few months, and you may be scratching your head.

Developing user documentation and online help

In addition to your programming documentation, you need to develop user documentation. You have two basic choices: paper-based documentation or electronic (online) documentation.

Online help is standard fare in Windows applications. Fortunately, your Excel applications can provide online help — even context-sensitive help. You can develop help files and display them by using the Windows standard WINHELP.EXE program. Although developing online help requires quite a bit of additional effort, this may be worthwhile for a large project. To simplify the process, I suggest that you acquire any of several software products designed for creating Windows help files.

Distributing the application to the user

You've completed your project, and you're ready to release it to the end users. How do you do this?

It depends. You could simply hand over a disk, scribble a few instructions, and be on your way. Or, you might install the application yourself. Another option is to develop an official setup program that automatically installs your application. You can write such a program in a traditional programming language, purchase a generic setup program, or write your own in VBA.

If you use the registered version of the Power Utility Pak (see the coupon in the back of this book), you'll see an example of an installation routine written entirely in VBA.

You also need to consider the issue of providing support for your application. In other words, who gets the phone call if the user encounters a problem? If you aren't prepared to handle routine questions, you need to identify someone who is. In some cases, you might specify that the developer handles only highly technical problems or bug-related issues.

Updating the application when necessary

After you distribute your application, you're finished with it, right? You can sit back, enjoy yourself, and try to forget about the problems you encountered (and solved) during the development of your application. In rare cases, yes, you may be finished. More often, however, the users of your application will not be completely satisfied.

Sure, your application adheres to all of the *original* specifications, but things change. After seeing an application work, users often think of other things the application could be doing. That's right, I'm talking about *updates*.

When you need to update or revise your application, you'll appreciate the fact that you designed it well in the first place and you fully documented your efforts. If not, well . . . you learn from your experiences.

Learning More

So concludes Part VI. You now have some general guidelines to help you develop effective Excel applications that will be used by others.

Part VII covers some of the more advanced features of Excel programming.

Part VII
Advanced Stuff

The 5th Wave   By Rich Tennant

"ALL RIGHT, NOW, WE NEED SOMEONE TO PLAY THE PART OF THE GEEK."

In this part . . .

The three chapters in Part VII deal with topics you may or may not find useful. But remember, things that seem completely irrelevant today may become very important next week. These chapters cover working with the Windows API (Application Programming Interface), automating tasks that use lists, and a grab-bag of other topics.

Chapter 24

Using the Windows API

. . . .

In This Chapter

▶ An overview of the API functions available courtesy of Microsoft Windows

▶ Why you may need to access the Windows API functions

▶ Several useful examples that show how to use the Windows API functions

. . . .

*A*lthough VBA is powerful, it can't do everything. In this chapter, I explain how you can unleash even more raw power by accessing the *Application Programming Interface* (API), one of the tools built into Windows. (Make sure you wear your safety goggles.)

What Is This API Business?

Many novice Excel programmers are amazed to discover that VBA can use code from other files that have nothing to do with Excel or VBA (at least *I* was amazed when I discovered this fact). For example, your VBA code can access the DLL (Dynamic Link Library) files that Windows and other programs use. As a result, your VBA program can do things that would otherwise be beyond the language's scope.

The Windows API is a set of functions available to Windows programmers. When you call a Windows function from VBA, you're accessing the Windows API. Hundreds of such functions are available.

Fortunately, Microsoft was kind enough to give VBA the capability to use many of the Windows API functions.

Accessing the Windows API

Before you can use a Windows API function in your VBA code, you must declare the function at the beginning of the VBA module. By declaring the function, you let VBA know that it needs to work with the information in another file. The procedure for declaring an API function is a bit tricky. You must declare the API function precisely, or it won't work — it may even cause Excel to crash.

Because the system often crashes when you work with the Windows API, you should save your work frequently — *very* frequently.

Declaring an API function

When you declare an API function, you give VBA three pieces of information:

- ✔ The name of the API procedure you want to use
- ✔ The name of the library in which the procedure is located
- ✔ The procedure's arguments, if any

After you declare a procedure in your module, you can use it in your code.

An example

By now, you're probably completely confused. An example will help clear up matters.

Remember, you use an API call to perform an action that is otherwise impossible using only VBA code. Assume that your application needs to find out the path of the Windows directory. You could search all day, but you won't find a function in Excel or VBA to do the trick. However, knowing how to access the Windows API saves the day.

The following is an example of a Windows API function declaration:

```
Declare Function GetWindowsDirectoryA Lib "KERNEL32" _
    (ByVal lpBuffer As String, ByVal nsize As Integer) _
    As Integer
```

The GetWindowsDirectoryA function returns the name of the Windows directory. This function takes two arguments: *lpBuffer,* a string; and *nSize,* an integer. After you call this function, lpbuffer contains the name of the Windows directory (stored as a string), and nsize contains an integer representing the length of that string.

After inserting this Declare statement at the top of your module, you can access the function by calling the GetWindowsDirectoryA function. The following example shows how you call the function and display the result in a message box:

```
Sub ShowWindowsDir()
    Dim WinPath As String
    Dim WinDir As String
    WinPath = String(145, Chr(0))
    WinDir = Left(WinPath, GetWindowsDirectoryA _
        (WinPath, Len(WinPath)))
    MsgBox WinDir
End Sub
```

It's important to remember that you don't have to understand everything that's going on in order to use an API function in your code. In most cases, you copy the declaration and the code from another source (at least that's what *I* do).

Creating a wrapper function

You can create a VBA function that serves as a *wrapper* for an API function. In other words, you create your own VBA function that calls the API function. This action is particularly useful if you use the API function several times in your code. You can simply call your wrapper VBA function, which is easier than dealing with the API function at multiple places in your code.

Here's an example of a wrapper VBA function:

```
Function WINDOWSDIR() As String
'    Returns the Windows directory
    Dim WinPath As String
    WinPath = String(145, Chr(0))
    WINDOWSDIR = Left(WinPath, GetWindowsDirectoryA _
        (WinPath, Len(WinPath)))
End Function
```

After declaring this function, you can call it from another procedure, like this:

```
Msgbox WINDOWSDIR()
```

And, as shown in the following example, you can even use the function in a worksheet formula:

```
=WINDOWSDIR()
```

Compatibility Concerns

If you use Windows API functions in your code, you need to be aware of a potentially serious compatibility issue. For example, if you develop an Excel for Windows 95 application that uses API calls, you can't run the application with Excel 5. That's because Excel for Windows 95 is a 32-bit application (and uses 32-bit API calls) and Excel 5 is a 16-bit application (and uses 16-bit API calls). The two versions are not compatible.

But don't despair, you can write code that works with both Excel 5 and Excel for Windows 95. The trick is to declare both the 16-bit and the 32-bit versions of the function. Then write code that determines which version of Excel is being used and calls the appropriate API function.

Start by declaring the 16-bit and the 32-bit API functions:

```
'    32-bit API declaration
    Declare Function GetWindowsDirectoryA Lib "KERNEL32" _
      (ByVal lpBuffer As String, ByVal nsize As Integer) _
      As Integer

'    16-bit API declaration
    Declare Function GetWindowsDirectory Lib "KERNEL" _
      (ByVal lpBuffer As String, ByVal nsize As Integer) _
      As Integer
```

Here's the wrapper function:

```
Function WindowsDir()
'    Returns the Windows directory
    Dim WinDir As String * 255

'    Determine whether Excel is 16-bit or 32-bit
    Select Case Left(Application.Version, 1)
        Case "5" '16-bit
            WLen = GetWindowsDirectory(WinDir, Len(WinDir))
        Case Else '32-bit
            WLen = GetWindowsDirectoryA(WinDir, Len(WinDir))
    End Select
    WindowsDir = Left(WinDir, WLen)
End Function
```

I determine which version of Excel is running by examining the first character returned by the Application.Version property. If the property returns *5,* 16-bit Excel 5 is running. Otherwise, a 32-bit version of Excel is running. Based on this result, the wrapper function calls the appropriate API function.

The following subroutine calls the WindowsDir function and displays the result, as shown in Figure 24-1:

```
Sub ShowWinDir()
    MsgBox WindowsDir()
End Sub
```

Figure 24-1:
The
WindowsDir
function
display.

To use this technique, you must know how to declare both the 16-bit and the 32-bit versions of a particular API function.

A Few More Examples Using Windows API

This section presents three more examples that use Windows API calls. These examples work only with Excel for Windows 95. In other words, I don't use the dual-declaration technique I describe in the preceding section. Also, I don't go into a lot of detail about how these examples work. My purpose in this section is to introduce you to the *types* of things you can do by using API calls. If you find these examples helpful, you can use them verbatim in your own projects.

Detecting the Shift key

Assume you've written a VBA macro that is executed from a toolbar button. In addition, assume that you want the macro to perform differently if the user presses the Shift key when clicking the button (several of Excel's built-in toolbar buttons operate like this). After digging around a bit, you discover that VBA code can't detect whether the user is pressing the Shift key.

However, you can detect this by using the GetKeyState API function. This function tells you whether a particular key is pressed. It takes a single argument, nVirtKey, which represents the code for that key.

The following code demonstrates how to detect whether the Shift key is pressed when the Button_Click subroutine is executed (Button_Click is the macro that executes when you click the toolbar button):

```
Declare Function GetKeyState Lib "user32" _
   (ByVal nVirtKey As Long) As Integer

   Const VK_SHIFT As Integer = &h10

Sub Button_Click()
   Dim Shifted As Boolean
   If GetKeyState(VK_SHIFT) < 0 Then Shifted = True _
      Else Shifted = False

   Select Case Shifted
      Case True

'        Statements to execute if Shift key
'        is pressed

         Case False

'        Statements to execute if Shift key
'        is not pressed

      End Select
End Sub
```

Notice that I define a constant for the Shift key and then use this constant as the argument for the GetKeyState function. If GetKeyState returns a value less than zero, the Shift key is pressed. If GetKeyState returns a value greater than zero, the Shift key is not pressed. Then I use a Select Case structure to take action based on the value returned by GetKeyState.

Determining the current video mode

This example uses the GetSystemMetrics Windows API function to determine a system's current video mode. If your application needs to display a certain amount of information on one screen, knowing the display size can help you scale the text accordingly.

```
'32-bit API declaration
Declare Function GetSystemMetrics Lib "user32" _
  (ByVal nIndex As Long) As Long

Public Const SM_CXSCREEN = 0
Public Const SM_CYSCREEN = 1

Sub DisplayVideoInfo()
    vidWidth = GetSystemMetrics(SM_CXSCREEN)
    vidHeight = GetSystemMetrics(SM_CYSCREEN)

    Msg = "The current video driver is: "
    Msg = Msg & vidWidth & " X " & vidHeight
    MsgBox Msg
End Sub
```

Figure 24-2 shows the message box returned by this routine on a system running in 1024-×-768 resolution.

Figure 24-2:
The video
display
mode
message
box.

Removing the Excel control menu

Most windows have a control menu at the extreme left of their title bar. In Windows 95, this menu takes the form of the application's icon. Clicking the control menu displays a menu with commands that let you manipulate the window's size and close the application.

You can remove the Excel control menu to make it less likely that the user will manipulate Excel's window. You can do this by using the Windows API. This example requires three functions:

```
Private Declare Function FindWindow Lib "user32" _
  Alias "FindWindowA" (ByVal lpClassName As Any, _
  ByVal lpWindowName As String) As Long
```

(continued)

(continued)

```
Private Declare Function GetWindowLong Lib "user32" _
    Alias "GetWindowLongA" (ByVal hWnd As Long, _
    ByVal nIndex As Long) As Long

Private Declare Function SetWindowLong Lib "user32" _
    Alias "SetWindowLongA" (ByVal hWnd As Long, _
    ByVal nIndex As Long, ByVal dwNewLong As Long) As Long
```

The following subroutine disables the control menu in the Excel window:

```
Sub RemoveControlMenu()
    Const WS_SYSMENU = &h80000
    Const GWL_STYLE = -16

    Dim WinStyle As Long, hWnd As Long
'   Get the window's handle
    hWnd = FindWindow(O&, ByVal Application.Caption)
'   Get current style
    WinStyle = GetWindowLong(hWnd, GWL_STYLE)
'   Change style
    WinStyle = WinStyle And (Not WS_SYSMENU)
    x = SetWindowLong(hWnd, GWL_STYLE, WinStyle)
'   Change Excel's caption as a reminder
    If Not Application.Caption Like "*>>*" Then
        Application.Caption = Empty & _
        " <<Microsoft Excel has no Control Menu>>"
    End If
End Sub
```

After removing the menu, the subroutine displays a message in the title bar.

After you execute this routine, clicking the control menu has no effect. The routine also disables the buttons on the right side of the title bar. The net effect is that the user can no longer use these controls to change the size of Excel's window.

When you remove the control menu, you can still change the state of the Excel window by double-clicking the title bar. Also, VBA commands still work. For example, you can maximize Excel's window by using the following command:

```
Application.WindowState = XlMaximized
```

To restore the control menu to normal, execute the RestoreControlMenu
routine:

```
Sub RestoreControlMenu()
    Const WS_SYSMENU = &h80000
    Const GWL_STYLE = -16

    Dim WinStyle As Long, hWnd As Long
'   Get the window's handle
    hWnd = FindWindow(0&, ByVal Application.Caption)
'   Get current style
    WinStyle = GetWindowLong(hWnd, GWL_STYLE)
'   Change style
    WinStyle = WinStyle Or WS_SYSMENU
    x = SetWindowLong(hWnd, GWL_STYLE, WinStyle)
'   Restore Excel's caption to normal
    Application.Caption = Empty
End Sub
```

Learning More

This chapter introduces you to the concept of using Windows API functions
from within your VBA code. Many programming reference books list the
declarations for common API calls and often provide examples. Usually, you can
simply copy the declarations and use the functions without really understanding the details.

In the next chapter, I discuss some methods that help you automate tasks that
use worksheet lists.

Chapter 25

Automating Tasks That Use Lists

∙∙

In This Chapter

▶ A brief overview of worksheet lists

▶ VBA techniques for automating work you do with lists

▶ A realistic example of developing a macro to automate a daily update task

∙∙

*E*xcel helps you work with data stored in lists (also known as tables or worksheet databases) by providing such features as sorting, autofiltering, and pivot tables. In this chapter, I discuss several topics related to working with worksheet lists, with an emphasis (of course) on automating these tasks by using VBA.

About Excel Lists

A list in a worksheet has the following features:

✔ The list is structured as a rectangular range of cells.

✔ The top row is usually a *header row,* with text that describes the contents of each column.

✔ Each row (or *record*) is made up of columns (or *fields*).

You probably have lots of experience working with lists. For example, you know that Excel can automatically detect a list. This means you don't have to select the list before you perform operations such as sorting or autofiltering.

A few words about getting data

Spreadsheet users continually face the problem of getting data into their spreadsheets. You can solve this problem in several ways:

✔ **Enter the data manually.** This method works fine for a small amount of data, but entering large amounts of data gets old very fast — and is prone to errors.

✔ **Copy the data via the Clipboard.** If the data can be read into another software program, you can probably transfer it to your worksheet by using the Windows Clipboard.

✔ **Import the data.** Excel can import several types of data files, including other spreadsheet formats, dBASE files, and various types of text files.

✔ **Connect to an external database.** You can use the MS Query add-in to perform queries on database files and bring the query results right into your spreadsheet.

VBA Table Techniques

In this section, I describe some useful techniques you can use when working with tables. To help you get your bearings, I base the examples in this section on the list shown in Figure 25-1. This list is relatively small, but the same principles apply regardless of the list's size. The list consists of five fields and 16 records. Each record describes the regional sales performance of a product (the table lists data for four regions and two products).

	A	B	C	D	E
1	**Month**	**Region**	**Product**	**Quantity**	**Sales Amt**
2	January	North	Sprockets	509	30031
3	January	East	Sprockets	433	25547
4	January	South	Sprockets	379	22361
5	January	East	Widgets	322	14490
6	January	West	Sprockets	244	14396
7	January	North	Widgets	145	6525
8	January	South	Widgets	132	5940
9	January	West	Widgets	79	3555
10	February	East	Sprockets	509	30031
11	February	North	Sprockets	492	29028
12	February	West	Sprockets	332	19588
13	February	East	Widgets	433	19485
14	February	South	Sprockets	301	17759
15	February	North	Widgets	189	8505
16	February	South	Widgets	165	7425
17	February	West	Widgets	132	5940
18					
19					
20					

Figure 25-1: The examples in this section use the data in this list.

Lists, by their very nature, tend to vary in size. For example, assume that you use a list to track sales data and you update the data monthly or weekly. In such a case, the number of records in the list changes every time you update the worksheet. Writing VBA code to manipulate the list can therefore get a bit tricky.

Selecting a list

You can use several techniques if your VBA code needs to select all the data in a list. Perhaps the simplest method is to use VBA's CurrentRegion property, which returns a Range object that represents the range bounded by any combination of blank rows and blank columns. As long as you know the address of one cell that's definitely inside the list, this technique works reliably. Here's an example:

```
Sub SelectList()
    Sheets("Sales").Activate
    Range("A1").CurrentRegion.Select
End Sub
```

This routine starts by activating the sheet that contains the list. Then it selects the current region around cell A1. Because cell A1 is definitely in the list, the entire list is selected.

To select the current region manually, choose the Edit⇨Go To command, and click the Special button. In the Go To Special dialog box, select the Current Region option, and click OK.

Naming data in a list

You often need to provide a name for your list. But because the size of the list varies, you need a way to automatically update the name definition after adding (or deleting) rows. The following code assigns the name SalesTable to the list (which the routine assumes to begin in cell A1):

```
Sub UpdateListName()
    Sheets("Sales").Activate
    Range("A1").CurrentRegion.Name = "SalesTable"
End Sub
```

Notice that this subroutine doesn't select the list — that's not necessary. However, this code ensures that the proper worksheet is active.

Determining the number of rows in a list

If you write a subroutine that adds data to the end of your list, you need to be able to identify the next empty row in the list. If you know that the list begins in row 1 and no extraneous data follows the list, you can use a simple function like this:

```
Function NextEmptyRow()
    NextEmptyRow = Application.CountA(Sheets("Sales") _
        .Range("A:A")) + 1
End Function
```

This function uses Excel's COUNTA worksheet function to count the number of nonempty cells in column A and then adds one to this value.

The preceding function does not return the correct value if the list doesn't begin in row 1, or if you have additional data below the table in column A.

The following function returns the next empty row number for a list, regardless of where the list is located and where it begins. This function takes one argument: a single-cell Range object that is known to be within the list.

```
Function NextEmptyRow(OneCell As Range)
    NumRows = OneCell.CurrentRegion.Rows.Count
    NextEmptyRow = OneCell.CurrentRegion.Rows(NumRows).Row + 1
End Function
```

This function starts by assigning the total row count of the current region around the cell to a variable, NumRows. The next statement determines the row number of the last row in the list and then increments it by one.

For example, assume that your list begins in cell A12 and you need to know the next empty row. You can get that row number by passing the known cell to the NextEmptyRow function, like this:

```
MsgBox NextEmptyRow(Sheets("Sales").Range("A12"))
```

The message box displays the row number of the next blank row beneath the list that contains cell A12.

Sorting a list

The easiest way to automate the sorting of a list is to start by recording your actions while you sort. Then you may need to modify the recorded code to make it more general.

Excel records the following code when I sort the sales list in descending order by the Sales Amount field:

```
Sub Macro1()
    Selection.Sort Key1:=Range("E2"), Order1:=xlDescending, _
        Header:=xlGuess, OrderCustom:=5, MatchCase:=False, _
        Orientation:=xlTopToBottom
End Sub
```

Look up the Sort method in the online help, and you see that it's a rather complicated method. In fact, the Sort method has 10 arguments (all optional).

Notice that the Sort method is based on the Selection. This fact could be a problem, because you can't assume that the cell pointer is within the table you want to sort. Therefore, you need to make a slight modification. Here's the modified macro:

```
Sub SortTable()
    Sheets("Sales").Range("A1").Sort _
        Key1:=Sheets("Sales").Range("A1").Range("E1"), _
        Order1:=xlDescending, Header:=xlGuess, _
        OrderCustom:=5, MatchCase:=False, _
        Orientation:=xlTopToBottom
End Sub
```

Rather than use Selection, I change the macro so the Sort method works on a fully-qualified specific range — cell A1 in the Sales sheet (which is known to be within the list). I also change the Key1 argument so it refers to the fully-qualified cell. After you make this change, the list is sorted regardless of which sheet is active and regardless of the cell pointer's location.

Autofiltering a list

If you want to create a macro to perform autofiltering, my best advice (once again) is to record your actions while you perform this task. The macro recorder generates the following routine when I use autofiltering to display only the records for the Northern region:

```
Sub Macro1()
    Selection.AutoFilter
    Selection.AutoFilter Field:=2, Criteria1:="North"
End Sub
```

Notice that the AutoFilter method is recorded twice: first, when I select the Data⇨Filter⇨AutoFilter command; and second, when I actually select the filter. The first statement is not necessary.

Again, some cleanup ensures that the list is filtered regardless of the cell pointer's location. You need to modify the macro to select the Sales sheet and then perform the autofiltering using cell A1 as the base. Here's the modified macro:

```
Sub FilterNorth()
    Worksheets("Sales").Activate
    Range("A1").AutoFilter Field:=2, Criteria1:="North"
End Sub
```

Creating a pivot table

One of the most impressive Excel features is the pivot table. You should take advantage of this feature whenever possible. In most cases, you create the pivot table manually and then create a macro that updates the pivot table when necessary. For example, if you create a pivot table based on a list, you should update the pivot table when you add or delete data.

Figure 25-2 shows a pivot table I created from the Sales list. I use the Region field for a page field, which means the pivot table will display data for a single region, or for all regions combined.

The question is, how can you automate the process of refreshing the pivot table when the size of the source data list changes? The answer involves recording your actions. Add a new row to the list, turn on the macro recorder and then perform the actions necessary for updating the pivot table and specifying the new data. When I do this using the Pivot Table Wizard, the macro recorder generates the following code:

```
Sub Macro1()
    ActiveSheet.PivotTableWizard SourceType:=xlDatabase, _
      SourceData:="Sales!R1C1:R18C5", _
            TableDestination:="R3C1", _
      TableName:="PivotTable1"
End Sub
```

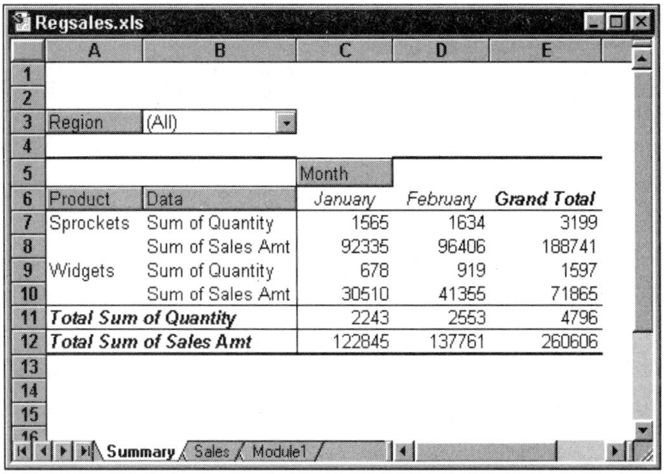

Figure 25-2:
This pivot
table uses
the data in
the Sales
table.

Again, this method results in a rather complicated single-statement procedure.
The PivotTableWizard method has nine arguments. The argument of interest
here is SourceData. You need a way to pass a new value for SourceData — one
that includes the current range, which comprises the sales table.

Here's the revised subroutine:

```
Sub UpdatePivotTable()
'    Create object variable for the table
     Set DataRange = Sheets("Sales").Range("A1").CurrentRegion

'    Activate the pivot table sheet
     Sheets("Summary").Activate

'    Update the pivot table
     ActiveSheet.PivotTableWizard SourceType:=xlDatabase, _
        SourceData:=DataRange, TableDestination:="R3C1", _
        TableName:="PivotTable1"
End Sub
```

First, the routine creates an object variable (DataRange) that consists of the
table on the Sales sheet. Notice that I use the CurrentRegion property to define
the range. Next, the routine activates the Summary sheet (the sheet that has the
pivot table). Next, I modify the previous statement to use DataRange as the
SourceData argument.

This subroutine now updates the pivot table regardless of the size of the sales
table.

Importing data

A common Excel activity — and one you might consider worthy of being automated — is importing data. Excel can import various types of files, including text files. If Excel can't determine how to import the data in a text file, its Text Import Wizard walks you through the process.

Recording your actions while importing a file can be very illuminating — or maybe the word is *confusing.* For example, here's the code Excel generates when I use the Text Import Wizard to import the simple text file shown in Figure 25-3:

```
Sub Macro1()
    Workbooks.OpenText Filename:="C:\XLFILES\textfile.txt",
            Origin:= _
        xlWindows, StartRow:=1, DataType:=xlDelimited,
            TextQualifier _
        :=xlDoubleQuote, ConsecutiveDelimiter:=True,
            Tab:=False, _
        Semicolon:=False, Comma:=False, Space:=True,
            Other:=False, _
        OtherChar:=".", FieldInfo:=Array(Array(1, 1), Array(2,
            1), _
        Array(3, 1), Array(4, 1), Array(5, 1))
End Sub
```

Figure 25-3:
A simple
text file to be
imported
into Excel.

```
textfile.txt - Notepad
File  Edit  Search  Help
Month      Region    Product   QuantitySales Amt
January    North     Sprockets    509     30031
February   East      Sprockets    509     30031
February   North     Sprockets    492     29028
January    East      Sprockets    433     25547
January    South     Sprockets    379     22361
February   West      Sprockets    332     19588
February   East      Widgets      433     19485
February   South     Sprockets    301     17759
January    East      Widgets      322     14490
January    West      Sprockets    244     14396
February   North     Widgets      189      8505
February   South     Widgets      165      7425
January    North     Widgets      145      6525
January    South     Widgets      132      5940
February   West      Widgets      132      5940
January    West      Widgets       79      3555
```

You can see that this is a rather complex piece of code (and it's only one VBA statement), which uses the OpenText method of the Workbooks collection. As you can see in the online help, this method has 13 arguments.

This lengthy statement starts to make sense when you examine it in terms of the options you specify in the Text Import Wizard. Each argument corresponds to one of the options in the Text Import Wizard.

Most of these arguments are quite straightforward, though you might find the FieldInfo argument a bit puzzling. This argument is an array that consists of one element for each field. Each array element consists of another array element. Confusing? You bet. The good news is that you don't have to understand it: The macro recorder does the work for you.

After you record this macro, you can open other identically formatted text files with a single command — no need to deal with the Text Import Wizard.

A Real-Life Example

Here are some automation techniques in action. In many cases, you need to perform some type of data analysis on a regular basis. For example, you may need to create a report from sales data you receive at the end of the month.

Unlike some examples in this book, this scenario isn't a figment of my imagination: I receive a daily e-mail message from my Internet World Wide Web (WWW) server that lists the number of times each file on my Web site was accessed the previous day, as well as the number of bytes transferred. I save this message as a text file and then import it into Excel. I add this new data to my master database and use a pivot table to summarize the information.

Figure 25-4 shows an example of the file I import. The text file consists of one line for each file I have at my Web site. Each line shows the number of times the file was accessed, the number of bytes transferred, and the filename.

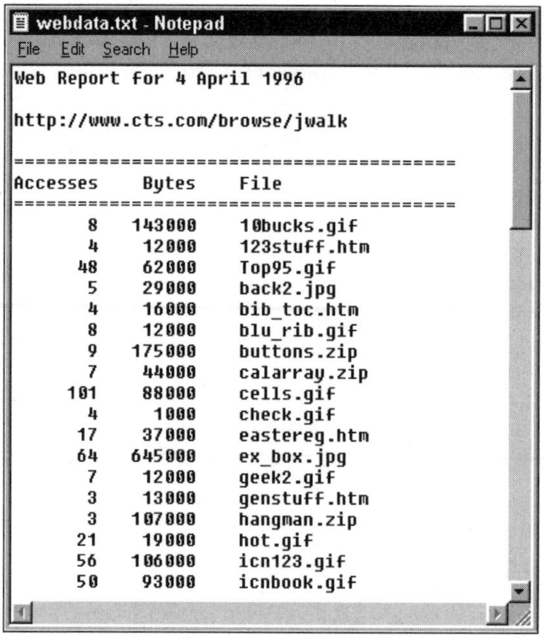


```
Web Report for 4 April 1996

http://www.cts.com/browse/jwalk

========================================
Accesses     Bytes     File
========================================
       8    143000     10bucks.gif
       4     12000     123stuff.htm
      48     62000     Top95.gif
       5     29000     back2.jpg
       4     16000     bib_toc.htm
       8     12000     blu_rib.gif
       9    175000     buttons.zip
       7     44000     calarray.zip
     101     88000     cells.gif
       4      1000     check.gif
      17     37000     eastereg.htm
      64    645000     ex_box.jpg
       7     12000     geek2.gif
       3     13000     genstuff.htm
       3    107000     hangman.zip
      21     19000     hot.gif
      56    106000     icn123.gif
      50     93000     icnbook.gif
```

Figure 25-4: I can import this text file into Excel.

Overview

In this example, I demonstrate how to

1. **Record a macro to import a text file.**
2. **Modify the macro so it copies the imported data to my master database.**
3. **Modify the macro so it automatically updates the range name I use for the database.**
4. **Modify the macro so it updates my pivot table.**

Figure 25-5 shows part of my master database — the file I update each day with the new data. It consists of six fields: Date, Accesses, Bytes, File, and Extension.

The file I import doesn't contain a date on each line (I provide this manually, as you'll see). Also, I separate each filename from its extension so I can use the file type as a field in the pivot table.

In the following sections, I describe how I develop my automated updating system.

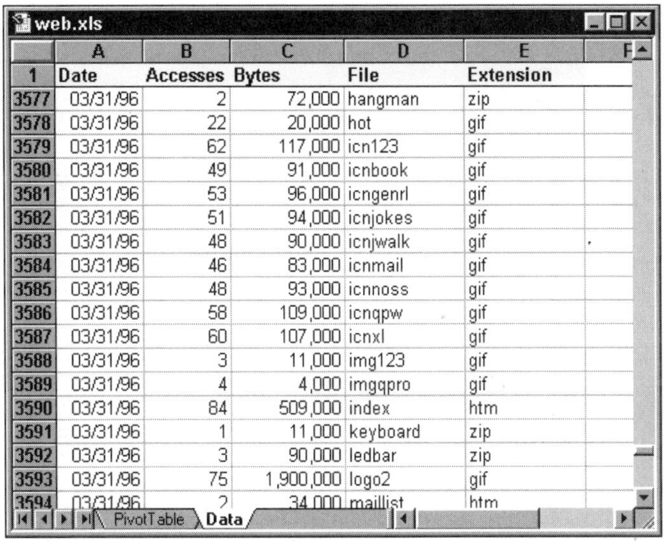

web.xls

	A	B	C	D	E	F
1	Date	Accesses	Bytes	File	Extension	
3577	03/31/96	2	72,000	hangman	zip	
3578	03/31/96	22	20,000	hot	gif	
3579	03/31/96	62	117,000	icn123	gif	
3580	03/31/96	49	91,000	icnbook	gif	
3581	03/31/96	53	96,000	icngenrl	gif	
3582	03/31/96	51	94,000	icnjokes	gif	
3583	03/31/96	48	90,000	icnjwalk	gif	
3584	03/31/96	46	83,000	icnmail	gif	
3585	03/31/96	48	93,000	icnnoss	gif	
3586	03/31/96	58	109,000	icnqpw	gif	
3587	03/31/96	60	107,000	icnxl	gif	
3588	03/31/96	3	11,000	img123	gif	
3589	03/31/96	4	4,000	imgqpro	gif	
3590	03/31/96	84	509,000	index	htm	
3591	03/31/96	1	11,000	keyboard	zip	
3592	03/31/96	3	90,000	ledbar	zip	
3593	03/31/96	75	1,900,000	logo2	gif	
3594	03/31/96	2	34,000	maillist	htm	

Figure 25-5: This database tracks the number of times each WWW file is accessed.

Recording the Text Import Wizard

Because importing the text file is critical to this process, I start with this step. The best way to create a macro for importing a text file is to turn on the macro recorder and let Excel write the code for you.

In my case, I specified the following options in the Text Import Wizard:

- Use a delimited file.
- Start importing at line 8 (ignore the header information).
- Use space and period as the delimiters. (By using the period as a delimiter, the import process separates the filename from its extension, storing these items in two columns.)
- Skip the first column. This column is blank because the data does not start flush left on each line.

Here's the recorded macro:

```
Sub Macro1()
    Workbooks.OpenText Filename:="C:\XLFILES\webdata.txt", _
        Origin:=xlWindows, StartRow:=8,
            DataType:=xlDelimited, _
        TextQualifier:=xlDoubleQuote,
            ConsecutiveDelimiter:=True, _
```

(continued)

(continued)

```
        Tab:=False, Semicolon:=False, Comma:=False,
            Space:=True, _
        Other:=True, OtherChar:=".",
            FieldInfo:=Array(Array(1, 9), _
        Array(2, 1), Array(3, 1), Array(4, 1), Array(5, 1))
End Sub
```

I test the macro, and it works just fine. Figure 25-6 shows how the imported data appears in Excel.

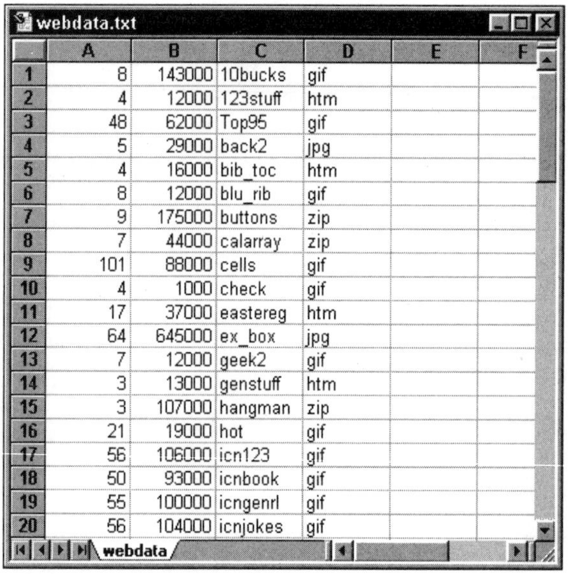

webdata.txt

	A	B	C	D	E	F
1	8	143000	10bucks	gif		
2	4	12000	123stuff	htm		
3	48	62000	Top95	gif		
4	5	29000	back2	jpg		
5	4	16000	bib_toc	htm		
6	8	12000	blu_rib	gif		
7	9	175000	buttons	zip		
8	7	44000	calarray	zip		
9	101	88000	cells	gif		
10	4	1000	check	gif		
11	17	37000	eastereg	htm		
12	64	645000	ex_box	jpg		
13	7	12000	geek2	gif		
14	3	13000	genstuff	htm		
15	3	107000	hangman	zip		
16	21	19000	hot	gif		
17	56	106000	icn123	gif		
18	50	93000	icnbook	gif		
19	55	100000	icngenrl	gif		
20	56	104000	icnjokes	gif		

webdata

Figure 25-6: The imported data.

Getting the date

The imported file doesn't include the date on each, line although I need this information for tracking purposes. Therefore, I modify the macro to display an input box asking me for a date. The input box provides a clever twist. I usually update my master file on the same day I receive the data, although the data is for the previous day. Therefore, my code sets the default date as the previous day's date.

Here's the code I wrote:

```
TheDate = Format(Now() - 1, "mm/dd/yy")
    TheDate = InputBox("Enter the date:", , TheDate)
```

Notice that the default date is today's date (obtained from the Now function) minus one — *yesterday*. Figure 25-7 shows the input box in action.

Opening the master workbook

When I import the text file, it always appears in a new workbook.

To make this macro as easy as possible, I also wrote code that opens the master workbook (named WEB.XLS). I wrote a custom function (BookOpen) to determine whether the workbook is already open. If so, I don't reopen it.

```
Function BookOpen(BookName)
'    Returns True if the specified workbook is open
    For Each book In Workbooks
        If book.Name = BookName Then
            BookOpen = True
            Exit Function
        End if
    Next book
    BookOpen = False
End Function
```

Here's the code I wrote to open the master workbook:

```
    MasterBook = "web.xls"
    If Not BookOpen(MasterBook) Then _
        Workbooks.Open Filename:="c:\xlfiles\" & MasterBook
```

Copying the imported data

I now have code to import the text file, get the date, and open the master workbook if it's not already open. The next step is to write code to copy the imported data to the master workbook, beginning in the first blank row. The data is copied beginning in column 2, because column 1 holds the date.

Here's the entire macro, including the code I wrote to copy the data:

```
Sub UpdateWebData()
'    Import the file
    Workbooks.OpenText Filename:="C:\XLFILES\webdata.txt", _
        Origin:=xlWindows, StartRow:=8,
            DataType:=xlDelimited, _
        TextQualifier:=xlDoubleQuote,
            ConsecutiveDelimiter:=True, _
        Tab:=False, Semicolon:=False, Comma:=False,
            Space:=True, _
        Other:=True, OtherChar:=".",
            FieldInfo:=Array(Array(1, 9), _
        Array(2, 1), Array(3, 1), Array(4, 1), Array(5, 1))

'    Get the date
    TheDate = Format(Now() - 1, "mm/dd/yy")
    TheDate = InputBox("Enter the date:", , TheDate)

'    Copy the data
    Range("A1").CurrentRegion.Copy

'    Open the master workbook if it's not open
    MasterBook = "web.xls"
    If Not BookOpen(MasterBook) Then _
        Workbooks.Open Filename:="c:\xlfiles\" & MasterBook

'    Determine first blank row
    Workbooks(MasterBook).Activate
    Sheets("Data").Activate
    FirstBlank = Application.CountA(Range("A:A")) + 1

'    Paste the data beginning in column B
    Cells(FirstBlank, 2).Select
    ActiveSheet.Paste

'    Determine the last row pasted
    LastUsed = Application.CountA(Range("B:B"))

'    Enter the dates in column A
    Range(Cells(FirstBlank, 1), Cells(LastUsed, 1)).Value = _
        TheDate
End Sub
```

Examine this code closely to see how it works. I specify the data to be copied by using the CurrentRegion property. After the master workbook is opened, it becomes the active workbook. I then use the Excel COUNTA function to determine the first blank row. I activate column 2 of the first blank row, and paste the data. Then I determine the last row that was pasted, again using COUNTA — but this time counting the nonblank cells in column B. Then I enter the date into the range that consists of the empty cells in column A, directly to the left of the copied data. Whew!

Updating the pivot table

The master workbook also includes a worksheet with a pivot table. Figure 25-8 shows how the pivot table looks.

	A	B	C	D	E	F	G	
3	Extension	zip ▾						
4								
5			Date					
6	Data	File	02/14/96	02/15/96	02/16/96	02/17/96	02/18/96	02/
7	# Accesses	xlpowr2a	7	33	48	33	25	
8		xlpatern	0	4	2	1	1	
9		xlguitar	2	3	1	1	3	
10		wiz-demo	2	6	5	2	3	
11		timeline	2	1	6	4	3	
12		tidechrt	2	1	5	3	0	
13		spinedit	0	0	0	0	0	
14		sel-demo	0	0	0	0	0	
15		salesdb2	0	0	0	0	0	
16		qpwpoker	0	0	0	0	0	
17		pupreg	0	0	0	9	7	
18		pptsetup	0	0	0	0	0	
19		powrcopy	0	4	6	1	2	
20		password	1	1	1	1	0	

Figure 25-8: This pivot table summarizes the data.

I add the following code to the end of the subroutine. This code updates the pivot table by using the same technique I describe earlier in this chapter:

```
'    Update the pivot table
    Sheets("PivotTable").Activate
    Set DataRange = Sheets("Data").Range("A1").CurrentRegion

    ActiveSheet.PivotTableWizard SourceType:=xlDatabase, _
        SourceData:=DataRange, _
        TableDestination:="R3C1", _
        TableName:="PivotTable1"
```

Conclusions

I've used this macro for several weeks, and it works fine. It saves me quite a bit of time — more time than I spent creating it.

If I were developing this for someone else to use, I would add some error-handling features. For example, what if WEB.XLS doesn't exist? Or, what if the worksheet does not have enough room to handle all the pasted data (this will eventually happen, but I'll figure out how to handle it).

If you'd like to become a statistic in my WEB.XLS workbook, point your Web browser to:

```
http://www.cts.com/browse/jwalk
```

Learning More

This chapter presents some techniques to help you automate tasks that deal with worksheet tables. The example I present is typical of those performed thousands of times every day. You will, of course, have to adapt it to your own needs.

In the next chapter, I discuss some additional techniques that may be useful for some projects.

Chapter 26

Other Useful VBA Techniques

● ●

In This Chapter

▶ An introduction to user-defined data types

▶ How to launch other applications from Excel

▶ How to send Excel data to Microsoft Word

▶ Things to remember when creating applications for people in other countries

● ●

The preceding 25 chapters cover quite a bit of material. But guess what? I still have lots more to tell you. This chapter introduces some additional VBA techniques that may come in handy at some point in your career.

User-Defined Data Types

Data used in VBA and Excel comes in several varieties, known as *data types*. For example, you can work with data types like text strings, integers, Boolean variables, and dates. If you don't declare your variables, VBA uses the default *variant* data type. In this section, I describe how to create your very own data types.

A user-defined data type can ease your work with some types of data. For example, assume that you need to keep track of the following information for your customers:

  ✔ Company name

  ✔ Contact person's name

  ✔ A three-digit region code

  ✔ Total sales for that customer

You may think that you need four separate variables to keep track of all this data. Think again. Here's a better way to keep track of data: a user-defined data type.

Here's how to create a user-defined data type named CustomerInfo. Enter the following code into a VBA module. This code should appear before the first procedure is defined:

```
Type CustomerInfo
    Company As String
    Contact As String
    RegionCode As Integer
    Sales As Long
End Type
```

This new data type has four components (two strings, an integer, and a long). After you create a user-defined data type, you use a Dim statement to declare a variable as that new type. The following example shows how you usually define an array:

```
Dim Customers(1 to 100) as CustomerInfo
```

Each of the 100 elements in this array has four components (as specified by the user-defined data type, CustomerInfo). You can refer to a particular component of a customer record by connecting the variable name (and its array index) with the data type component, separated by a dot. Here's an example.

```
Customers(1).Company = "Acme Explosives"
Customers(1).Contact = "W. Coyote"
Customers(1).RegionCode = 302
Customers(1).Sales = 150677.54
```

And, of course, you can get the data from a worksheet. Figure 26-1 shows a worksheet that contains customer information. The following code reads the data (seven customers) into the Customers array:

```
Sub GetData()
    i = 1
    For Row = 2 To 8
        Customers(i).Company = Sheets("Clients").Cells(Row, 1)
        Customers(i).Contact = Sheets("Clients").Cells(Row, 2)
        Customers(i).RegionCode = _
            Sheets("Clients").Cells(Row, 3)
        Customers(i).Sales = Sheets("Clients").Cells(Row, 4)
        i = i + 1
    Next Row
End Sub
```

	A	B	C	D	E
1	**Company**	**Contact**	**RegionCode**	**Sales**	
2	International Widgets Inc.	Jane Walters	134	14,450.32	
3	XYZ Corporation	Mike Jones	45	2,394.43	
4	MicroHard Corporation	Richard L. Harris	221	7,882.33	
5	NEC & NEC Products, Inc.	Judy Kramer	223	2,199.00	
6	JWalk & Associates	John Walkenbach	134	1.29	
7	Flagship Productions	Tom Peterson	45	33,092.00	
8	Eversharp Pencils	Karen Roth	221	1,893.44	
9					
10					
11					

clients.xls — Module1 \ Clients

You also can work with an element in the array as an entire unit. For example, the following statement copies the information from Customers(1) to Customers(2):

```
Customers(2) = Customers(1)
```

The preceding statement is equivalent to the following block of statements:

```
Customers(2).Company = Customers(1).Company
Customers(2).Contact = Customers(1).Contact
Customers(2).RegionCode = Customers(1).RegionCode
Customers(2).Sales = Customers(1).Sales
```

Here's another example of a user-defined data type; this one describes computer systems:

```
Type ComputerData
    Manufacturer As String
    ProcessorType As String
    RAM As Long
    NumDrives As Integer
    MonitorSize As Integer
    HasModem As Boolean
    WhenPurchased As Date
    Price As Long
End Type
```

After you define this data type, you can create an array to store data. For example:

```
Dim Computers(1 to 50) as ComputerData
```

After you assign values to the array, you can work with the data by using all the standard VBA techniques. Here's some code that calculates the total purchase price of all the computers in the array:

```
TotalCost = 0
For i = 1 To 50
    TotalCost = TotalCost + Computers(i).Price
Next i
```

The user-defined data type feature is quite flexible, and you can make your user-defined data types as complex as you like (this example is rather wimpy). In addition, you can define as many custom data types as you need. Check out the online help for more details.

Launching Other Programs

You might want your VBA code to start another program. You can do this by using VBA's Shell function.

The following example starts the Windows Control Panel application and displays the Date/Time dialog box, which lets you adjust the system's date and time:

```
Sub ChangeDateandTime()
    On Error GoTo NotFound
    AppFile = "CONTROL.EXE Date/Time"
    x = Shell(AppFile, 1)
    Exit Sub
NotFound:
    MsgBox "Cannot start " & AppFile, vbCritical, "Error"
End Sub
```

This example takes advantage of the fact that you can activate a Control Panel's icon by including the title of the icon on the command line.

Figure 26-2 shows the Date/Time dialog box displayed from VBA.

The Shell function returns a task identification number of the application. You can use this number later in your routine to activate the task. The second argument for the Shell function determines how the application is displayed (*1* specifies normal size, with the focus).

If the Shell function is not successful, it generates an error. Therefore, the routine uses an On Error statement to display a message if the file cannot be found or some other error occurs.

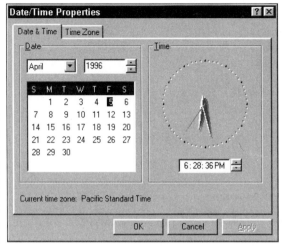

Figure 26-2:
Running a
Windows
Control
Panel
application
from VBA.

The Shell function runs the application *asynchronously*. This means VBA does not pause while the launched application is running. If more statements follow the Shell function in your routine, VBA executes those statements while the new program is active — in most cases, that's *not* what you want. To avoid this scenario, you should usually avoid placing other statements after the Shell function.

If the application you want to start is one of several Microsoft applications, you can use the ActivateMicrosoftApp method of the Application object. For example, the following procedure starts Word for Windows:

```
Sub StartWord()
    Application.ActivateMicrosoftApp xlMicrosoftWord
End Sub
```

If Word is already running when you execute the preceding procedure, Word is activated. The other constants available for this method are

- ✔ xlMicrosoftPowerPoint
- ✔ xlMicrosoftMail
- ✔ xlMicrosoftAccess
- ✔ xlMicrosoftFoxPro
- ✔ xlMicrosoftProject
- ✔ xlMicrosoftSchedulePlus

Windows 95 offers a new command, Start, which you can use as an argument for the Shell function. The Start command starts a Windows application from a DOS window. I discovered that you need only specify a filename — the Shell function executes the program associated with the filename extension, and loads the specified file at the same time. For example, the following statements start the installed World Wide Web browser application (that is, the application associated with the HTM extension) and load an HTML document named HOMEPAGE.HTM:

```
WebPage = "c:\webstuff\homepage.htm"
Shell ("Start " & WebPage)
```

Automating a Word Session

You've probably already discovered that Excel and Microsoft Word work very well together. The example in this section demonstrates how to control Word from within Excel.

The MakeMemos procedure creates three customized memos in Word (using data stored in a worksheet) and then saves each memo to a file. This procedure uses a technique known as OLE automation.

To execute the MakeMemos procedure, you must use Word for Windows 6.0 or a later version.

The MakeMemos subroutine starts by creating an object called Word. The routine cycles through the three rows of data in Sheet1 and uses WordBasic commands (Word's macro language) to create each memo and save it to disk.

The following lines of code demonstrate how to write a make memos procedure in VBA.

```
Sub MakeMemos()
'    Creates memos in Word by using OLE automation

'    Start Word and create an object
     Set Word = CreateObject("Word.Basic")

'    Information from worksheet
     Set Data = Sheets("Sheet1").Range("A1")
     Message = Sheets("Sheet1").Range("Message")

'    Cycle through all records in Sheet1
     Records = _
          Application.CountA(Sheets("Sheet1").Range("A:A"))
```

```
For i = 1 To Records
    ' Update status bar progress message _
    Application.StatusBar = "Processing Record " & i
    ' Assign current data to variables
    Region = Data.Offset(i - 1, 0).Value
    SalesAmt = Format(Data.Offset(i - 1, 2).Value, _
        "#,000")
    SalesNum = Data.Offset(i - 1, 1).Value

    ' Determine the filename
    SaveAsName = UCase(Region & ".DOC")

    ' Send commands to Word
    With Word
        .FileNewDefault
        .Insert "M E M O R A N D U M"
        .InsertPara
        .InsertPara
        .Insert "Date:" & Chr(9) & _ _
            Format(Date, "mmmm d, yyyy")
        .InsertPara
        .Insert "To:" & Chr(9) & Region & " Manager"
        .InsertPara
        .InsertPara
        .Insert Message
        .InsertPara
        .InsertPara
        .Insert "Units Sold:" & Chr(9) & SalesNum
        .InsertPara
        .Insert "Total Amount:" & Chr(9) & _ _
            Format(SalesAmt, "$#,##0")
        .InsertPara
        .InsertPara
        .Insert Application.UserName
        .StartOfDocument
        .EndOfLine 1
        .Bold
        .CenterPara
        .FileSaveAs SaveAsName
    End With
Next i
```

(continued)

```
(continued)
'    Reset status bar
     Application.StatusBar = ""

     Msg = Records & " memos were created and saved." & _
          Chr(10)
     Msg = Msg & "Activate Word now?"
     Ans = MsgBox(Msg, vbYesNo + vbQuestion)
     If Ans = vbYes Then _
          Application.ActivateMicrosoftApp xlMicrosoftWord
End Sub
```

Figure 26-3 displays the results of the MakeMemos procedure: a word document and the Excel worksheet that provides the data.

To learn more about controlling Word from Excel, consult the online help (search for *OLE Automation*).

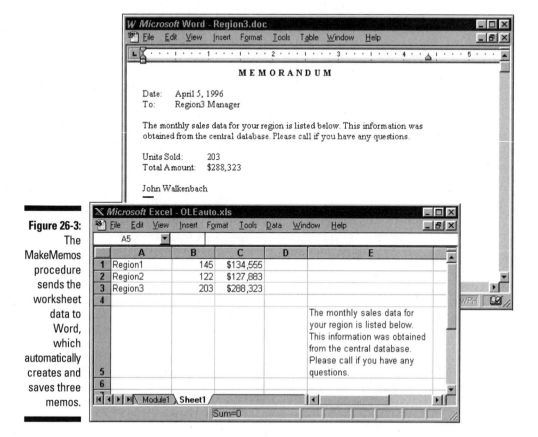

Figure 26-3: The MakeMemos procedure sends the worksheet data to Word, which automatically creates and saves three memos.

International Issues

If you create applications for use by people in other countries, you should be aware of a few issues:

- ✔ Not everyone uses the English language version of Excel.
- ✔ Not everyone uses A1 cell notation. Some people prefer the old R1C1 notation.
- ✔ Not everyone uses a period as a *decimal separator*. In some countries, they use a comma.
- ✔ Not everyone uses a comma as a *thousands separator*. In some countries, they use a period.
- ✔ Not everyone uses a comma as a *list separator*. In some countries, they use a semicolon.
- ✔ Not everyone uses the (illogical) U.S. date convention (for example, April 1, 1996). Most countries use the more logical style of placing the day first (such as 1 April, 1996).

Using local properties

If your code displays worksheet information (such as a range address), you should use the local language. For example, the following statement displays the address of the selected range:

```
MsgBox Selection.Address
```

For international applications, a better approach uses the AddressLocal property rather than the Address property:

```
MsgBox Selection.AddressLocal
```

An even better approach ensures that the reference style (A1 or R1C1) matches the style the user has selected. You can accomplish this task with the following statement:

```
MsgBox Selection.AddressLocal _
    (ReferenceStyle:=Application.ReferenceStyle)
```

Several other properties have *local* versions (refer to the online help for details):

Property	Local Version	What It Does
Address	AddressLocal	Returns an address
Category	CategoryLocal	Returns a function category
Formula	FormulaLocal	Returns a formula
Name	NameLocal	Returns a name
RefersTo	RefersToLocal	Returns a reference

Identifying system settings

You can't always assume that the end user's system is set up like the system on which you develop the application. For international applications, you need to be aware of the following settings:

- ✔ **Decimal separator:** Separates the decimal portion from the rest of a value.
- ✔ **Thousands separator:** Delineates every three digits in a value.
- ✔ **List separator:** Separates items in a list.

You can determine the current system settings by accessing the International property of the Application object. For example, the following statement displays the decimal separator (which isn't always a period):

```
MsgBox Application.International(xlDecimalSeparator)
```

You can access 44 other international settings by using the International property. Check out the online help for details.

Here's an example that writes a value to a cell by combining an integer with a decimal — but it first determines the decimal separator in use on the system:

```
Sub WriteValue()
    DecSep = Application.International(xlDecimalSeparator)
    IntegerPart = 123
    Decimalpart = 45
    Sheets("Sheet1").Range("A1") = IntegerPart & DecSep _
            Decimalpart
End Sub
```

If the decimal separator is a period, this routine enters *123.45* into cell A1. If the decimal separator is a comma, it enters *123,45* into the cell.

Changing date and time settings

If your routine writes formatted dates (and the workbook will be used in other countries), make sure the routine writes the date in the correct format. The following routine shows one way to write a formatted date. This routine uses VBA's Format function to write the date in the specified format. For example, the routine may write 04/01/96 to the specified cell:

```
Sub WriteDate()
    Today = Now()
    Sheets("Sheet1").Range("A1") = Format(Today, "mm/dd/yy")
End Sub
```

A non-U.S. user might be confused by this date, interpreting it as January 4 rather than April 1. You can avoid such confusion by using named formats, which use the format that the user is accustomed to. Here's an example:

```
Sub WriteDate()
    Today = Now()
    Sheets("Sheet1").Range("A1") = Format(Today, "Short
            Date")
End Sub
```

This routine writes the current date into cell A1, using the Windows *Short Date* format.

Excel provides several other named date and time formats, as well as quite a few named-number formats. The online help describes all of these (search for *named date/time formats* or *named numeric formats*).

Learning More

This chapter concludes Part VII. Although I don't go into great detail, the information in this chapter can help you get started. As always, you can get more details from the online help.

Part VIII is coming up: The Part of Tens.

Part VIII
The Part of Tens

In this part...

For reasons that are historical — as well as useful — all the books in the *. . . For Dummies* series have chapters with lists in them. This book is no exception. The next four chapters contain my own Top Ten lists that deal with tricks, frequently-asked questions, spreadsheet evaluation criteria, and other Excel resources. David Letterman has nothing to worry about.

Chapter 27
Top Ten VBA Tips and Tricks

*T*his chapter contains a list of 10 clever tricks I've developed (or acquired from other users) over the years.

Getting VBA Help, Fast

When working in a VBA module, you can get instant help regarding a VBA object, property, or method. Just move the cursor to the word that interests you and press F1.

Undoing and Redoing a Series of Changes in a VBA Module

VBA has an undocumented feature that's often very useful: multiple levels of undo and redo. Press Alt+Backspace to undo a change, and F4 to redo it. Unlike using the Undo and Redo commands in a worksheet, you can use these commands repeatedly. For example, if you delete 10 lines by using 10 separate delete operations, you can get each line back in turn by press Alt+Backspace 10 times.

Moving Quickly to the Next or Previous Procedure in a Module

If your module contains many different procedures, you can quickly jump to the next or the previous procedure in the module by pressing Ctrl+Down or Ctrl+Up, respectively.

Hiding a Sheet So the End User Can't Unhide It

If you want to prevent end users from viewing a particular sheet, set its Visible property to xlVeryHidden. There's no menu command to accomplish this; you can only change this property by using VBA. After you do this, the sheet does not appear in the list of hidden sheets. The only way you can *unhide* the module is by using VBA to set the Visible property to True.

This method is not completely foolproof, but it prevents almost all users from viewing the hidden sheet.

Reducing the Size of a Workbook

In many cases, you can significantly reduce the size of a workbook — especially a workbook with modules you've edited heavily — because Excel does not do a good job of cleaning up its symbol table. To clean up the mess Excel leaves behind, insert a new module and use the Clipboard to copy the heavily edited VBA code into the blank module. Then delete the original module. Save the workbook, and you usually find that it's much smaller than it was.

This technique won't copy any toolbars stored in the module. You also lose any options you set with the Macro Options dialog box.

Preventing Execution of the Auto_Open Macro

If your workbook has an Auto_Open macro (a macro Excel executes automatically when the workbook is opened), you can prevent Excel from running this macro by pressing Shift while you open the workbook.

Disabling Shortcut Menus

The Excel right-click shortcut menus are handy, but the program doesn't provide an option for turning off these menus if you don't want them. However, the following VBA routine disables all the shortcut menus:

```
Sub DisableShortcuts()
    For sc = 1 To 25
        ShortcutMenus(sc).Enabled = False
    Next sc
End Sub
```

Formatting the Text in a Custom Dialog Box

Although you can't format a label object in a custom dialog box, you have two good alternatives for getting the text to look just right. One approach is to use a text box in your dialog box. Although you usually use text boxes in worksheets, they work perfectly well in dialog boxes. And, you can format text boxes any way you like.

The other alternative is to use a linked picture. Create the text you want to display in a worksheet range, and copy the range to the Clipboard. Then activate your dialog sheet, hold down Shift, and choose the Edit Paste Picture Link command. This action creates a picture object that displays the current contents of the linked range, including all its formatting.

Protecting Your Secret Formula

If you develop Excel add-ins that you distribute to other users, remember that an add-in can usually be converted back to its original XLS source file. Therefore, be careful if you use any proprietary formulas or techniques. Bottom line? An add-in is not as secure as an encrypted file. To foil all but the most sophisticated hackers, password-protect your workbook's structure before creating an add-in.

Finding the Excel For Windows 95 Secret Doom-like Window

Try this:

1. **Open a new, empty workbook.**

2. **Activate a worksheet, and scroll down to row 95.**

3. **Click the row heading to select the entire row 95.**

4. **Press Tab.**

5. **Choose the Help⇨About Microsoft Excel command.**

6. **In the dialog box Excel displays, press Ctrl+Shift while you click the Tech Support button.**

   A new (and very unexpected) window appears.

7. **In the new window, use the arrow keys to explore.**

If you haven't seen the faces, you haven't fully explored this window.

Chapter 28

Top Ten VBA Questions (and Answers)

*I*n this chapter, I answer the most frequently asked questions about VBA. These questions appear time after time on the online services I monitor.

1. **When I execute my macro, everything that happens flashes on the screen. Can I execute the macro without showing what's happening?**

   Yes. Insert the following statement to turn off screen updating:

   ```
   Application.ScreenUpdating = False
   ```

   Using this statement has a nice side effect: your macro usually executes much faster.

2. **Is there a utility I can use to translate my XLM macros into VBA?**

   No existing utility does this, and it is very unlikely that anyone will ever write a utility for this purpose. Such conversions must be done manually. However, because Excel 95 can execute XLM macros, you don't really need to convert them. And even if someone were to develop such a utility, the resulting code probably would not be as efficient as the original XLM macros.

3. Is it possible to display messages in the status bar while a macro is running? I have a lengthy macro, and it would be helpful to display its progress in the status bar.

Yes, you can assign the text of a progress message to the StatusBar property of the Application object. Here's an example:

```
Application.StatusBar = "Now processing File " & FileNum
```

When your routine ends, return the status bar to normal with the following statement:

```
Application.StatusBar = False
```

4. Can I stop Excel from showing messages while my macro runs? For example, I'd like to eliminate the warning message that appears when my macro deletes a worksheet.

The following statement turns off most of the Excel warning messages:

```
Application.DisplayAlerts = False
```

5. Is there a VBA command to select a range from the active cell to the last entry in a column or a row? (In other words, how can a macro accomplish the same thing as Ctrl+Shift+down-arrow or Ctrl+Shift+right-arrow?)

The VBA equivalent for Ctrl+Shift+down-arrow is

```
Range(ActiveCell, ActiveCell.End(xlDown)).Select
```

For the other directions, use the following constants:

- XLToLeft
- XLToRight
- XLUp

6. How can I make my VBA code run as fast as possible?

Here are a few tips:

- Make sure you declare all your variables (use Option Explicit at the beginning of each module to force yourself to declare all variables).
- If you reference an object more than once, create an object variable by using the Set keyword.
- Use the With...End With construct whenever possible.
- If your macro writes information to a worksheet, turn off screen updating by using Application.ScreenUpdating = False.

7. **Calling a custom dialog box worked fine — until I converted the XLS file to an XLA add-in. Now, I get an error message whenever I try to access the custom dialog box by using the Show method. What's wrong?**

   You need to qualify the reference to the dialog sheet with a reference to its workbook. This makes the dialog box callable when any workbook is active. The general way to do this is by using ThisWorkbook. Here's an example:

   ```
   ThisWorkbook.Dialogsheets("Dialog1").Show
   ```

8. **My custom dialog box has several buttons that all call the same macro. How can the macro determine which button the user clicked?**

   Use Application.Caller. This property returns the name of the control that called the macro.

9. **I'm not able to print anything when a custom dialog box is displayed. Is this right?**

   I'm not sure if it's right, but that's the way it is. You must dismiss your dialog box before using the PrintOut method or the PrintPreview method. One solution is to assign the Print button on your dialog box to a macro that sets a Boolean variable (for example, PrintIt = True). When the dialog box is dismissed, check the value of the Boolean variable to determine whether the user clicked the Print button.

10. **I added a custom button to a toolbar, but the tool tip continues to display *Custom*. How can I get it to show something more meaningful?**

    The tool tip for a toolbar button is actually the Name property of the button. The only way you can change the Name property is by using VBA macro code. Here's an example that displays *Process Data* as a tool tip for the first button on a toolbar named MyBar:

    ```
    Toolbars("MyBar").ToolbarButtons(1).Name = "Process Data"
    ```

Chapter 29

Top Ten Signs That You Purchased a *Bad* Spreadsheet

• •

1. A sticker on the box reads, *Now Supports Negative Numbers!*

2. It's part of a software suite called Office Schmoffice.

3. User testimonials are written in Latin.

4. Pressing F1 for help plays a sound file named BIGLAUGH.WAV.

5. The product advertisements feature Beavis and Butthead as celebrity spokespersons.

6. The Setup routine displays *Another Sucker* as the default user name.

7. The user manual is written in long hand — and mimeographed.

8. The phone number listed for technical support is 555-1212.

9. The only way to get a hard copy of your work is by photographing the screen.

10. When you press F9, a message box tells you to dig out your calculator.

Chapter 30

Top Ten Excel Resources

● ●

● ●

*Y*ou've reached the final chapter in this saga (were you surprised by the ending?) If I've done my job, you now know enough to develop some useful programs in Excel — and I hope you've acquired a deeper appreciation for the product.

But this book is only an introduction. For those who hunger for more, I've compiled a list of additional resources. You can learn new techniques, communicate with other Excel users, download useful files, ask questions, access the extensive Microsoft Knowledge Base, and lots more.

Several of these resources are online services or Internet resources. These types of resources tend to change frequently. The descriptions are accurate at the time I'm writing this, but I can't guarantee that this information will remain current.

The VBA Online Help System

I hope you've already discovered VBA's online help system. In Excel 95, it's better than ever — and amazingly thorough. It's there and it's free, so use it.

Microsoft Product Support

Microsoft offers a wide variety of technical support options (some for free, others for a fee). For complete information on how to contact Microsoft for technical support, choose Help⇨About Microsoft Excel. Then in the dialog box Excel displays, click the Tech Support button. You'll find details on various ways to get help directly from Bill Gates (well, probably one of his employees).

My Book, Excel for Windows 95 Power Programming With VBA, 2nd Edition

Sorry, but I couldn't resist the opportunity for a blatant plug. I have received tons of positive feedback on my book, *Excel 5 For Windows Power Programming Techniques* (published by IDG Books Worldwide, Inc.). The new edition, *Excel For Windows 95 Power Programming with VBA,* 2nd Edition, should be available in the summer of 1996.

The book covers all aspects of Excel application development in detail, with lots of useful examples on the companion CD-ROM.

Usenet Newsgroups

One of my favorite Internet hangouts is the Usenet newsgroup, comp.apps.spreadsheets. Although this newsgroup deals with all spreadsheets, most of the traffic focuses on Excel.

Internet Web Sites

Several World Wide Web sites contain Excel-related material. A good place to start your web surfing is my very own site, which is named **The Spreadsheet Page**. Once you get there, you can check out my material and then click some links to visit other Excel-related sites. The URL is:

```
http://www.cts.com/browse/jwalk
```

Internet Mailing Lists

Two Internet mailing lists deal with Excel:

- **EXCEL-G**: Excel General Q & A List
- **EXCEL-L**: Excel Developers List

To subscribe to one of these lists, send e-mail to:

```
LISTSERV@PEACH.EASE.LSOFT.COM
```

The subject line of the message doesn't matter. In the body of your message, include the following information:

```
SUB listname Your Name
```

For example, if your name is Bill Gates and you want to subscribe to the Excel Developers List, send e-mail with the following text in the message body:

```
SUB EXCEL-L Bill Gates
```

You'll receive return mail that describes the list and provides complete instructions.

The CompuServe Excel Forum

If you subscribe to CompuServe, you should definitely check out the Excel Forum (**Go Excel**). You'll find lots of files to download, plus a lively (and very informative) question-and-answer forum.

America Online

If you're an America Online subscriber, the Applications forum has many Excel files you can download.

The Microsoft Network

The Microsoft Network is Microsoft's initial foray into the world of online services. As I write this, Excel-related content on The Microsoft Network is rather skimpy. However, I expect this to change. If you're a subscriber, check out the available Excel information. After logging on, do a global search for *Excel,* and you'll get a list of pointers to various areas.

My E-Mail Address

I'm always happy to try to answer questions that readers submit (time permitting). All I ask is that you be very specific, and avoid broad questions such as, "I need a macro to track my company's sales. What should I do?"

To contact me directly, use the following e-mail address:

```
jwalk@cts.com
```

Index

• E •